CANADIAN FINANCIAL ACCOUNTING CASES

Camillo Lento, CA, CFE, Ph.D.
Assistant Professor (Accounting)
Faculty of Business Administration
Lakehead University

Jo-Anne Ryan, CA, Ph.D.
Assistant Professor (Accounting)
Chair of Business Programs, Orillia Campus
Faculty of Business Administration
Lakehead University

WILEY

Library and Archives Canada Cataloguing in Publication

Lento, Camillo, 1981-
    Canadian financial accounting cases / Camillo Lento,
JoAnne Ryan.—Canadian ed.

ISBN 978-11-18362-44-0

    1. Accounting—Case studies. I. Ryan, JoAnne, 1968-
II. Title.

HF5636.L46 2012   657'.044   C2012-904210-2

Production Credits

Acquisitions Editor: Zoë Craig
Vice President and Publisher: Veronica Visentin
Marketing Manager: Anita Osborne
Editorial Manager: Karen Staudinger
Production Manager: Tegan Wallace
Developmental Editor: Daleara Hirjikaka
Editorial Assistant: Laura Hwee
Cover and Interior Design: Tegan Wallace and Joanna Vieira
Cover Image: Jordan Law
Typesetting: Thomson Digital
Printing and Binding: ePAC

Questions from the Uniform Final Examination have been reprinted (or adapted) with permission from the Canadian Institute of Chartered Accountants, Toronto, Canada. Any changes to the original material are the sole responsibility of the author (and/or publisher) and have not been reviewed or endorsed by the CICA.

Printed and bound in the United States of America

 3 4 5 6 7 EP 16 15 14 13 12

John Wiley & Sons Canada, Ltd.
6045 Freemont Blvd.
Mississauga, Ontario L5R 4J3
Visit our website at : www.wiley.ca

ABOUT THE AUTHORS

Camillo Lento is an Assistant Professor in the Faculty of Business Administration at Lakehead University's Thunder Bay, Ontario, campus. Camillo earned his Ph.D. in Accounting from the University of Southern Queensland (Australia), and a Master of Science in Management and Honours Bachelor of Commerce from Lakehead University. Camillo is a Chartered Accountant (Ontario), a Certified Fraud Examiner, and a student member of the Canadian Institute of Chartered Business Valuators.

Camillo teaches various financial accounting and auditing courses, including contemporary issues in accounting theory, advanced topics in accounting, intermediate accounting, and introductory accounting. In addition, he has been a seminar leader, examination marker, and case reviewer for the ICAO's School of Accountancy over the past five years.

Camillo is a Contributing Editor for *Canadian MoneySaver* magazine and has authored numerous articles on personal tax planning matters. His tax planning articles have also been featured in *The Globe and Mail's Report on Business*, *Canada Business* (on-line), and *Money Sense*.

Camillo has more than 10 years' experience working with a mid-sized public accounting firm. His public practice experience includes a variety of assurance engagements, the valuation of privately owned businesses, corporate and personal tax compliance, the assessment of personal injury damages, and business interruption claims.

Jo-Anne Ryan is an Assistant Professor at Lakehead University's Orillia, Ontario, campus, where she teaches graduate and undergraduate courses in financial and managerial accounting. She is currently the Chair of Business Programs at the campus. She has an HBComm in Accounting from Laurentian University and is a Chartered Accountant (Ontario), having articled with KPMG LLP. She earned a Ph.D. in Accounting from the University of Birmingham, United Kingdom.

Jo-Anne has over 14 years of experience in the classroom, having taught at both Nipissing University and Lakehead University. She has been a facilitator at the ICAO's School of Accountancy for over six years. She has received several awards for excellence in teaching. Her academic research focuses on the use of investor relations websites to transmit accounting information to stakeholders and the impact of emerging technologies on organizations, auditors, and education.

Outside the classroom, Jo-Anne has been a guest speaker at several Rotary functions and has volunteered her time on several boards and at charity events. She has also been involved in her local district Chartered Accountants' associations.

ACKNOWLEDGEMENTS

Camillo would like to thank his fiancée, Angela, and family for all of their support.

The authors would like to thank the following for their valuable contributions to *Canadian Financial Accounting Cases:*

Stephanie McGarry
Laura Simeoni
Sara Stonehouse
Irene Wiecek

The authors would like to thank the following reviewers for their valuable suggestions:

Robert Ducharme, University of Waterloo
Jocelyn King, University of Alberta
Heather Sceles, Saint Mary's University
Rik Smistad, Mount Royal University

TABLE OF CONTENTS

INTRODUCTION | 1

THE CASE FOR CASES

Accounting is not just about memorization, calculations, and bookkeeping. Although these things are crucial building blocks, the key skill to be learned is problem solving within the Canadian and global financial reporting environment.

Case analysis is an important tool for developing problem-solving skills for financial reporting. At the introductory level, short case studies expose the students to a realistic situation and stress the importance that numbers do not always fit neatly into formulas. At the intermediate and advanced levels, more complex cases encourage integrated thinking. Not only do cases mirror real-life decision-making, they encourage critical thinking and help develop professional judgement. Furthermore, they allow students to test their true knowledge of journal entries and accounting theory by attempting to apply the latter in real-life situations.

Cases can be used to help students develop higher levels of knowledge as measured by Bloom's taxonomy.[1] For example, consider Table 1.1, which applies Bloom's taxonomy to accounting education.

TABLE 1.1 – BLOOM'S TAXONOMY AS IT APPLIES TO ACCOUNTING EDUCATION			
Bloom Taxonomy – Category	**Example of Category**	**Example of Financial Accounting Knowledge**	**Educational Tools Available**
Knowledge	Recall data or information	Debits increase assets and decrease liabilities. Credits increase liabilities and decrease assets.	Matching (e.g., terms to definitions) True and False questions
Comprehension	Understand the meaning, translation, interpolation, and interpretation of instructions and problems. State a problem in one's own words.	Identifying the accounting issue.	Multiple choice questions Exercises and problems on individual topics
Application	Use a concept in a new situation or unprompted use of an abstraction. Apply what was learned in the classroom into novel situations in the workplace.	Recording journal entries.	Recording journal entries Exercises and problems on individual topics
Analysis	Separate material or concepts into component parts so that its organizational structure may be understood. Distinguish between facts and inferences.	Applying technical GAAP knowledge to specific situations.	Exercises and problems on individual topics Cases (e.g., applying technical knowledge to case facts to analyze accounting issues)

---

[1]Bloom, B. S. (1956). *Taxonomy of Educational Objectives, Handbook I: The Cognitive Domain*. New York: David McKay Co Inc.

Synthesis	Build a structure or pattern from diverse elements. Put parts together to form a whole, with emphasis on creating a new meaning or structure.	Understand how various accounting issues come together to make a significant impact on the users and preparers.	Cases (e.g., calculate or revise the EPS estimate based on an analysis of various individual accounting issues)
Evaluation	Make judgments about the value of ideas or materials.	Develop professional judgement. Selecting between alternatives that are equally valid and within the boundaries of GAAP.	Cases (e.g., require students to analyze alternatives and make a recommendation based on the users and reporting landscape)

In order to solve problems, memorized knowledge of journal entries and generally accepted accounting principles are important. However, Table 1.1 reveals that a student who has memorized this information has only climbed up half the mountain. Students must also be able to apply the knowledge in situations where there is uncertainty. This is where cases become important in developing problem-solving skills, critical thinking, and professional judgment.

WHAT'S IN A CASE?

What makes a case, a case? Many people have different views on this. Most cases involve some sort of real-life scenario where there are one or several issues or problems. You would be expected to identify the issues, understand the implications of the issue, analyse the issue, and then recommend a course of action. The cases may involve quantitative analysis, qualitative analysis, or both analyses.

What makes a case more challenging is the "required" information. Some cases will specify what you should do (e.g., calculate the future tax expense or identify which amortization method the company should use). Others leave the "required" section more open by requesting that you discuss the issues. In the latter, you must decide, for instance, if the future tax expense needs to be calculated in the first place or whether the choice of amortization methods is even an issue. Therein lies the challenge. What is the issue? How should the case be approached?

A successful accountant should not only be able to solve problems that have been identified for her, but more importantly, she should be able to identify the problems in the first place.

It is rare in real life that someone will present you with a problem and provide all the facts needed to solve it. In many cases, identifying the problem and gathering relevant information is a large part of the task.

Accountants are also required to communicate their findings and recommendations back to their manager, their partners, and their clients. Cases require you to determine who the report or memo needs to be addressed to, and how to write this in an appropriate and professional manner.

You must also learn to consider the impact of the environment on your decision-making, including the people involved, such as the financial statement preparers and users. Different people think in different ways depending on their own perspectives. What is right or good for one person may not be right or good for another. For instance, assume that two people are discussing the weather. Both comment that they hope the weather will be good tomorrow. One might be thinking that she hopes it stays sunny because she has to drive to Montreal. The other might be thinking that he hopes it snows because he plans to do a lot of skiing. They both want "good weather" but each one has a completely different definition of what "good weather" is at that time. "Good" financial reporting might mean one thing to one person and a completely different thing to another.

Cases sensitize you to these things. Because this way of thinking is often different from what you are used to, you may have problems analyzing cases at first. However, you will eventually catch on and find that the study of accounting is more fulfilling as a result of the use of cases. It is easier to approach this material with a completely open mind than trying to make it fit into a preconceived notion of accounting that may be more narrowly focused.

With cases, there is rarely a single acceptable answer or recommendation. There may be several, even for the same issue. The important thing is how you support your answer or recommendation.

For the most part, each case has a common set of learning objectives with the intent of developing problem-solving and critical thinking skills, and professional judgement. The common learning objectives are as follows:

» To develop an ability to identify and assume an assigned role;

» To be able to identify and rank the importance of explicit issues;

» To understand the importance of hidden (undirected) issues that arise from a detailed analysis;

» To identify accounting issues (GAAP compliance issues), assess their implications, generate alternatives, and provide recommendations within the bounds of GAAP to meet the client's needs;

» To understand how accounting standards impact financial measures (ratios, covenants, etc); and

» To prepare a coherent report and integrated analysis that meets specific user needs.

In addition to the above noted learning objectives, each case will have its own additional learning objectives that are based on the specific technical accounting issues in the case.

THE PURPOSE OF THIS CASEBOOK – STUDENTS AND INSTRUCTORS

The purpose of this casebook is to use cases to:

» Develop problem-solving skills, critical thinking abilities, and professional judgement; and

» Promote an understanding of the decision usefulness approach to accounting.

Accordingly, all of the cases require the student to understand the implications of financial reporting decisions on the users of the financial statements. A thorough user analysis is required for each case.

For the instructor: The casebook provides a wide variety of cases that can be used in several classroom settings. Some cases are short, and focus on a few issues. These cases are well suited to be used as in-class discussion tools. Other cases are longer, more complicated, and deal with several issues. These cases are more suited to be used as assignments or exams.

Each case comes with a full suggested solution and many have been classroom tested. The solutions highlight key *CICA Handbook* sections, key areas addressed in each case, and a difficulty level to assist instructors in choosing the appropriate case.

In addition, a section of this book is devoted to cases on business valuations. These cases can be used to help facilitate the instruction of business valuation concepts in the classroom. The business valuation cases focus on both asset-based and earnings-based approaches, and range from easy to difficult in terms of complexity.

For the student: The cases allow you to assume a wide variety of roles and place you in different settings. Common reporting objectives, such as a focus on the debt to equity ratio, management bonuses, and purchase price calculations, are coupled with less common reporting objectives, such as government grant applications, debt versus equity investment decisions, and assessing the creditworthiness of a company. Why is this important? As professionals, you will be faced with daily issues and decision making. While it is not possible to provide you with this practice in actual situations, these cases will enable you to go beyond the numbers and integrate the quantitative applications you learn in your textbooks with the qualitative issues that ultimately occur in management decision making.

Ultimately, the goal of this casebook is to enhance the learning in introductory, intermediate, and advanced accounting courses by exposing the students to situations that cannot be addressed in standard financial accounting textbooks.

CONCLUSION

This chapter presents the case for cases by introducing the purpose of, and need for case analysis. Before attempting to analyze a case, students are encouraged to read the following five chapters. Chapters 2 to 4 present the fundamental concepts required to properly analyze a case in financial accounting. Specifically, the following chapters are organized as follows:

- » Chapter 2 – The Financial Reporting Landscape
- » Chapter 3 – Accounting Issues
- » Chapter 4 – The Case Approach
- » Chapter 5 – A Walk-Through Example of Case Analysis
- » Chapter 6 – What Happens after the Case Is Written: The Debrief

THE FINANCIAL REPORTING LANDSCAPE | 2

The *CICA Handbook* (Parts I and II) provides some guidance on the objective of financial reporting. Essentially, both reporting frameworks suggest that the objective of financial reporting is to "communicate information that is useful for the purpose of making resource allocation decisions." Essentially, this can be called the decision usefulness approach.

However, this general statement leaves much to be determined. For example, who are the users? What resources are being allocated? How are the decisions being made? What models are being used to make the decisions? How can decisions about management's stewardship be made? The purpose of this chapter is to help answer some of these questions.

The general definition of reporting objectives may seem concerning given that accounting estimates and policy choices are generally based on the overall reporting objective. In practice, the reporting objectives are often very specific and narrowly defined. For example, a reporting objective may be to maximize net income for some specific purpose. Alternatively, a reporting objective may be to aid in the prediction of cash flows.

The following is a discussion of some of the main users of financial statements, along with their needs. In addition, management's potential reporting objectives are explored. This chapter wraps up by discussing the constraints by which financial reporting objectives may be achieved.

USERS AND THEIR NEEDS

There are unlimited numbers of potential users and uses of financial statements. Recall the definition of relevance. Relevant information impacts a user's decision. Relevant information provides both feedback value (confirming past events) and predictive value (aiding in assessing future events).

Table 2.1 presents a brief summary of the most common users and their needs:

TABLE 2.1 – USERS AND THEIR USES OF FINANCIAL STATEMENTS	
Users	**User Needs**

Banks and other creditors	• Predictive
	  o Cash flow prediction for debt repayment.
	• Feedback
	  o Compliance with covenants (debt to equity ratio covenant, working capital covenant, etc.).

Potential equity investors	• Predictive
	  o Cash flow prediction for dividend payments.
	• Feedback
	  o Performance evaluation (time series analysis over time and cross-sectional analysis against competitors).

Current equity investors	• Predictive
	o Cash flow prediction for dividend payments.
	• Feedback
	o Assessment of management stewardship.
Governments and funding agencies	• Predictive
	o Determine whether future funds should be provided.
	• Feedback
	o Assessment of the use of funds provided (effectiveness and efficiency of funds provided).
Tax authorities	• Starting point for the assessment of taxable income.
Suppliers	• Determine creditworthiness for extending credit for supplies.
Employees	• Predictive
	o Cash flow prediction for bonuses.

PREPARERS AND THEIR REPORTING OBJECTIVES

The preparers of financial statements may have different objectives than the users of financial statements. Generally, the preparer refers to the senior management of the company, as opposed to the accounting staff.

The following is a summary of some of the major financial reporting objectives of senior management:

1. **Income tax minimization:** Management of private entities that do not have any major creditors may have a primary reporting objective to minimize income taxes. Minimizing income taxes would help maximize shareholders' wealth.

2. **Income smoothing:** Management may try to smooth net income in order to reduce the company's perceived riskiness. Smoothing net income will also help management meet performance targets year over year.

3. **Maximizing net income:** Management may try to maximize net income for various reasons. For example, management may have a bonus based on net income (e.g., 10% of net income) and thereby try to maximize their personal wealth by maximizing net income. Alternatively, management may try to maximize net income in order to show strong financial performance to maximize an IPO price.

4. **Minimizing net income:** Management may try to minimize net income for various reasons. One reason may be that the company is experiencing significant political costs. For example, large banks or oil companies may want to minimize net income in order to avoid political backlash or the potential for increased regulation/taxes. Alternatively, management may try to minimize net income in order to maximize net income in future periods. This is also known as taking a "big bath" as the books are cleaned up to allow for strong future profits. Consider management that is facing a poor year and will not earn a bonus. Management may decide to minimize net income by taking excess impairment writedowns and large contingencies in order to reduce future amortization and expenses, thereby increasing the possibility of earning future bonuses.

5. **Contract compliance:** Management may be confronted with various contracts that are tied to financial statement metrics. For example, loan covenants may restrict the ability to raise additional debt by limiting the debt to equity ratio. Working capital loans may be based on a percentage of accounts receivable and inventory. Not-for-profits that are charitable may be required to distribute a certain percentage of their net income. Government funding may require companies to incur a certain amount of wage expense.

CONSTRAINT – THE BASIS OF FINANCIAL REPORTING

It is important to keep in mind that preparers cannot meet their own needs or user needs without considering the constraints on financial reporting. In general, one of the following constraints will be present:

» Part I GAAP – International Financial Reporting Standards (IFRS): publicly accountable enterprises will be constrained by IFRS, and have no choice to adopt a different reporting framework.

» Part II GAAP – Accounting Standards for Private Enterprises (ASPE): non-publicly accountable enterprises (e.g., private corporations) can either choose ASPE or IFRS. If a framework is not prescribed by the user (e.g., the bank), then management must assess which framework will provide the most benefit considering the costs.

» Part III GAAP – Accounting Standards for Non-Profit Organizations (ASNPO): not-for-profit enterprises can choose ASNPO or IFRS. Again, if a framework is not prescribed by a funding government or contributor, then management must assess which framework will provide the most benefit considering the costs.

» Basis Other Than Generally Accepted Accounting Principles (GAAP): It is possible that financial reporting must comply with some other basis. For example, compliance with a specific contract for reporting lease revenues, or rate-regulated utilities, which have their own specific reporting standards.

HOW DO REPORTING OBJECTIVES IMPACT CASE ANALYSIS?

The reporting objective is of upmost importance to a case analysis. The reporting objective determines the overall purpose of financial reporting, which leads to an understanding of the implication of accounting issues. They often provide the motivation for *why a company reports the way they do*. In most cases, this is done while following the constraints on financial reporting (i.e., appropriately following their applicable financial reporting section). Unfortunately, history has shown us that there are times when this is not the case. What is important to remember is that reporting objectives can be used to select between alternative choices within GAAP. Management can remain ethical and still present fair financial statements if they select accounting policies and estimates that are within GAAP but meet their specific reporting objectives.

CONCLUSION

This chapter discusses the components of the financial reporting landscape. Specifically, this chapter first presents the most common users and uses of financial statement. Next, the constraints to financial reporting (e.g., IFRS, ASPE, ASNPO) were discussed. The chapter concludes by discussing why an understanding of the financial reporting landscape is important to case analysis.

The next chapter presents the issues in financial accounting by introducing the concepts of recognition, measurement, presentation, and disclosure, as they relate to financial accounting.

3 | ACCOUNTING ISSUES

Most issues can be boiled down to four simple categories:

» **Recognition** – when should something be included in the financial statements?

» **Measurement** – how should the item be measured when it is initially recognized? How should it be measured going forward?

» **Presentation** – how should the item be presented in the financial statements?

» **Disclosure** – how much detail, if any, should be included in the notes?

Your issue identification statements should normally include at least one of recognition, measurement, presentation, or disclosure as the issue.

It is also important to note that the *CICA Handbook* sections, in both IFRS and ASPE, are organized in the same categories noted above.

RECOGNITION

Recognition is the process of including an item in the financial statements of an entity. Recognition consists of the addition of the amount involved into statement totals together with a narrative description of the item (e.g., inventory, sales, etc.) in a statement.

In general, the recognition criteria under ASPE are as follows:

1. The item has an appropriate measurement basis and a reasonable estimate can be made of the amounts involved; and

2. For items involving obtaining or giving up future benefits, it is probable that such benefits will be received or given up.

Examples of a recognition issue could be as follows: (1) Should revenue be recognized in the current period or future period? (2) Should a contingent liability be recognized in the current period? (3) Should development costs be recognized as an intangible asset?

MEASUREMENT - INITIAL AND SUBSEQUENT

Measurement, or valuation, is the process of determining the amount at which an item is recognized in the financial statements. There are a number of measurement bases on which an amount can be measured; however, the two major measurements bases are:

» Historical costs: Financial statements have historically been prepared primarily using the historical cost basis of accounting whereby transactions or events are measured at the amount of cash or cash equivalents given up or received.

» Fair value: Recently, fair value measurements have become much more common whereby an item is measured at its fair value, which can be measured as the value in an open market or the value-in-use (discounted cash flows).

Measurement decisions must be made for items in two timeframes:

» Initial measurement: How should the item be measured when it is first recognized in the financial statements?

» Subsequent measurement: How should the item be measured at the end of each reporting period after it has already been recognized? For example, capital assets can be measured at either their amortized cost (net book value) or their fair value.

Examples of measurement issues are as follows: (1) How should the inventory be measured? (2) How should the asset retirement obligation be measured? (3) How should the goodwill be measured?

PRESENTATION

Presentation is the process of determining how an item should be classified in the financial statements. In general, an item can be presented as an asset, liability, equity, revenue, gain, expense, or loss.

An example of a major presentation issue is whether a complex financial instrument should be presented as either debt or equity. An additional example is whether an operating segment should be presented as discontinued operations.

DISCLOSURE

Disclosure generally focuses on two areas:

1. Providing more details on an item that has been recognized in the financial statements
2. Providing information on an item that has not met the recognition criteria and is not included in the financial statements

An example of an issue with disclosure is as follows: Should the contingent liability be disclosed in the notes?

As you can see, each accounting issue identified may require a combination of discussion, alternative generation, and recommendation that will include the four categories: recognition, measurement, presentation and disclosure. Case studies are useful in presenting issues that require you to address these, thereby giving you valuable experience.

CONCLUSION

The purpose of this chapter is to introduce the four main issues in financial accounting: recognition, measurement (initial and subsequent), presentation, and disclosure. All issues in accounting cases can essentially be boiled down into one of the four categories.

Chapter 4 presents the case approach and brings together the concepts discussed in Chapters 1 to Chapter 3.

4 | THE CASE APPROACH

In order to answer a case study satisfactorily, we must first understand the environment within which the analysis takes place. A good question to ask is as follows: Is there anything about the environment or any background information that might cause us to identify different issues, or to view the issues differently, or to respond differently?

POINTS FOR CONSIDERATION

1. **Identify the role that you are playing.**

   Usually, most cases require that you assume a role. Who are you in the case? From whose perspective will you be answering the case? As in our previous weather example, different people have differing opinions and views on things.

   If your role is that of an independent advisor (e.g., a chartered accountant hired by the shareholders), you might think differently than an employee who works for the company. As an employee, you might be concerned with keeping your job and, therefore, would want to keep your boss happy by giving her what she wants. As an outside professional, hired by the shareholders, you might focus more on keeping the shareholders happy. Keeping the boss happy and keeping the shareholders happy might not result in the same course of action.

   Consideration should also be given to ethics and legal liability. Outside consultants who offer advice might later be sued if the advice is relied on and results in a loss to the company, shareholders, or other users. Therefore, outside consultants must assess the risk of each engagement. For higher risk engagements, they might take a more conservative position and give more conservative advice.

   Many situations involve ethical dilemmas where the individual must make decisions that either will harm himself or harm others and a choice must be made. Sometimes, doing the right thing may result in personal loss. Humanize the analysis by thinking about what you would do in the situation. For instance, accruing a large loss might result in lower net income and, hence, a lower bonus for the controller. On the other hand, not accruing the loss may mislead users.

   Remember that the financial statements are a reflection of the success/failures of the company and of management in that they reveal whether management is fulfilling its stewardship function. Therefore, in preparing the statements, management might be concerned about disclosing negative items.

   TIP – Put yourself in the shoes of the person whose role you are playing. Think about how you would react in a situation and what factors would influence your decision. Would you put your own needs ahead of other users?

   TIP – Preparers of financial information may be biased and this must be considered in any analysis.

2. **Assess the financial reporting landscape.**

2.1 Identify the users of the information and the users' needs.

Who will be using the information required in the case? What will they be using it for? Also, more broadly, who will be affected by the financial reporting decisions being made and how will they be affected? This will make a difference in your analysis. Different users have different information needs and since the overall reporting objective is to provide information that is relevant to users, this user focus is critical. Again, anyone affected by the information should be considered. Chapter 2 of the case book considers different stakeholders in the financial reporting environment.

TIP – For any question that requires professional judgement, always ask two questions: (1) who wants to know? and (2) why do they need this information i.e., what decision will they use this information for? That way you may consider tailoring the information to help the users make their decisions.

TIP – Although ideally, the main objective of financial reporting is to provide information to users that is useful for decision making, this does not always happen due to personal and corporate biases.

TIP – A good analysis will always look at the impact of the decision-making on the affected parties.

2.2 Identify constraints.

Are there any factors that will limit the possibilities? Is there a legal requirement to follow IFRS? Would ASPE be a more suitable framework for reporting? Are there time constraints on obtaining information? Is all the required information available? Generally, if a company has shares or debt that are traded publicly, then there is an IFRS constraint. Private entities may choose to follow ASPE or IFRS.

TIP – If the question does not make it clear as to whether a GAAP constraint exists, then look to the main users. Normally, users would want GAAP financial statements since they are more reliable and comparable.

TIP – Acknowledging constraints up-front will help to keep you focused on the relevant analysis.

2.3 Consider the business environment and company.

Is the economy in a recession or is the real estate market in a slump? This will affect your analysis as the company might be more prone to bias if it is trying to stay afloat in a sinking environment. Looking at other companies in the industry will give some background on how other companies are faring in the current times.

TIP – The environment will give some clues as to how information might be biased.

It is important to understand what the company does. How does it earn its revenues? Which costs must be incurred to earn revenues? What are the business risks? What is the financial history of the company; i.e., have revenues been steadily increasing over time, or decreasing? What about profits? Does the company turn a profit every year? Were the results of this year predictable? What are the key ratios that are considered to be important in the industry? How does the company's ratios compare to industry norms and its own historical ratios? All this data provides a backdrop for the analysis.

TIP – Insight into the way the company operates and what is important to the company helps you understand why they might find certain financial reporting issues more sensitive than others and will help in understanding what is at stake in the decision.

2.4 Based on the above, determine the overall financial reporting objective.

This is a summation of the financial reporting landscape assessment. It helps to focus the analysis and conclude in a manner that is consistent with the environment. For instance, assume that your role is a chartered accountant and that you will be providing information to a bank so it can make a lending decision. Your tendency will be to offer conservative advice and disclose more information (especially about risks and potential losses), rather than less. Hopefully, this will reduce the risk of a potential lawsuit should the bank suffer a loss. It will also give the bank the information needed to make a decision.

This is only one position or conclusion, and you might think that there are other overriding factors that are more important.

TIP – The conclusion or recommendation is a matter of judgement and there is usually no right or wrong answer, although certain cases may lean toward a certain interpretation.

TIP – Once the financial reporting objective is outlined, try to be consistent in your recommendations where there are multiple issues. For example, if you conclude conservatively on the first issue, the other issues should also reflect the conservative approach unless you explain why.

3. Identifying the issues.

3.1 An issue is a financial reporting problem that needs resolution.

Resolution is usually not straightforward but rather is arrived at through careful analysis of relevant alternatives. In financial reporting, keep in mind that most issues will relate to how to account for something or how to present it in the financial statements. Focus on relevant issues only.

TIP – Although there might be issues that need to be addressed in other areas, such as tax or management accounting issues, try to keep focused on the financial reporting issues. Having said this, in real life, all important issues would be addressed.

TIP – For more complex issues, the issue may not be any clearer than …How do we account for the transaction?

In cases involving complex issues, the following will help to clarify how to proceed with the analysis. (1) Draw a diagram of the exchange, including all parties involved. This will illustrate the legal form. (2) Try to answer the question: "What did the company give up and what did it get?" (3) Attempt a journal entry or at least part of one. (4) Try to identify economic substance. Note that management intent often gives a key to this.

3.2 Identifying issues requires technical knowledge.

You cannot hope to spot an issue if you do not know GAAP. For instance, suppose a friend comes to you with the observation that his dog is shedding hair. He asks you if this is a problem. Is it? Unless you know something about dogs, and that particular breed, you will not be able to answer. The shedding might be perfectly normal if it happens every year and occurs in the spring. However, if this is a breed that normally does not shed hair at all, it may mean that the dog is sick. The point is that in order to spot a problem or an issue, you need to have specific knowledge in that area.

In the area of accounting, the specific knowledge you need to know is GAAP; the general principles, the available alternatives, the rules. Only then can you recognize if GAAP is not being followed, or advise a client how to account for something. Keep in mind that GAAP is not always legally required, or required by users of the financial information. In the latter case, you would be governed by providing the most useful information. This requires knowledge of what useful information is. It also helps to use common sense, as well, which is part of professional judgement.

TIP – Sometimes, if you cannot figure out the issues in the case, perhaps you need to reread the technical material assigned for that or preceding weeks. After going over the material, reread the case again.

3.3 Understand the company's business.

What does the company do? How does it earn revenues? What costs must it incur? What are the business risks? All these questions and others must be understood. It is critical that you understand the business and the environment before you can offer any advice. Therefore, spend a few minutes figuring this out. This might include drawing quick timelines of the earnings process or diagrams of the business relationships; e.g., who owns who.

TIP – If you do not understand the business, how do you ever hope to advise on how the business should be represented in the financial statements?

3.4 Issues involve choices.

Try to see if there is more than one way to look at a problem (i.e., from different perspectives). Look carefully at the preparer of the financial information (usually management) and the users of the information. Does good financial disclosure mean the same thing to management as it does to the shareholders? Often not. In the past, companies have often held the belief that the shareholders need only be told limited amounts of information. Furthermore, management might have a tendency to disclose only things that make the company and itself look good. Shareholders, on the other hand, may think that more information is better, especially information about risks and potential losses.

If you can see differing viewpoints, there is likely an issue (i.e., one has a different idea of what the best accounting or presentation is than the other).

TIP – Look at the people in the case. Honestly attempt to put yourself in their shoes. This may sound silly, but you will find it to be one of the keys to successful case analysis. How would you feel about what is going on? How would you react? What would be important to you? After all, it could be you in the situation. If you see that the parties in the case may see things differently (remember the weather example) then there is a potential issue.

TIP – Keep your issue and alternatives basic. Most issues can be boiled down to a few simple categories:

» Recognition - Should I recognize something on the financial statements or not?

» Measurement/valuation - What amount should I recognize? How do I measure the transaction?

» Presentation/disclosure/classification - Where should the item be shown, and in how much detail, if any?

3.5 Some issues may be more important or less important.

It is essential to rank the issues and tackle the more important ones first.

An issue is generally more important if it involves large amounts, especially those that affect the calculation of net income (or some other sensitive number on the financial statements) or a sensitive financial ratio. This is a numeric application of the concept of materiality. Which numbers/ratios are more sensitive? That depends on the situation. Net income is almost always sensitive. That is, if net income changes by a material amount, it will usually affect user decisions. Other numbers/ratios are determined to be sensitive because the users will focus on them in that particular scenario. For instance, if the company has a loan, and part of the terms of the loan are that the working capital ratio be at least 1:1, then current assets and current liabilities would be sensitive numbers and anything that affects those numbers would potentially be an issue (e.g., classification of items between current and long term).

TIP – Rank issues and deal with the most relevant and material issues first.

TIP – Look for sensitive numbers or ratios in the case. If you see a potential reporting issue that affects these numbers, then you likely have an issue.

4.   Analyze the issues.

Once identified, the issues must be analyzed in a meaningful way such that the conclusions/recommendations are relevant, especially within the context of the environment.

4.1 Develop relevant alternatives.

Only relevant alternatives should be looked at in your analysis. This is perhaps the most common mistake. Most students think in terms of right and wrong, black and white. When students are first introduced to case analysis, many are unable to look at an issue from more than one perspective. The tendency is to skip the assessment of the environment, skip the analysis, and give the "right" answer. Resist this urge!

Once enlightened that there may be more than one way of looking at the question, students often go to the other extreme and look for alternatives or different perspectives, even where none exist. Eventually a happy medium is reached and they analyze only relevant alternatives. Be patient. Although to some of you, case analysis is intuitive, for many, this skill must be developed and it takes time.

What is a relevant alternative? A relevant alternative is one that is applicable given the reporting environment. It must make sense. There is no use suggesting an alternative if it is completely impractical or if it is impossible given the constraints. For instance, if GAAP is a constraint, do not suggest a non-GAAP approach as an alternative. It is not an option.

TIP – In order to train students to look at both sides of an issue or alternatives, we encourage them to start out an analysis with the words "on the one hand" and include "on the other hand" at some point later in the analysis. Otherwise the temptation to only look at one alternative is too great.

TIP – Looking at the issue from different perspectives is the key to identifying alternatives. Consideration should be given to the parties in the case. Imagine yourself as one party, and then as another. Would they see things differently?

TIP – Relevance is a function of the environment. Continue to ask yourself if your comment is pertinent to this specific case.

4.2 Consider qualitative and quantitative analysis.

Some cases lend themselves more to qualitative analysis, or quantitative analysis, or both. You must be sensitive to this. Cases with numbers in them may lend themselves more to quantitative analysis. However, just because numbers are provided does not automatically mean that the information is relevant. Any calculations that you do must contribute something to the overall analysis. Do not just perform numerical analysis blindly.

Whether to present numbers in the case itself is an interesting dilemma that illustrates one of the shortcomings of cases studies. In real life, you will always have numbers available to you—tons of them! You must choose which ones are relevant and then do the appropriate calculations to support or refute your analysis. You may choose to do many supporting calculations, or none at all. But usually, at a minimum, you should look at the numerical impact of the proposed alternative on net income and other sensitive financial statement numbers/ratios.

With cases, however, the authors of the cases cannot include all the numerical information that you would have access to in real life. They must choose selective information to include in the case and, by doing so, it might be construed that they are making a statement that these numbers should be considered in the analysis. However, keep in mind that the numbers could be a "red herring" and also that time wasted on irrelevant number crunching is time that could have been spent on productive, qualitative analysis.

TIP – Just because numbers are included in the case does not mean that you should overemphasize quantitative analysis.

TIP – Keep focused by asking yourself the following questions: Will these calculations support or refute my analysis? Will they help in making the final decision? Will they provide additional information to help determine what the problem is and to arrive at a solution?

TIP – Try to strike a good balance between qualitative and quantitative analysis, assuming that quantitative analysis is warranted in the situation.

TIP – Remember that it is easy to get bogged down in numbers. If you are doing a case on a test, allocate some time for numerical analysis and stick to it closely. If you are not finished after the allotted time, then stop anyway, even if you know that the calculations are incorrect. In a test situation, it has been our experience that it is easier to go astray on quantitative analysis than qualitative. Also, once you go off on the wrong track, it's easy to get entrenched and waste valuable time. You become unable to pull yourself away from the calculations. Therefore, the best solution is to allot time and stick to it, no matter what!

TIP – Often some key numerical analysis opens up a deeper or more complex issue and might help explain certain things in the case. Issues may be disguised such that unless certain revealing analysis is performed, the issues will not reveal themselves and the resulting analysis may be shallow and without substance. To obtain a better answer, you may be expected to delve into the deeper level of analysis. This is difficult and comes with practice.

TIP – In most cases, a minimal quantitative analysis would include showing the impact of an alternative on key financial statement numbers and ratios.

While developing alternatives, and providing a balance of quantitative and qualitative analysis, the following additional points should be considered.

4.3 Keep your analysis case-specific.

Any discussions should make reference to the particulars of the case. Do not just regurgitate GAAP!

TIP – Try to start your sentences with the following "in this case….". This will force you to focus on case specific analysis.

TIP – Reread your analysis every couple of paragraphs. If any given paragraph or sentence does not have case-specific facts in it, reconsider your wording. One test to determine this is whether you could use that sentence/paragraph in another case analysis with the same issues ... without altering a word! If so, then you know that the sentence is generic and not specific to the case. Sometimes these types of sentences are unavoidable in that they are useful to set up a discussion. However, try to limit these to a minimum.

4.4 Incorporate technical knowledge.

You must indicate that you know the technical material (i.e., GAAP) by making reference to it in the analysis. This does not mean that you should be quoting reference sources or the *CICA Handbook* by section number; however, you should be making specific reference to the key underlying principles.

TIP – Incorporate references to GAAP in your analysis; e.g., revenues should be recognized when the goods are shipped since this represents the point at which the risks and rewards of ownership have passed. This illustrates your knowledge of GAAP in a case context.

4.5 Do not blindly regurgitate case facts.

Having discussed the importance of including case facts in the analysis, we will now stress the importance of not blindly regurgitating them, otherwise known as "dumping." The idea is to work selective case facts into your analysis, as opposed to just repeating case facts as a kind of introduction to the analysis.

There may only be a subtle distinction there but the former results in a much tighter, more focused analysis. For instance, in a revenue recognition question, instead of taking up space by regurgitating the company's present policy word for word, you might say the following: "At present, the company's policy of recognizing revenue before shipment is a very aggressive policy since the risks and rewards of ownership generally do not pass until goods are shipped." Please note how we have worked several items into that sentence. We have incorporated case-specific facts, displayed knowledge of GAAP, and made a judgemental statement or gave an opinion about the policy.

TIP – Try to make each sentence insightful, combining case facts and knowledge of GAAP with your analysis.

5. Provide recommendations/conclusions.

Recommendations should follow analysis of each individual issue. They should also be consistent with the overall financial reporting objective. For instance, if your role is the external chartered accountant providing information about a company to a bank, you may decide to offer advice that is conservative. Therefore, you would conclude, given alternatives, that revenues should be recognized later and costs recognized earlier.

CONCLUSION

In summary, this chapter shows how the first step is to understand your role and the financial reporting landscape. Next, you can properly identify, analyze, and make recommendations to the reporting issues. The following approach is suggested:

1. *Issue:* Identify the reporting issue and state why it is an issue.
2. *Implication:* Determine the implications of the issue for the users of the financial statements. It is good to use both quantitative and qualitative analysis to fully understand the implication. Be specific, and make use of case facts.
3. *Alternatives:* Generate viable and reasonable alternatives that are within GAAP. It is usually not useful to generate alternatives outside of GAAP because they are not available options. The case facts will help you generate alternatives.
4. *Recommendation:* Based on the user needs, make a viable recommendation to address the reporting issue. Be specific.

Your recommendation must flow logically from your analysis. Because the users' needs form the major criteria to evaluate the alternatives, they also provide the support for your recommendation. The case approach is summarized in Figure 4.1.

Figure 4.1 – The Case Writing Framework

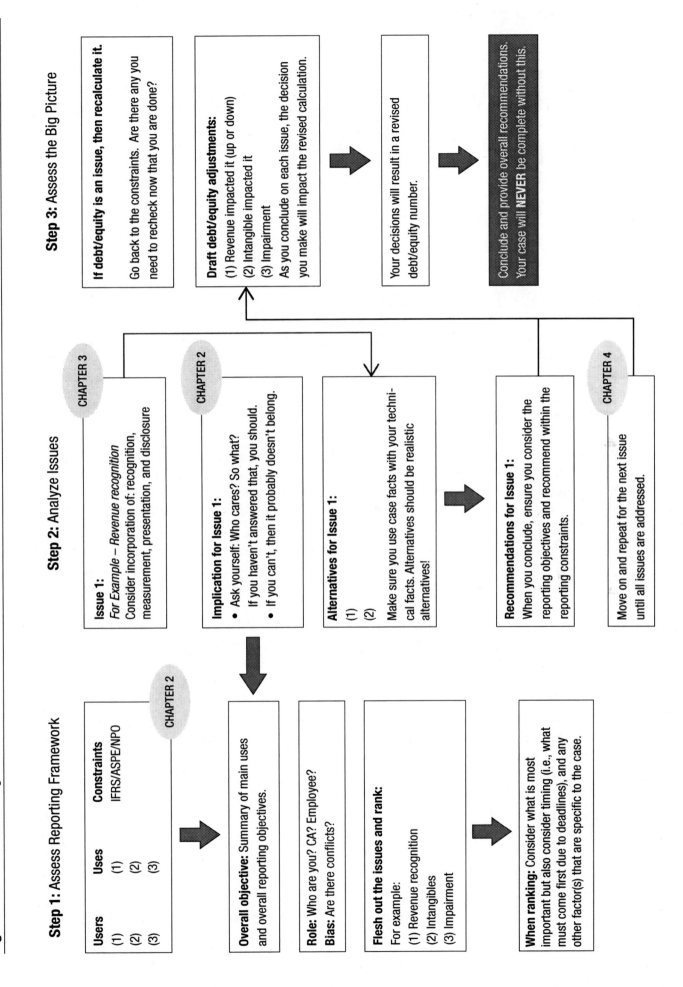

5 | A WALK-THROUGH EXAMPLE OF CASE ANALYSIS

THE CASE – THE CHALLENGE

Let's look at the sample case of Bronwyn Boats. This case was chosen as it is of moderate length and difficulty so as not to either complicate or oversimplify case analysis. Read the case through to get a feel for what it involves.

BRONWYN BOATS LIMITED

Bronwyn Boats Limited (BB) has been in the yacht-building business for the last 20 years. Basically, Bob, the owner, builds high-priced, customized boats that take on average two years to build. His reputation is such that Bob has never had to advertise. Rather, potential customers contact him, having heard of Bob through word of mouth. Bob has never had a dissatisfied customer and prides himself on high quality workmanship.

In the past, Bob has always done his accounting on a cash basis; that is, expenses and revenues were recorded when cash changed hands. Also, Bob has never had to externally finance the boat construction since the business has always retained sufficient cash to internally finance the next boat to be built. Last year, however, Bob stripped all the excess cash from the business when he purchased his dream "cottage," a mansion on Lake Muskoka.

As a result of this, Bob found that he did not have enough cash to finance the construction of the next boat to be built and had to go to the bank for a loan. The bank told Bob that it would be happy to lend him the money as long as it could take his cottage as security. Also, the bank informed Bob that it wanted ASPE financial statements (accrual-based) and required that the debt to equity ratio not exceed 2:1. Bob reluctantly agreed to pledge his cottage as security and promised ASPE financial statements.

Bob was not very worried about repayment of the loan since he had just received some very large orders. As a matter of fact, he had to hire several assistants to help him get the boats built on time. Bob also rented an additional barn in the local area so that he could work on the boats at the same time. The barn that he normally rented was not big enough to house all the boats. Bob also hired a secretary to help keep up with the filing and the paperwork.

For the first time, Bob had a customer who placed a large order and signed a written contract. Bob felt that the contract was required due to the size of the boat and the expensive special materials that had to be ordered. All other agreements were verbal. The key terms of the contract are:

- » Purchase price: $500,000
- » Delivery date: June 30, 2016 (approximately two years)
- » Down payment: $50,000 upfront; $100,000 on June 30, 2015; rest on delivery

»	Insurance:	Bob must cover the cost of insurance while the boat is being built. (Bob just included this as a cost of building the boat and passed it on to the customer anyway).
»	Acceptance:	Purchaser can test the boat prior to making the last payment made. Purchaser can refuse to accept it if not satisfied (within reason).

At December 31, 2013, Bob had completed about two thirds of the work on the boat and was ahead of schedule. However, on the other boats, work was behind and they were only 10% complete.

Bob has come to you, his friend, a professional accountant, for advice on how to prepare the financial statements.

CASES VERSUS QUESTIONS

This case could have been a straightforward question on revenue recognition. It could have simply asked the following question and not bothered to create a scenario: When should revenues be recognized?

The above type of directed question asks for regurgitation of memorized facts (i.e., revenues should be recognized when the risks and rewards of ownership have passed from the seller to the buyer and when measurability and collectibility are reasonably assured).

Instead, the question is complicated by disguising it within a scenario or case. Firstly, revenue recognition must be identified as an issue and once identified, the question then becomes when should revenues be recognized in this scenario? The memorized knowledge must be applied to the facts of this specific situation. You must recall revenue recognition principles and ask yourself the following questions:

» What are the risks and rewards of owning/building a boat?

» When do they pass to the buyer?

» When is the earnings process substantially complete?

» Can revenues and costs be measured?

» What are the costs associated with these revenues?

» Are there any collectibility problems?

The trick here is to identify the issue and then to apply knowledge instead of merely regurgitating memorized information. That is the true test of whether you have absorbed and understood the material.

TACKLING THE CASE

For most students, the initial challenge is being able to identify the issues. Then, once that is mastered, the challenge becomes how to analyze the issues in a meaningful way that will result in a reasonable recommendation or conclusion.

There are many different ways to approach case analysis, but most have a similar underlying structure that may be adapted in different situations. The material that follows is one method of case analysis.

APPLYING THE CASE ANALYSIS

Assessment of the Financial Reporting Landscape

With Bronwyn Boats Limited (BB), who are you? From what perspective will you be discussing the case? What is the reporting environment? Are there any constraints that will limit your analysis? These items will all affect your answer.

<u>Your Role</u>

It would appear that you are a professional accountant and friend of Bob's. How will that affect your analysis? As a professional accountant, you would want to ensure that your advice is professional, unbiased, and sound. However, you would want to make sure that any advice you gave would not leave you open to future lawsuits (e.g., if someone like the bank relied on the financial statements and suffered losses).

<u>Identify the Users and User Needs</u>

Who are the main users of the financial statements? What decisions (uses) will the users be making? An understanding of the users and their needs will help you further identify issues, and to rank the importance of issues (e.g., some issues will impact users decisions more so than other issues).

In this case, it appears that the bank is going to be one of the main users. What does the bank want? Does that matter? Again, yes it does. The bank is going to be using the financial statements to assess financial performance of BB and compliance with the debt to equity ratio. Therefore, knowing that the bank would rely on the statements in order to advance funds to Bob, you would likely be conservative in your advice to Bob.

In addition, Bob will be using the financial statements in order to determine BB's compliance with the loan agreement. What does Bob want? Does this matter? Of course it matters. He is the one who has hired you to do the job and is a friend of yours. Bob does not appear to know what he wants; however, he likely wants the statements to look good so that the bank will give him the financing he needs.

Would the fact that you are friends with Bob affect your answer? Perhaps. You might be tempted to give Bob the answer that he wants although this would be weighed against your professional responsibility and the bank's reliance on the statements. What would you do in this situation?

Remember that, ideally, the objective of financial reporting is to provide information that is useful to users. The bank is the key user of these financial statements. They will use the statements to determine whether to lend money to Bob. They will, therefore, want reliable information using the accrual basis of accounting, since net income is presumably the best indicator of future profits and the ability of the company to pay off the loans.

In conclusion, you will likely be conservative in any advice given to Bob (assuming that you have decided as a professional not to let your friendship influence the advice given).

<u>Constraints</u>

Can you make any accounting recommendation that will maximize the debt to equity ratio? Are there any constraints on how the statements will have to be presented? Are the statements constrained by the recommendation of IFRS (Part I GAAP), ASPE (Part II GAAP), ASNPO (Part III GAAP), or some other reporting framework?

In this case, ASPE will be a constraint since the bank will want reliable information. Since ASPE is a constraint, you will have to follow the accrual basis of accounting.

Identifying the Issues

The overall issue is how to prepare the financial statements since this is the first time they will be presented on an accrual basis. Remember to keep focused on financial reporting issues.

Bob has a simple operation. He generates revenues by building boats and incurs costs in the process. He obtains the contracts up-front, and then builds each boat according to the qualifications specified in the contracts. A key business risk is that customers can refuse the boat at the end if they are not satisfied. However, Bob has never had any problems.

Recall that accounting issues can be boiled down into four groups: recognition issues, measurement issues, presentation issues, and disclosure issues. Therefore, the issues here would appear to be fairly straightforward:

1. When to <u>recognize</u> revenues, and
2. When to <u>recognize</u> the costs associated with the revenues as expenses.

Why are these issues? Firstly, there appears to be some choice as to when revenues could be recognized. The earnings process is not a traditional one whereby goods are produced, sold, and then shipped. Here goods are sold first, then paid for, produced, and finally delivered. Also, there is the question of whether costs can be deferred or whether they should be recognized immediately since it is not clear which costs relate directly to the revenue-generating activity.

The preceding paragraph requires knowledge of ASPE/IFRS. If it is not clear to you, then read the chapter in your accounting textbook on revenue recognition, or better yet, refer to the *CICA Handbook* section.

Assess the Implications of the Issues

How do the accounting issues impact the financial statement users? For example, does the period that revenue is recognized impact the users? How about the expense recognition? If the issue identified has no implication, it is most likely not an issue!

In this situation, earlier recognition of revenue will positively impact the debt to equity ratio.

Analyzing the Issues

The analysis of issues requires the development of reasonable alternatives that are within the confines of the identified constraints (ASPE, IFRS, etc.).

Revenue Recognition

Usually for revenue recognition questions, it is wise to go over the earnings process. Draw a timeline depicting the process. This helps to identify alternative points where revenues may be recognized. Keep in mind that Bob likely wants to recognize revenues earlier (more aggressive treatment) in order to make the statements look better (benefits the debt to equity ratio). Also, remember that you would rather wait to recognize revenues since you are adopting a more conservative stance. Since ASPE is fairly flexible, there is some judgement in determining when the revenues may be recognized and there will be a more aggressive and a more conservative position.

You will likely present both to Bob since he will want to see the more aggressive stance and since you know that you will recommend the more conservative one. Alternatives that require waiting until cash is collected are not really relevant here since no information has been given to indicate that there are collection problems.

Make sure that your discussion is case-specific and try to incorporate knowledge of ASPE. For revenue recognition, the following concepts should be worked into the solution:

» Risks and rewards of ownership
» Critical event
» Earnings process
» Costs/revenues measurable
» Revenues reasonably collectible.

Ensure that the recommendation is consistent with the overview. For instance, in this case, earlier recognition is justifiable, but probably not as early as Bob would like. Therefore, the recommendation will be to conclude on the conservative side.

Costs

The key issue is whether the costs should be expensed immediately or deferred or treated as inventory costs to be matched to revenue when recognized. Deferral of costs will presumably help maximize net income, and therefore, positively impact the debt to equity ratio. Key technical knowledge to be worked into the answer is as follows:

» Matching principle-costs with revenues

» Direct costs versus indirect costs

» Inventoriable costs versus period costs.

Again, keep the discussion case-specific by making reference to the facts of the case whenever possible.

The recommendation will depend on the conclusion for revenue recognition since the costs must be matched with the revenues. This is not so much of an issue if the revenues are recognized bit by bit, as the boats are completed, since all costs will be recognized in the period incurred anyway along with a corresponding portion of revenues. However, if the conclusion is to wait until the boats are delivered, this would be a bigger issue since costs that vary directly with the production could be deferred.

For both costs and revenues, the answer given is only one suggested solution. Numerous others would also be acceptable, including ones with different financial reporting objectives, different alternatives, and different conclusions. That is the beauty of case analysis. As long as the answer makes sense and the position taken is defensible within the context of the case, the answer is acceptable. Work toward a defensible position!

SUGGESTED SOLUTION

Assessing the Financial Reporting Landscape

User Analysis

Users	Objectives	Constraints
Bob	Performance evaluation / obtain bank loan	ASPE
The bank	Evaluation loan repayment / covenant compliance	ASPE
CRA	Tax determination purpose	ITA

The main user of these financial statements will be the banker who will provide the financing to Bob. The banker will look for the ability to repay the loan and a successful business. Bob will want to maximize revenues and profits. ASPE is a requirement since the bank has requested it. Bob must switch from cash-based to accrual accounting.

As a professional, you are aware that the statements will be used by the bank to make a decision as to whether a loan should be granted and, therefore, if there is exposure. If the statements are overly aggressive and make the business look better than it really is, there is the risk that the bank will rely on the information and later suffer a loss if Bob is unable to pay. If this is the case, there is the potential for the bank to sue you.

Therefore, although you would like to help Bob get the loan, you must consider your professional obligations. Any advice that you give will be conservative, emphasizing full disclosure such that the bank has the information that it needs.

BRONWYN BOATS LIMITED: REPORT TO BB MANAGEMENT REGARDING THE FINANCIAL ACCOUNTING ISSUES

Revenue Recognition

Issue: When should revenue be recognized?

Implication: The timing of revenue *recognition* will impact the debt to equity ratio, and the financial performance of BB. Early recognition will be more favourable.

Analysis and Alternatives

In order to determine when the earnings process is substantially complete (critical event) and when the risks and rewards of ownership pass, the earnings process must first be identified as follows:

- » Agreement/contract signed/down payment.
- » Supplies purchased.
- » Construction.
- » Deposits.
- » Boat completed.
- » Delivery.
- » Purchaser tries out boat to see if satisfied.
- » Final payment.

Alternative 1 - Recognize Revenues Earlier

- » Earlier recognition would be supported by the following:
  - The agreement is made up-front (i.e., the boat is pre-sold).
  - Some cash is received up-front as evidence of the contract.
  - Bob has never had a dissatisfied customer.
  - Bob is very experienced and is capable of finishing the boat once a customer is found.
- » Therefore, we might conclude that the signing of the initial agreement is really the critical event in the earnings process. At this point, revenues are measurable, being agreed to, and costs are estimable, given that Bob has been in business a long time and knows what it will cost. Many of the boats use special materials, which Bob appears to order up-front anyway.
- » There is no information that would indicate collectibility is not reasonably assured and it appears as though Bob has always been able to collect in the past.

Alternative 2 - Recognize Later

- » On the other hand, the following would support later recognition:
  - Purchaser has the right to not purchase the boat if not satisfied (really, the contract is just conditional).
  - Bob insures the boat up to this point, indicating that he still has the risks and rewards of ownership.
  - The customer does not really indicate acceptance until the final payment.
- » Measurement is not necessarily estimable since the sales price may change if Bob has to alter the original plan for the boat or the purchaser is not satisfied. Costs may also not be estimable since each boat is different and Bob will not know what the price of materials is or their availability until he actually purchases them.

Alternative 3 - Recognize Revenues as the Boats Are Constructed

» This is more like a continuous earnings process since the earnings process is made up of many significant events.

- • It makes sense to recognize revenues before delivery due to the binding contracts and Bob's past reputation.

- • A percentage of revenues and profits could be recognized as costs are incurred.

- • Total costs are estimable since Bob has had a great deal of experience.

» In this case, Bob would prefer earlier recognition to make the financial statements look better, especially since the bulk of the boats under construction are only 10% completed.

» The bank might not be so concerned that revenues are recognized later if they can see the contracts in order to assess cash flows. The problem is that most of the agreements are verbal and, therefore, the bank will not be able to verify them.

<u>Recommendation</u>

Given all of the above, it would seem more desirable to recognize the revenues earlier rather than later. Although this may be less conservative, it is justifiable due to Bob's track record (he has been in the business 20 years and has never had a dissatisfied customer). Likely, revenues will be recognized bit by bit based on percentage complete, since full recognition prior to the boat being built might be considered to be too aggressive. There is still uncertainty as to whether Bob will indeed finish the boat and that the customer will be satisfied.

Full note disclosure of the revenue recognition policy will be made so that the bank is aware of its impact.

Costs

<u>Issue:</u> When should costs be *recognized* as an expense?

<u>Implication:</u> The timing of expense *recognition* will impact the debt to equity ratio, and the financial performance of BB. Later recognition will be more favourable.

<u>Analysis</u>

Bob must decide which costs are period costs, which are deferrable, and which are inventoriable. If the costs are inventoriable, they will be recognized when the revenue is recognized, which is more desirable than showing them as period costs, especially in years with little or no revenues.

The following costs would clearly be inventoriable since they were incurred directly in the production of the boats: payroll for assistants working on the boats, and materials used for the boats.

There are other costs that may be inventoriable. To back up a bit, the boats would be considered inventory and the *CICA Handbook* states that inventory should be costed using absorption costing, which includes an applicable share of overhead. Although the latter is not clearly defined, Bob could easily consider capitalizing overhead costs that vary with production, such as rent and presumably heat, light, and power for the barn. If Bob was not constructing the boats, he would not incur these costs. Therefore, there is a direct relationship.

Other costs, such as the secretary's salary, are more clearly period costs and do not relate even indirectly to the construction of these specific boats.

<u>Recommendations</u>

In conclusion, it would be in Bob's best interest to treat any costs that vary with construction, such as direct labour, materials, and variable overhead (like the incremental rent on the barn), as inventoriable costs. These costs would be recognized on the income statement when revenues are recognized under the matching concept.

Earlier revenue recognition would require **estimation of some of these costs**, especially if the 10% complete boats were recognized as sales. This might pose some estimation problems. Recognition of revenues, bit by bit based on percentage complete, makes this a non-issue since the percentage of revenues recognized would only be based on actual costs incurred to date (as a percentage of total estimated costs).

Other Issues

» Regardless of when the revenues are recognized, Bob should consider providing the bank with information on the sales orders taken, as this will help the bank assess future cash flow.

CONCLUSION

This chapter walked you through a typical case and how you should analyze it after you write your answer. The next chapter details what happens after the case is written.

The case analysis is adapted from "The Case Primer" accompanying Kieso, Weygandt, Warfield, Young and Wiecek: *Intermediate Accounting*, Ninth Canadian Edition (Toronto, ON: John Wiley & Sons Canada, Ltd., 2010).

6 | WHAT HAPPENS AFTER THE CASE IS WRITTEN: THE DEBRIEF

WHAT'S A DEBRIEF AND WHY DO IT?

Any student who has gone through the accounting professional designation process will tell you that debriefing the cases that you have written is just as important as writing the case to begin with. Why? Well let's focus away from cases and think about how we learn accounting to begin with (or at least how we should be learning accounting!). We begin with the fundamental accounting concepts, such as reading about what the accounting equation is all about, what journal entries are, and what debits and credits are. We then generally complete some technical questions in the area, come back to class, and check our answers against the suggested answers. Why does this generally result in a better learning experience? When you check your answers against the suggested solutions, you find out where you went wrong. If you are really doing this the right way, you'll then go back and find out why you went wrong. By doing this, you are more likely to do the question better the next time.

Debriefing your cases after you have written them is just as important. In some ways, debriefing is even more important for cases than for problems. Recall that cases are not just about the numbers. The calculations are just one component of the case. You need to be able to identify the issues, generate and discuss alternatives, and provide recommendations.

So what is debriefing? Consider an elite sports athlete. They train hard physically during the off season, and before games they'll study the tapes of opposing teams to try to get tips about how best to approach the upcoming game. They prepare beforehand so that when it comes to game time, they give themselves the best opportunity to perform well. Now, what do they do after the game? Well, the weekend athlete is more apt to shower and move on with their day. But the athlete who wants to be better will analyze their performance. They'll reflect on what they did well and what they could have improved upon. They'll reflect on the feedback given to them by their coaches: Could they have run faster? Was their accuracy off? In summary, they'll debrief their performance so that they can learn about what they did well and what they didn't do well so that next time, they'll hopefully be better. That's what we do when we debrief a case. Writing a case is only half the learning experience. The other half is learning about what we did right and where we can improve so that the next time we write a case, we can do a little better. Learning to do a good job at debriefing will improve your case writing over time.

DEBRIEFING A CASE

Debriefing can be performed in different ways by different individuals. Ideally, you should develop your own approach to debriefing that is suited to your unique learning style.

However, there are some common elements to debriefing a case. Debriefing is not merely reading the solution and re-writing your response. Although these could be considered components of debriefing, they are very of little use in isolation. Rather, debriefing should be a much more proactive and reflective process, which includes:

» Understanding the main issues in the case, and where in the case the concepts are that give rise to these issues

» Evaluating your performance to determine what was done well and what was done poorly

» Determining actions to correct the identified weaknesses with your case writing skills

Although there is no single approach or standard methodology to debriefing a case, we suggest the following as a possible approach:

1. Summarize your feelings about the case.

2. Read the solution and teaching notes.

3. Compare your response against the solution and identify any deficiencies.

   (a) Determine if the deficiencies are related to case writing skills (e.g., reading, issue identification, ranking).

   (b) Determine if the deficiencies are related to technical skills (e.g., lack of GAAP or GAAS knowledge, etc.).

4. Re-write and edit your response (e.g., using track changes) so that it is sufficient to meet the expectations.

5. Prepare and update your list of technical weaknesses and required corrective actions.

Your correct actions should be a function of the weakness identified. For example, consider the following:

» Did not understand an issue?

   • This could be a technical issue if you lack the technical knowledge required to fully understand the issue in the case.

» Did not see an issue?

   • This could suggest that the weakness is with your reading skills. Go back and try to identify what words in the case are the triggers for the issue.

» Saw an issue but did not address it?

   • This could be the result of various weaknesses. It could be an issue with ranking and time management. Try to develop and stick to a time budget. In addition, it could be a technical issue in that you did not have the technical knowledge to adequately deal with the issue.

» Identified and addressed, but incorrectly?

   • This is more than likely a technical issue. Consider reviewing the technical material in your textbook of the *CICA Handbook*.

As a general rule of thumb, the debriefing process should take between one to two times the writing time of the case.

Experiment with a debriefing system that works for you but try to be consistent with it. Remember that the cases are often a prelude to the examinations. Consider creating an electronic list that tracks the issues and technical questions that you are exposed to, and an honest assessment of how you did. This list can then be used as your starting point for your final examination preparation.

CONCLUSION

Good case writing takes practice and like anything you practise, you get better when you sit back and assess what you did. If you spend the time to determine where you had problems, not only will your case writing skills improve, but you will also find that your overall examination writing skills will improve.

Section 2: Introductory Cases

Barrie Trucking Company

Barrie Trucking Company (BTC) was privately incorporated in 1983 and services the Greater Toronto Area and the Highway 11 corridor in Ontario. BTC is in the "less than load" business, making its money by filling the trucks with several smaller loads and delivering them to and from Toronto.

Recently, the financial controller for BTC retired, leaving the owner, Klaus Bauer, looking for a new one. After several months of interviews, Klaus made an offer to you for the position and with a hefty pay raise and substantial benefits, you accepted. This is your first week on the job, it is now December 31, and you need to make all of the property, plant, and equipment journal entries today that haven't been done as of yet. BTC's year end is December 31.

The following events require your attention:

» On July 1, BTC purchased land south of Toronto that has the potential to be another loading terminal. In addition to the land, the purchase also included two transport trailers and one cube van. The total purchase price was $880,000 and was paid half in cash and the balance as a five-year loan. The loan carries an 8% interest rate with equal annual principal payments (every July 1). Interest is also paid annually on July 1. Appraisers have valued the land at $1 million, the two transport trailers at $160,000 each, and the cube van at $90,000. Although the transaction has taken place and possession has transferred, no entry has been made. The expected useful life of the trailers and the van are estimated at six years each. BTC amortizes its trailers on a straight-line basis. Residual value is estimated at $3,000 for each trailer and zero for the van.

» On August 1, BTC sold one of its buildings in Northern Ontario for $220,000. The building originally cost BTC $180,000 and had accumulated amortization of $90,000 at the time of the sale. Amortization of $6,000 that had accumulated up to August 1 had not been recorded in the books. The proceeds were received in cash.

» On January 1, the previous controller determined that trucks with a cost of $550,000 and accumulated amortization of $110,000 would actually have an estimated useful life of nine more years with no residual. The previous estimated useful life had been 10 years, with two years having already passed (so the useful life of nine years is from January 1 and beyond).

» A customer list from ABC transport was purchased by BTC on September 1 for $50,000 cash. It is expected that the list will generate revenues for the next four years.

» BTC has internally developed a strong customer list of its own. The owner, Klaus, has stated that this list is worth about $150,000 if sold.

» A warehouse terminal and land in the Muskokas was purchased on November 1 for $350,000 cash. The land is valued at $250,000 and the terminal at $100,000. BTC amortizes terminals at 8% per year using the declining balance method.

» BTC has an administrative building just west of Ottawa that is recorded on its books at $800,000. The building was purchased five years ago and has been amortized over 20 years. On December 31, it was determined that there was a major soil issue around the building, which will make it difficult to sell. It is estimated that the building's fair value and value in use is now 50% of its original cost, with an estimated $10,000 in costs to sell.

Additional information:

>> BTC records its amortization to the nearest month. In other words, an asset purchased October 1 would have its amortization prorated (3/12ths).

>> No entries have been made to reflect any of the transactions above.

Required

Prepare journal entries, with supporting documentation, for the issues above. State any assumptions that you make.

Credit Decisions
and the Balance Sheet

You just started your new position as a junior credit analyst with a large Canadian bank. For your first assignment, you have been asked to review the balance sheets of Design Your Sign Inc. and Info Tech Systems. Both companies have applied for a $100,000 small business loan. However, given current credit conditions, only one company will be awarded the loan.

You manager has given you a brief background on the operations of each company and the purpose of the loan:

» Design Your Sign Inc.: The company designs and prints corporate signs, business cards, letterheads, etc. Although the company is relatively new, it has been able to secure deals with various local businesses. The loan will be used to purchase additional equipment to expand operations.

» Info Tech Systems: The company has been researching and developing a new accounting software package for small business users. The new software has significant improvements over current packages in terms of functionality and the user interface. The company has already made sales to local businesses. The loan will be used to continue to develop the software, and to begin full scale marketing.

Your manager has provided you with a copy of each company's balance sheet (Exhibit I). Although she is aware that you do not have any other financial statement information at this time, your manager has asked you to prepare a brief report that outlines your key insights from an analysis of the balance sheets. In your report, you should consider the potential strengths and weaknesses (risks) of both companies.

Required

Prepare the report.

EXHIBIT I – BALANCE SHEETS

DESIGN YOUR SIGN INC.
BALANCE SHEET
AS AT DECEMBER 31, 2014

Current assets			**Current liabilities**		
Accounts receivable	$22,750		Bank overdraft		$22,575
Inventory	35,000		Accounts payable		17,750
	57,750				40,325
			Non-current liabilities		
Non-current assets			Long-term debt		82,750
Land and buildings	125,750				
Intangible assets	15,000		**Shareholders' equity**		
	140,750		Share capital		25,000
Total assets	$198,500		Retained Earnings		50,425
					75,425
					$198,500

INFO TECH SYSTEMS LTD.
BALANCE SHEET
AS AT DECEMBER 31, 2014

Current assets			**Current liabilities**		
Cash	$12,750		Accounts payable		$15,575
Accounts receivable	55,750		Accrued liabilities		7,000
	$68,500				$22,575
			Non-current liabilities		
Non-current assets			Long-term debt		152,750
Property and equipment	$12,750				
Intangible assets	98,950		**Shareholders' equity**		
	111,700		Share capital		5,000
Total assets	$180,200		Retained Earnings		(125)
					4,875
					$180,200

Equity Investments and the Income Statement

You have just accepted a position as an equity analyst with a small private equity firm. Your firm's investment mandate is to invest only in businesses that operate in the City of Moncton.

You have been assigned to the micro-business unit of the private equity firm for the first year of employment. The micro-business unit makes buy and sell recommendations on very small businesses (revenues under $500,000). Your first assignment is to perform a comparative analysis of the profitability of two potential equity investments. Your manager has given you a brief background on the operations of the two companies:

» Touch Plus Ltd. (TPL): TPL just completed the research and development of a new touch screen technology for mobile devices. The new technology is both more sensitive and durable than the current technology on the market. Touch Plus Ltd. has just signed a major contract to provide the screens to a major producer of mobile devices. The founder of the business would like to sell a 50% interest in the business for $100,000 in order to finance further expansion of operations.

» Wash Your Car Inc. (WYCI): WYCI is a self-service, coin-operated car wash located in a busy residential area. The company provides all of the services of a typical car wash, including soap, wax, and vacuum. WYCI has been long established and enjoys the loyalty and repeat business of many local residents. The current owner is getting up in age and would like to sell his 100% ownership interest in the business for $100,000 to pursue retirement. The current year's income statement is consistent with prior years.

One of the first tasks in the analysis of the potential equity acquisition is an assessment of each company's current and future profitability. Your manager has provided you with copies of each company's income statement (Exhibit I). Next, you are to calculate the expected return on investment for each company. You have been asked to discuss any other issues that you believe are relevant to the investment decision.

Required

Prepare the report.

EXHIBIT I – INCOME STATEMENTS

TOUCH PLUS LTD.
INCOME STATEMENT
FOR THE YEAR ENDED DECEMBER 31, 2014

Revenue	$ 375,000
Cost of goods sold	86,250
Gross profit	288,750
Other expenses	
Advertising	35,400
Office expense	22,750
Research	195,000
Wages and salaries	40,000
Total other expenses	293,150
Income before taxes	(4,400)
Income taxes	0
Net income	$ (4,400)

WASH YOUR CAR INC.
INCOME STATEMENT
FOR THE YEAR ENDED DECEMBER 31, 2014

Revenue	$375,000
Cost of service provided	163,125
Gross profit	211,875
Other expenses	
Advertising	5,200
Office expense	17,400
Repairs and maintenance	85,000
Wages and salaries	50,000
Total other expenses	157,600
Income before taxes	54,275
Income taxes	8,413
Net income	$ 45,862

Gamma Systems Ltd.
An Introduction to Financial Statement Information

Gamma Systems Ltd (GSL) was created by Jesse Gemmel, a third-year undergraduate business student. Unable to find work in a business setting, Jesse started up his own business during the summer months. Jesse was able to secure the services of his uncle, Pierre Chalut, to incorporate the company.

Prior to attending university, Jesse was involved in various athletic activities. In addition, Jesse has taken many kinesiology courses during his undergraduate studies. Jesse has always had a passion for fitness and athletics, and spends more time in the gym than in class! Therefore, Jesse is trying to turn his passion into his business by incorporating GSL with the purpose of developing and distributing fitness-related products.

GSL began operations in April 2014, and continued until the end of August 2014, at which point Jesse had to return to university to complete his degree. Jesse invested $2,500 of his savings into GSL, and also took out a loan of $1,000 from his father.

During its first summer of operations, GSL designed and sold DVDs for beginners. Jesse recorded the videos with the help of a friend, a professional videographer, who was paid $750 by GSL. The videos focus on basic stretches, workouts, and diet tips. The DVD cover was designed by a professional in the community for $500. Jesse purchased 250 high quality DVDs for $5 each, including the jewel case, and made copies of his video on his personal computer and packaged the videos to be ready for sale. Jesse incurred $200 in printing costs for the front and back covers. All expenditures were paid for with cash as Jesse did not have a credit card or any credit history.

A total of $2,000 was used to purchase new gym equipment for the video shoots. The equipment can be used for at least another three years to produce videos. In addition, GSL spent an additional $400 on the appropriate software to copy the videos.

Jesse promoted the video at local gyms, and virally on YouTube and Facebook. During the course of the summer months, GSL sold all 250 copies of the DVD for $30 each. A local gym has purchased 100 copies of the DVD to give away to its members, but promised to pay GSL in December 2014.

It is now September 1, 2014, and Jesse is reflecting upon the first five months of GSL's operations. Given that the new semester is about to begin, and tuition payments are coming due, Jesse would like to know how GSL performed. He is fairly excited because GSL sold $7,500 worth of DVDs, which he believes could be used to cover his tuition and book costs. As of today, Jesse received $1,500 from GSL for his services, which he paid himself at the end of August.

Required

As Jesse's best friend, who is majoring in accounting, you have been asked to prepare a report on GSL's financial performance over the past five months. Specifically, Jesse has asked you to consider the following:

(a) Prepare GSL's balance sheet and income statement.

(b) Given that GSL is a corporation, how could Jesse receive funds from the corporation?

(c) What does the accounting information say about Jesse's management abilities? If he did not start-up GSL, he could have found a summer job at a grocery store and earned $3,000.

(d) GSL is applying for a bank loan in the near future to expand operations and develop a new video. How can the accounting information be used by the bank to decide whether credit should be provided to GSL? The bank has said that it will only provide a loan if the business has twice as much equity than debt.

(e) Jesse would like to know if the bank will accept the financial statements as prepared by GSL, or whether the statement will need to be audited. What benefit does an audit provide to the bank?

Iced Confections Inc.

Your partner, Paddy O'Flaherty, has just dropped a mountain of files and other paperwork on your desk and left instructions for you. You notice at the top of the instruction sheet, that he has marked the request *urgent*. As a result, you put your other work aside and begin to sift through the information.

Your firm has been a consultant for Iced Confections Inc. (ICE), a publicly traded company located in Windy Bay, Nfld, and founded by James McCormick. ICE manufactures the famous McCormick's beverage, Icy Bay Lemonade. Your firm has been their consultant for five years. ICE's year end is December 31. You are the brand new lead consultant for ICE. You were not originally assigned to ICE but you were given the task after the original consultant suddenly left for a job in the Caribbean.

ICE is currently in the process of a major expansion and it is looking into financing alternatives for the acquisition of manufacturing equipment to be used in its lemonade-making facilities.

ICE is currently in a cash crunch, although its sales and production have expanded considerably over the past 10 years. All of its other key ratios are in good order, which is allowing ICE to look at a variety of ways to finance its next expansion. The founder and major shareholder, James, is concerned about maintaining a healthy current ratio and debt to equity ratio as he believes this will be important in the future and the minority shareholders have shown some concern over these ratios in the past.

Your firm has been hired by ICE to assist it in exploring the various alternatives as described in Exhibit I. They would like your detailed analysis. This analysis should incorporate calculations, impact on financial statements, and more qualitative impacts as you deem appropriate in the circumstances (such as impact to corporate structure, overall leverage, advantages, and disadvantages).

In addition, in order to fully understand the situation, ICE would like you to prepare journal entries for the first year for alternatives one, two and three and the potential impact they will have on ICE's ratios.

You have been made aware that the auditors will be arriving in a few months and ICE has asked you to ensure that all accounting recommendations are followed. In addition, ICE has a few other items that it would like you to comment on prior to the auditors' arrival. See Exhibit II.

Required

Prepare the draft report to ICE.

EXHIBIT I – ICE DETAILS

Machine Details

» The equipment in question is an A24ISOK – Type II Beverage Bottling Machine capable of bottling 100 cases of lemonade per minute. The fair value of this machine is $1 million.

» The machine is expected to have a useful life of 10 years after which it could be sold for $50,000.

» Technological obsolescence is a factor in this type of machine as manufacturers are always making them better, stronger and faster.

» *Note: You may assume that the purchase or receipt of the equipment, the debt or lease payment, and so on all take place on January 1, 2014.*

[handwritten: Chpt 7]

Acquisition Arrangement #1

» ICE could finance the purchase of the machine by issuing bonds

» $1,000 bonds would be issued totalling $1 million, for 10 years and a stated interest rate of 8%

» The current market value for similar bonds is 6%

» Interest would be paid semi-annually with the bonds being issued January 1, 2015

[handwritten: Chpt 9]

Acquisition Arrangement #2   *[handwritten: 442 for balance sheet breakdown.]*

» ICE could purchase the asset for $1 million and obtain a secured loan from its bank

» The terms of the loan calls for principal payments each year beginning January 1, 2015, of $100,000

» The interest is to be paid annually each January first and is fixed at 9%

» ICE is required to maintain a specified debt to equity ratio or the loan will become immediately payable

[handwritten: Chpt 9]

Acquisition Arrangement #3

» ICE could issue common shares or preferred shares to finance the acquisition of the machinery

» ICE is a public company with the founding member owning 51% of the common shares currently outstanding (currently there are 4.5 million shares outstanding in total)

» The current market price per share is $14

[handwritten: Chpt 10]

[handwritten: 1M ÷ 14 = 71 428.57 = 71 429 shares need to be sold. 2 205 000 need to be sold.]

EXHIBIT II – OTHER DETAILS

[handwritten: 4.5 M = 51% ... 6.40952%]

» During the year, a visitor to the facility slipped and fell on some spilled lemonade and broke their leg. They have subsequently sued ICE for $800,000. ICE's lawyers do not believe that the $800,000 lawsuit will be successful, but do believe that ICE will have to pay an amount between $300,000 and $600,000.

» ICE intends to put on a contest this year with a coupon attached to each lemonade product. Any customer who collects five coupons may send them to ICE and redeem them for an ICE T-shirt. ICE would like some guidance on how to account for this.

Muskoka Internet Café

Muskoka Internet Café (MIC) was established and incorporated on January 1, 2012, by Bruce Waiters and has just completed its third year of operations with a year end of December 31. Bruce was born in the Muskoka region and after completing his university degree in history, he decided to return to the area to set up his own business. After months of research, Bruce decided to open his business along the Gravenhurst waterfront. His research showed that there was tremendous potential in that area, especially during the summer tourist season, for a small café with an Internet service. Local cottagers without service suggested that they would find it appealing to check their email while shopping in the trendy area.

MIC runs out of 90 square metres (1,000 square feet) of space. It has one entrance into the café and patio doors leading out to a deck that overlooks the water. MIC pays $5,000 per month for the rental of the space. Bruce was able to negotiate with the landlord and was not required to pay the first month's rent in advance. All of his rental payments are current and up to date. For the last two years, MIC has had a very reliable accountant prepare its year-end financial statements and everything has been correct. This year, MIC's accountant retired and Bruce did the best he could recording his own financial information. For the information he was not sure about, he kept all of the required supporting documentation. Bruce hired your accounting firm to prepare his financial statements for the year and you were assigned the job. Bruce supplied you with his unadjusted trial balance and the information in Exhibit I to assist you.

Additional information:

» The amount currently sitting in prepaids arose due to the insurance policy last year. Bruce didn't know how to correct it, so he left it. This year's insurance policy was purchased on November 1 for $9,000. The policy runs from November 1 to October 31 of each year.

» Bruce has a note that he owed $900 in wages to his employees for the period ending December 31.

» The loan was incurred when the café was opened. The loan carries an interest rate of 8%. The interest is payable two months after year end and the principal is due in 2018.

» MIC will sometimes book special events with small organizations that are allowed to pay after the event has taken place. On December 29, a small company had a gathering at the café. The company was billed $1,089 and has 30 days to pay it. Bruce has not yet recorded this in his financial records.

» MIC declared a dividend of $5,000 on December 30.

» Bruce didn't know how to record amortization for the year and so left it for you to record. Amortization for all assets is charged using a straight-line method by taking the cost of the asset and dividing it by its expected useful life. The assets have expected useful lives as follows:

- Computers: 5 years
- Café equipment: 10 years
- Furniture and fixtures: 20 years

» The information shows that MIC owes $400 for a telephone bill and $300 for electricity for December. These amounts have not been recorded yet.

Required

Based on the information you have, prepare the adjusting journal entries, an adjusted trial balance, the statement of earnings (income statement), statement of financial position (balance sheet), and statement of retained earnings. After you have completed the statements, prepare the closing journal entries and the post-closing trial balance. Ensure you show all of your work, and prepare proper journal entries and properly formatted financial statements.

EXHIBIT I

MUSKOKA INTERNET CAFÉ
UNADJUSTED TRIAL BALANCE
DECEMBER 31, 2014

Account Name	Debit	Credit
Cash	35,000	
Accounts receivable	5,600	
Food inventory	21,000	
Merchandise inventory	62,500	
Prepaids	3,400	
Computers	30,000	
Accumulated amortization—computers		12,000
Café equipment	90,000	
Accumulated amortization—Café equipment		18,000
Furniture and fixtures	150,000	
Accumulated amortization—Furniture and fixtures		15,000
Accounts payable		18,000
Accrued liabilities		
Interest payable		
Dividend payable		
Long-term loan		220,000
Common shares		50,000
Retained earnings		22,000
Food revenue		468,500
Internet revenue		127,000
Merchandise revenue		103,000
Food expense	240,000	
Internet expense	54,000	
Electricity expense	65,000	
Telephone expense	20,000	
Interest expense	—	
Salary expense	200,000	
Insurance expense	9,000	
Supplies expense	8,000	
Depreciation expense	—	
Rent expense	60,000	
	1,053,500	1,053,500

Orillia Cement Company

Orillia Cement Company (OCC) is a medium sized company that specializes in providing cement for construction sites, primarily in the Central Ontario area. OCC had sales two years ago of $10 million and sales for the year just ended were $12 million. At present OCC is solely owned by Joel Tomatuk, who founded the private company in 1980. OCC follows the Accounting Standards for Private Enterprises. Despite its revenues, OCC operates with few administrative staff, currently employing 12 individuals in addition to Joel, who is there every day.

Joel is considering expanding his operations into Southern Ontario. In order to do so he will have to look into financing options. He is contemplating two debt options: traditional bank financing, or bonds. He is also considering selling some of his common shares to five of his friends and relatives. He is unsure of how these options would impact him and the current organization of his company.

In December of this year, one of OCC's trucks carrying cement was in an accident. The substance spilled into a local river, contaminating the water supply. OCC's lawyers have stated that the local residents have filed a lawsuit for $2 million. They expect that OCC will be found guilty but the settlement will be between $1.0 million and $1.8 million. OCC had let its insurance policy expire and therefore does not have any coverage.

On December 31, four of OCC's trucks were loaded with customer freight and sitting at OCC's loading docks. The goods were delivered to the customers on January 5 and 6, respectively. The revenue of $80,000 was recorded in the books on December 31.

Joel knows about the importance of internal controls but believes he needs a refresher. He had an individual from purchasing leave earlier this year and is now using the accounts payable person who also prepares the cheques to take care of all purchases. He is beginning to think that this is a good idea as it would save one salary. On the other hand, he does want to maintain controls and is interested in eliminating all potential problems. He would like your recommendations about how he should deal with this.

OCC purchased equipment on January 1 five years ago for $80,000 and estimated an $8,000 salvage value at the end of the equipment's 10-year useful life. On March 31 of this year, the equipment was sold for $21,000. The last entry to record depreciation was at December 31 of the prior year. No entries for the sale have been made yet.

OCC is a client of your accounting firm and you are the CA in charge of the engagement. The year end for OCC is December 31. It is now April 20 and you have been asked to provide a memo to your partner that can be used as the basis for discussion with Joel that addresses the issues that concern you and Joel. You must address all of the issues in depth and provide recommendations on how to account for them.

Required

Prepare the memo.

Play Tennis Now Inc.

Contributed by
Laura Simeoni, BComm, CA, CIA
Sysim Consulting Limited, Director and Professional Development and Training
Consultant Oakville, Ontario

Martina Fabcic's dream, ever since she was the national tennis championship in the under-14 girls' division, was to own and operate her own tennis club. After earning her business degree with a major in marketing, Martina decided to work for a local club as its general manager. She saw this as a stepping stone to her real dream. Martina was responsible for all operating aspects of the club except for the preparation of the monthly financial statements. These were prepared by the bookkeeper and audited annually by a local chartered accountant (CA) firm.

After five years at the local club, Martina decided it was time to start her own tennis club. She began to research the surrounding area in order to decide where to locate her new business. Within a year, Martina decided to open a new tennis club in a growing area in the north end of the city. She had $60,000 of her own savings and decided to invest $50,000 of it into the club. Based on her business knowledge and experience in the tennis industry, Martina estimated that she would need another $100,000. She approached a private investor, Mike Riggio, who had played professional tennis in his early years. He was keen to see a new club in the area and agreed to lend Martina the money with an option to buy into the club in five years. The terms of the loan requires Play Tennis Now Inc. to repay the full amount over the five years through monthly principal and interest payments. In addition, Play Tennis Now Inc. has to prepare and submit to Michael an audited set of financial statements within 60 days of year end. Also the terms require that the financial statements be prepared in accordance with Accounting Standards for Private Enterprises.

On February 1, Martina incorporated her business, Play Tennis Now, Inc. She then began the hard work of getting her office, staff, and facilities ready for opening day. On May 1, Martina successfully opened her doors to local tennis enthusiasts.

Now that the peak tennis season is over, Martina is thinking about the need to prepare her first set of annual financial statements. Although she is somewhat familiar with accounting processes based on her previous job, Martina did not have a good grasp of accounting policies suitable for this kind of business. She decided to contact her good friend, Professor Mark Phed, to ask for a reference for someone who could help her decide on the most appropriate policies for Play Tennis Now, Inc. Martina's friend teaches at the local university and was pleased to help Martina with this request. Professor Phed quickly thought of you, since you had recently earned the highest mark in his accounting class.

When Martina contacted you, you were excited to take on this role as accounting advisor. Here was a chance to earn some extra money and finally use all that accounting knowledge in a real situation. You agreed to meet with Martina to learn more about her tennis club.

On November 2, you met with Martina at her office at the back of the tennis club. A summary of your notes is found in Exhibit I.

Required

Assume the role of accounting advisor and top student. Provide Martina with your advice and recommendations on the accounting policies that would be appropriate for Play Tennis Now, Inc. for its first year end. Provide any other advice that you think may help Martina as she begins this new business venture.

EXHIBIT I – NOTES FROM MEETING WITH MARTINA

1. In order to promote the new club, Martina took out a full-page advertisement in the local paper. She paid $1,000 for this advertisement, which ran weekly in four local newspapers during the months of May and June. Martina felt that it was important to spend this amount of money and "get the word out" as the benefits could last over several years if players visited the club and then agreed to join as members.

2. On May 5, Martina had an open house. She offered healthy drinks and fruit trays for those people dropping in. It gave her a chance to meet potential players who would hopefully join the club. She had about 150 people drop in that day to meet her, the two office staff (the receptionist and the bookkeeper), and the tennis pro, Johnny Mac. The cost for the open house was about $250.

3. Martina explained that part of the $50,000 that she invested in the club was used to purchase office furniture, two computers, and some club house furniture such as two couches, and a table and chair set. In addition, tennis nets, tennis balls, and a ball machine were purchased. The ball machine will be made available to players, who can rent the machine on a first-come, first-served basis.

4. The funds received from Michael, the private investor, were primarily used to build four "hard courts," the most common tennis surface. The money not used for the building of the courts was set aside for ongoing court maintenance. Martina confirmed that she spent about $80,000 to build the courts. Of the amount remaining, $10,000 will be used to repaint the lines or resurface the courts about every 3 years. The remainder will be used for emergency repairs.

5. Martina explained that she had hired a web designer to set up a web page as well as an on-line booking system. In this way, members or potential members could easily access the site to learn more about the club or to book courts.

6. By mid-May, 100 people had joined the club. Per the terms of membership, each new member paid $900 for a non-refundable annual membership. The membership could be paid all upfront or at a monthly rate of $75.00 without any interest charges. The membership fee allows each player the right to book courts at any time. At the current time, Martina is not selling court time to non-members. In addition to the membership fee, court time is charged at $22.00 per hour for peak play and $18.00 per hour for non-peak play.

7. Martina introduced me to the tennis pro. He was well known among local tennis players. In order to encourage Johnny Mac to join the club, Martina included the following terms in his employment contract:

    (a) A fixed annual salary

    (b) A commission based on court bookings where the pro is asked to play in. These bookings can be made on-line or by other acceptable methods, i.e., call in or in-person bookings

    (c) A bonus if the club membership exceeds 250 members within one year of opening and remains at this level for 30 days after it is reached.

    Johnny Mac receives 12 equal monthly payments to cover his annual salary. Payments are made the last Friday of the month. The commission is paid one month after the commissions are earned since the amounts need to be verified against the on-line and manual booking systems.

    The bonus will be paid 10 days after the bonus is considered earned.

    Martina indicated that Johnny Mac was excited about the potential for this club. She felt that Johnny Mac would most likely earn his bonus given that the club had almost reached 50% of the total goal in the first two weeks of operations.

8. Martina also opened a small pro shop that carries tennis racquets, tennis balls, tennis clothing including tennis shoes, and other tennis accessories. Club members are particularly sensitive to new trends and models. Martina knows this is an opportunity for her to make additional profits over and above the membership and hourly bookings. She started out with an inventory level costing about $15,000 (estimated retail value $35,000). This should adequately service about 400 members.

9. The company's year end is March 31.

Pooches and Paws Grooming and Doggy Spa

Dustin Leibovitch has just completed his courses in dog care, training, and grooming and is excited about opening his new business, Pooches and Paws Grooming and Doggy Spa (PPG). PPG has been a dream for Dustin and he has come to you for some help on how to organize his financial affairs.

Dustin has received a $20,000 start-up loan from the Manitoba government under a recently announced new venture start-up program. He is allowed to use the loan to purchase equipment that he needs to run his business. He is not allowed to use the money for salaries (to him or any employees), rental, or any operating expenses (such as hydro). The loan does not have to be repaid for five years but interest of 4% must be paid annually. Dustin will begin to pay the loan back at a rate of $5,000 per year beginning in year six. There is an annual requirement by the government for financial statements. This is to make sure that PPG is performing satisfactorily.

In addition to the loan, Dustin provides you with the following information:

» Dustin intends on contributing $125,000 of his own savings to the business along with his computer. His computer is valued at $400.

» Although he hasn't signed the lease agreement yet, Dustin has agreed to rent space in a popular area just outside of the city. The space used to be a pet grooming centre, so little needs to be done to it except to add his equipment. The rental agreement calls for payments of $5,000 per month with the last month's rent being paid in advance (before he opens his grooming centre).

» Dustin is going to advertise in the local papers and on the radio. Advertising is expected to cost $8,000. Because Dustin does not have a credit history, he will have to pay half this amount in advance before any advertising runs. The other half is to be paid when it finishes. Dustin thinks that two months of advertising his new business is sufficient and then word of mouth should take over.

» Research shows that dog owners spend a significant amount of money on their pooches including grooming services and day care. Since he has no outside space, he won't have the ability to operate a day care. As a result, Dustin is going to concentrate on washing, trimming, and nails. There will be three packages offered for grooming. The gold package gives the pooch the full treatment, including wash, cut, style, and nails; the silver provides a wash and dry service and the bronze package gives them a good brushing but no wash. He will also offer a quick nail service that takes about 10 minutes and will carry a charge of $10.

» He also intends to stock his store with inventory items such as dog bowls, leashes, collars, and toys.

» In addition to the grooming at the store, Dustin will offer to do at-home training. The training packages will be 20 lessons, 10 lessons, or 5 lessons. Dustin isn't quite sure which one will be most popular and wants to be able to track them.

» Dustin knows he needs to buy the following equipment: Three pet table lifts, $5,000 each; grooming equipment, $10,000; three tables, $1,000 each; two bathtubs, $2,000 each; holding cage, $500; desk, $1,000. In addition, there will some other miscellaneous equipment costing approximately $10,000.

» Dustin expects to hire two part-time helpers. They would each average 15 hours per week for 50 weeks each year at an hourly rate of $13.50.

» In addition, Dustin expects to pay hydro and other utility costs of $500 per month and telephone/Internet charges of $200 per month. The only other real monthly expense he sees is liability insurance. The quote he received was $185 per month.

While Dustin is better at pet grooming than he is accounting, he knows he can rely on you. One thing he is sure about is that he doesn't want to risk losing the new Ford Explorer he just bought as his graduation present to himself.

He has asked you to prepare a short report that starts by providing recommendations on how he should structure his business from a legal/organizational point of view. Once this is done, he needs you to help him set up his accounting by going through the items and identifying which ones are assets, liabilities, expenses and revenues. Specifically on the revenues, he wants you to provide some recommendations on how he should record them; all in one account or several, and why. It may be best to start by setting up a statement of financial position and income statement that lists the names of all the accounts classified accordingly. He can hardly wait to get started and is awaiting your reply.

Required

Prepare the report.

Retro Candy Inc.

Retro Candy Inc. (RCI) began operations in 2011 in a small mall in Banff, Alberta. The store sells candy, specializing primarily in nostalgic candy and imported candy and chocolate from Europe. Charlie Sasaki is the owner of RCI and he typically reduces his overhead costs by working every day himself and employing a minimal number of employees.

For the last year of operations, Charlie has relied on Irma, one of his employees, to assist him with some of the accounting functions for RCI. Irma worked several days as a retail associate with RCE and for two days of the week she prepared cheques payable to suppliers and other creditors and entered all of the cheques and deposit information into a popular accounting software package. At the end of every month, Irma prepared the bank reconciliation that Charlie's year-end accountant requested. Since Irma was always in early and often agreed to stay late, Charlie also relied on her to purchase the candy from the suppliers and to accept the goods when they arrived, price them, and also place the candy on the floor. Charlie believed this was important as this allowed him to spend time on the floor talking to customers and, since Charlie knows little about accounting, provided him with a cost-effective way of keeping his books up-to-date.

In December, Irma tendered her resignation with RCI as she decided to go back to school. She agreed to work until January 31 and to enter the month-end information into the accounting package. She was not able to complete the bank reconciliation for the month of January.

Wanting to ensure that he had his information current and also desiring some recommendations on how to set up the accounting function going forward, Charlie has approached you. Charlie would like you to begin by preparing his January bank reconciliation. If you see any issues with the reconciliation, he would like you to note them.

After you have prepared the bank reconciliation, Charlie would like some brief recommendations on how he might improve the accounting process by discussing what risks he may have faced previously and how he can realistically implement any controls to mitigate those risks.

Below you will find both bank and book details for RCI. In addition to the tables in Exhibit I, you have been made aware of the following information:

» Assume that any mathematical errors you may find are on RCI's side not the bank's side.

» The bank balance per the bank statement as of the end of January was $166,094. The book balance was $167,000.

» RCI deposited $3,900 in the night deposit box on January 29 and $2,876 on January 30.

» The bank deducted $109 for service fees for the month of January. RCI has not yet recorded this amount.

» Cheque #98 payable to UK Candy Imports for $3,456 was mailed November 28 and has not yet been cashed.

Required

Prepare the bank reconciliation and provide the report to Charlie with your recommendations.

EXHIBIT I

Selected Details from the Bank Statement for January

Cheques recorded by the bank during the month of January (in the order they were recorded):

#126	$1,987	#114	$ 398
#121	198	#123	477
#109	500	#105	134
#101	321	#116	98
#117	1,201	#122	1,087
#128	958	#124	598
#129	390	#131	230
#118	632	#130	992
#133	124	#125	498
#119	45	#134	734
#135	821		

Selected Details from the Books of RCI

Cheques written and mailed during the month of January:

#114	$ 398	#115	$ 65
#116	98	#117	1,201
#118	632	#119	45
#120	345	#121	198
#122	1,087	#123	456
#124	598	#125	498
#126	1,987	#127	287
#128	958	#129	390
#130	992	#131	230
#133	124	#134	734
#135	821	#136	25
#137	164	#138	619
#139	1,001	#140	38

Sarah Smith Sporting

Contributed by
Laura Simeoni, BComm, CA, CIA
*Sysim Consulting Limited, Director and Professional Development and Training
Consultant Oakville, Ontario*

Sarah Smith has been an avid sports enthusiast since her early days of playing soccer for her city team. Sarah continued to play soccer throughout high school and university. She recognized during those early years of soccer that staying fit was a critical ingredient in performing well in any sport and for staying healthy in general. So it was no surprise when Sarah announced that she would pursue her dream of opening a fitness facility. Three years ago Sarah earned her degree in physical education. Sarah thought it would be useful to add to her skill set so she recently received a certificate in personal training. Once she completed the course she put all her energy into preparing a business plan and doing the ground work for her new business. Knowing Sarah's love for sports and fitness, her parents fully supported her business decision.

Sarah began to spread the news by "word of mouth" that she would soon open her own fitness and training facility. Sarah hired some high school students to deliver flyers that she designed and had printed at a local print shop. She paid the students a total of $500 to deliver the flyers to neighbourhoods within 10 kilometres of her business location. Her dream came true on February 1, 2014: Sarah Smith Sporting Ltd. (SSS) officially opened its doors to its first customers. The first 20 visitors received a one-year free membership. Sarah believed this would encourage the first 20 visitors to share their positive experience with their friends and encourage them to become new paid members.

Prior to opening on February 1, 2014, Sarah signed a five-year lease to rent the premises where she would conduct business. The premises had been previously used by a fitness club so all the necessary amenities, like a reception area, showers, and fitness rooms, were ready for use. On January 2, 2014, she paid the landlord a $1,000 security deposit for any damages that may be caused by her business while renting the premises. The security deposit would be returned at the end of the lease minus any costs to repair damage from other than normal usage. In addition, Sarah paid for the first month's rent in the amount of $500. She also gave the landlord 11 cheques, one for each month in the coming year. To comply with the terms of the lease agreement Sarah arranged for property and personal insurance for the period February 1, 2014, to January 31, 2015.

Sarah also purchased equipment such as mats, balls, skipping ropes, and hand weights. She spent a total of $3,000 for this equipment. Sarah is hoping the equipment will last more than one year as this will help to preserve cash in the company. She also purchased a computer and an "off-the-shelf" software package commonly used for businesses such as SSS.

In addition to the flyers that cost her $400 to design and print, Sarah advertised in a local newspaper. The advertising was going to run for four weeks starting February 14, 2014.

After studying various pricing structures at other fitness and training facilities, Sarah decided to offer the following pricing structure:

1. One year membership – paid in full on the date of joining: $500 per membership
2. One year membership – paid in two equal installments: $600 per membership paid one-half on the date of signing the membership contract and one-half six months later
3. One year membership – paid in 12 equal instalments: $720, the first one paid on the date of signing the membership contract. Monthly payments of $60 per month paid every 30 days from the first payment date.

The membership allows full use of the fitness facilities during all hours of operation.

Sarah plans to work at the club 7 days a week for 10 hours a day. Knowing she cannot operate the club alone, she hired one full-time trainer and one part-time trainer. In order to entice these two well known trainers she offered them each a signing bonus: $1,000 for the full-time trainer and $500 for the part-time trainer. In addition to their competitive salary she offered them a 5% bonus based on annual membership revenues. Sarah hopes that this will encourage the trainers to promote the business and bring in new members.

Sarah soon realized that all these costs were adding up quickly. She decided to approach a local bank where she had been a customer for several years. She asked the bank manager if she could borrow $10,000 to get the business started. The bank reviewed her business plan and felt comfortable with lending her the money given that Sarah had personally invested $20,000 into the business. The terms of the loan required Sarah to maintain a positive working capital and to provide monthly unaudited statements within 10 days of month end plus annual financial statements reviewed by a public accountant.

Given these bank requirements and having only studied first-year accounting, she decided to seek some accounting advice. Sarah texted you, a former university roommate who is now preparing for the chartered accountancy (CA) examinations, to ask if you could meet. You agree to meet Sarah on February 25 at the fitness facility.

Sarah has several questions about how to account for the recent business transactions. Specifically, she needs to understand what revenues and expenses will be reported in the first month end's financial statements. She wants to understand the alternatives if any exist. In addition she wants to understand what type of entity she should use for this business venture.

Required

Prepare the report for Sarah.

Summertime Golf Ltd.

Summertime Golf Ltd. (SGL) was founded by Mike Kostanski on January 1, 2012. SGL is a small private corporation selling golf equipment. After beginning in Victoria with revenues in the first year of operations of $300,000, SGL now has three locations on Vancouver Island. Revenues increased substantially during 2013. Mike is the majority shareholder. Mike's cousin Vinny owns some of the common shares after purchasing them this year.

It is now March 2014 and Mike has just left the office of one of the senior partners in the CA firm where you work. You are a CA in the firm and have been asked to assist the senior partner with this project. Mike had done his accounting on his own the past two years and thinks that he has done a really good job. He is looking to expand his operations but when he went to the bank in November 2013, they suggested he come to them with his financial statements at the end of the year. A friend of Mike suggested that he come and talk to your partner first and show her the statements. Mike is looking for a $100,000 loan in order to expand his operations and take advantage of the growing golf industry.

The bank suggested to Mike that they typically offer a loan to companies such as his at prime +2%. Prime is currently 1% and the bank stated that the loan they would provide Mike would be no larger than 25% of SGL's receivables and inventories as of December 31, 2013. He would be required to maintain a current ratio of at least 1.4:1 or the loan may become immediately payable.

Mike has provided your CA firm with his income statement for 2013 and his balance sheets for 2012 and 2013. He doesn't have his 2012 income statements but was able to tell you his 2012 revenues (see first paragraph) and his cost of goods sold was $160,000. He states that based on these statements, that it should be a slam dunk that he will get the loan.

In addition, although Mike believes he is doing a great job taking care of his own books, one of the things the bank mentioned was having an audit done and setting up accounting policies. As Mike stated in the meeting "my only sense of an audit is when those tax guys come in and make my life miserable looking for all the little pennies. Joke was on them last year as I managed to put $15,000 worth of cool home entertainment expenses through the business and they never even noticed. I'm looking at getting an IPad next." As a result of his meeting in 2013 with the bank, Mike would also like your help in establishing accounting policies for his young growing company. He would like your firm to evaluate his accounting issues and provide recommendations on how to account for these items given the current situation. He would also like to know what an audit does for him and what GAAP is all about.

After Mike leaves, your partner takes a deep breath first before she speaks.

"Okay, it looks like we have our work cut out for us here. I know what the bank is talking about and they take those industry stats Mike gave you in the attached material seriously. I need you to prepare a report for me that attempts to address several issues. First, let's examine those entries that Mike made in Exhibit I. If you see anything that doesn't look right, adjust the December 31, 2013 statements that he prepared in Exhibits II and III. Next, let's prepare a cash flow statement from your adjusted numbers and see where we sit. Also, we'll need to do some ratio analysis and make a preliminary determination as to how he is doing and whether we think he has a hope of getting a loan—after adjustments of course. For that matter, once you adjust the statements, you should probably go back to the conditions of the loan where they detail the maximum amount they will give him. Of course, all of this needs to be backed up by you so that I can go to Mike and discuss, so you will need a good solid report explaining why you are adjusting things. I also need you to address the other issues Mike talked about: you know the one about audit reports and setting up accounting policies. Take a stab at those as well; but put everything in a report to me. I can then look at it and see what the next steps are. We may wish to talk to him about other sources of financing that are available to him in addition to a traditional bank loan so perhaps include a short piece on that. Don't be afraid to provide me with your recommendations and a list of your concerns as you see them. If we are going to take him on as a client, I need another set of eyes to see what we are getting ourselves into. I need this all by tomorrow morning…so pay attention to your time."

Required

Prepare the report to the CA partner.

EXHIBIT I – SGL – YEAR TO DATE HIGHLIGHTS

» SGL inventory consists of items such as golf clubs, bags, balls, apparel, and other golf equipment. Information presented to you as of December 31 showed $346,000 in inventory at cost. Mike left you a note stating that the inventory actually has a market value of $356,000 and has adjusted his inventory on these preliminary, unaudited financial statements to this amount as he believes that his inventory should be represented on his balance sheet at fair market value given the high demand for golf. Mike tells you that he put the $10,000 difference to Revenue. "Has to be right," he said, "it's like I made money."

» During the year, SGL signed a contract with a company that owns 10 golf courses. SGL has agreed to supply them with golf equipment for the next 5 years. The contract included an $80,000 upfront amount in order for SGL to begin to acquire the equipment and takes effect February 1, 2014. The cash was received January 15, 2014, and Mike has recorded this forthcoming contract in his December 31, 2013 financial statements by debiting accounts receivable and crediting revenue.

» At December 31 of the year just ended, SGL recorded $65,000 of inventory on its books for miscellaneous golf equipment. The inventory was shipped FOB destination. It physically arrived at SGL on January 2.

» On December 28, 2013, SGL sold $25,000 of goods to a high-end golf course. The goods were delivered in January 2014 and Mike was responsible for the goods until the January 2014 delivery (i.e., if there was damage to the goods before then Mike would have to replace). The $25,000 was included in the $124,600 December 31 accounts receivable balance. The entry Mike made was a debit to Accounts Receivable and a credit to Revenue. He never removed the goods from inventory or made an entry to cost of goods sold.

» Assume that Mike's income tax rate is 30% and that income taxes and accounting for last year were done correctly. Mike has not set up any journal entry yet to record his taxes.

» SGL purchased the building in Victoria with money from the business for $300,000. This money was the capital that Mike brought in when he founded the company. He received the money as an inheritance so he doesn't have the ability to finance the next expansion himself. The building was expected to have a useful life of 30 years with no salvage or residual value. In addition, SGL purchased $50,000 of equipment at the start of business with an estimated useful life of eight years and no residual value. A friend of Mike's accurately recorded the purchase and amortization expense on a chart for Mike so you can assume that amortization expense on these assets has been recorded correctly.

» On July 1, 2013, Mike purchased $50,000 of equipment. He recorded the purchase of the equipment, but didn't know how to record the amortization so he left it. He expects the equipment to have a useful life of seven years and he thinks he can sell it for $2,000 after seven years.

» Mike informed you that he forgot to make a journal entry for a bundled purchase he made from someone going out of business. On October 1 he spent $30,000 and bought a specialized machine that allows customers to test the golf clubs before buying them and a used truck. The fair market value of the machine was $20,000 and of the truck was $15,000. He expects the machine to last eight years and the truck five years. All of this happened prior to year end. The owner of the equipment agreed to carry the loan. Terms of the loan are annual payments beginning September 30, 2014, of $10,000 each year plus 5% interest on the outstanding principal.

» SGL is leasing space in both Nanaimo and Victoria as of January 1, 2014. Mike signed two year leases at each location and SGL was required to place a deposit of $2,500 (for each location) which will cover their last month's rent at both of those locations. When asked, Mike informed you that he paid this amount on December 15 and expensed the $5,000, recording it under operating expenses.

» Golf continues to grow in Canada and is expected to continue to show strong growth despite the ongoing economic issues. Golf stores exist in most towns and cities and can be very competitive. Some ratios for the industry are as follows:

Key Ratios and Analysis:	2013	2012
Gross profit percentage of sales	45.5%	45.6%
Quick ratio	.95	.90
Current ratio	2:1	2:1
Total debt to equity ratio	1.85:1	1.21:1
Inventory turnover	3.23	3.11

EXHIBIT II

SUMMERTIME GOLF INCOME STATEMENT
DECEMBER 31, 2013

Sales	$975,000
Less: Cost of goods sold	467,000
Gross profit	508,000
Less:	
Amortization expense	16,250
Other operating expenses	296,670
Income before taxes	$195,080

EXHIBIT III

SUMMERTIME GOLF
MY BALANCE SHEETS
DECEMBER 31, 2013

	2013	2012
Assets		
Cash	$ 80,900	$ 43,400
Accounts receivable	124,600	27,250
Merchandise inventory	356,000	204,000
Property, plant, and equipment	400,000	350,000
Less: accumulated amortization	(32,500)	(16,250)
Total assets	$929,000	$608,400
Liabilities and Shareholders' Equity		
Accounts payable	$273,350	$249,400
Other accrued payables	80,570	76,000
Income taxes payable	0	3,000
Common shares	310,000	210,000
Retained earnings	265,080	70,000
Total liabilities and shareholders' equity	$929,000	$608,400

Additional Information:

» Mike noted to you that he paid himself a cash dividend of $70,000 this year for all the work he did and expensed it under other expenses.

» During the year he was able to convince his cousin Vinny to invest in SGL. Vinny purchased common shares and paid $100,000 cash.

Texas House Steakhouse

The Texas House Steakhouse (THS) is a bar and grill located in Saskatoon, Saskatchewan. THS is a regional restaurant created and operated by Kevin Masters, a former ranch farmer from Dallas, Texas. The company was established in 2010, and has experienced steady revenue growth since inception. The restaurant's success can be attributed to its variety of dishes.

Currently, there is only one THS restaurant located in downtown Saskatoon. Kevin is looking to expand the business by opening another restaurant in Regina. Kevin estimates that it will cost upwards of $1 million to open a new location in Regina. Kevin has approached Heather Fiorito, a managing partner at a venture capital firm in Regina, about the potential opportunity. Kevin has proposed two alternatives to Heather:

1. <u>Extend credit to the business:</u> Loan THS $1 million in debt financing. The debt would be secured by the building and equipment purchased with the funds. He would like the interest to accrue at 5% per annum, with the loan repayable with blended payments over a five-year term. In exchange for the low interest rate, the debt will be convertible to common shares at the rate of 9 common shares per $1,000.

2. <u>Purchase an ownership interest:</u> Purchase 10,000 shares in the business (50% interest) for $1 million. The funds will be used to start up the Regina location. Depending on the purchase price, any short-fall in the funds required will be obtained through traditional bank financing.

Of course, Kevin is aware of the fact that Heather can choose neither of the options and walk away from the opportunity.

In order to help make a decision, Kevin has provided Heather with the historical income statements (Exhibit I) and balance sheets since inception (Exhibit II). In addition, Heather had a long discussion with Kevin (notes from the meeting in Exhibit III).

Heather has asked you, a newly hired junior analyst, to prepare a preliminary report that provides a recommended course of action. Your report should be based on a thorough analysis of THS's historical financial performance. As it is one of your first assignments, Heather reminds you that a well-prepared report of this nature should include, at a minimum, the following:

» An analysis of the statement of cash flow for the five-year period

» An analysis of financial ratios and common-size financial statements (Note that common-size financial statements are financial statements that are expressed as a percentages. Normally, the income statement is expressed as a percentage of sales while the balance sheet is expressed as a percentage of total assets.)

» A preliminary valuation of the common shares (Note that a common share earnings multiple for similar franchise restaurants ranges from 4 to 6 times normalized net income. Note that normalized net income is an estimate of net income that will persist into the future. It is calculated as net income adjusted for any one-time or non-normal items.)

» Based on the estimated share value, the value of the conversion feature over the life of the bond

» A comparison of the rate of return on the equity versus debt investment.

Required

Prepare the report.

EXHIBIT I – HISTORICAL INCOME STATEMENT

Assets	2010	2011	2012	2013	2014
Current assets					
Cash and cash equivalents	$ 0	$ 0	$ 53,297	$ 76,969	$ 199,051
Receivables and recoverables	71,584	110,272	67,042	91,174	122,647
Inventory	107,663	129,680	76,408	114,630	139,310
Prepaid expenses	20,419	17,414	11,558	16,240	26,387
	199,666	257,366	208,305	299,013	487,395
Fixed assets (net)					
Land	165,000	165,000	165,000	165,000	165,000
Building	618,213	556,391	500,752	450,677	405,609
Computer and equipment	46,750	32,725	22,908	16,035	11,225
Furniture, fixtures, and equipment	94,500	75,600	60,480	48,384	38,707
Kitchen equipment	233,750	163,625	114,538	80,176	56,123
	1,158,213	993,341	863,678	760,272	676,664
	1,357,879	1,250,707	1,071,983	1,059,285	1,164,059
Liabilities					
Current liabilities					
Bank indebtedness	100,900	175,000	0	0	0
Deferred revenue	186,789	190,949	202,075	205,601	219,276
Payables and accruals	154,633	97,326	122,885	176,544	177,637
Income taxes payable	17,071	15,705	35,070	35,288	69,708
	459,393	478,980	360,030	417,433	466,621
Long-term debt					
Long-term debt	860,204	710,623	550,570	379,315	196,071
	860,204	710,623	550,570	379,315	196,071
Shareholders' equity					
Capital stock (10,000 shares issued)	10,000	10,000	10,000	10,000	10,000
Retained earnings	28,282	51,105	151,383	252,537	491,367
	38,282	61,105	161,383	262,537	501,367
	$1,357,879	$1,250,707	$1,071,983	$1,059,285	$1,164,059

EXHIBIT II – HISTORICAL BALANCE SHEET

	2010	2011	2012	2013	2014
Sales	$3,579,208	$3,675,730	$3,943,656	$3,964,108	$4,229,192
Cost of sales	2,290,693	2,315,710	2,464,785	2,497,388	2,579,807
Gross profit	1,288,515	1,360,020	1,478,871	1,466,720	1,649,385
Gross profit as % of sales	*0*	*0*	*0*	*0*	*0*
Expenses					
Administrative	209,117	214,608	293,408	302,173	318,119
Advertising	127,368	127,083	131,906	155,140	148,005
Amortization	92,538	164,871	129,664	103,405	83,608
Computer	3,074	5,464	6,944	4,687	6,844
Credit card	53,688	55,136	59,155	59,462	63,438
Bad debts	716	0	2,011	0	613
Equipment rental	25,269	12,271	1,456	1,726	2,206
Freight	16,035	16,210	17,253	17,482	18,059
Insurance	13,113	10,022	12,300	13,079	13,855
Interest and bank charges	5,021	4,248	3,421	2,536	1,588
Interest on long-term debt	63,556	53,770	43,299	32,095	20,108
Janitorial supplies	40,425	48,373	33,565	43,483	39,084
Office and restaurant supplies	144,962	132,242	133,784	124,079	129,500
Professional fees	3,909	4,186	4,299	4,683	4,481
Repairs and maintenance	74,152	75,952	48,455	49,564	47,560
Royalty fees	125,272	128,651	138,028	138,744	148,022
Taxes and licenses	1,682	1,682	1,682	1,682	1,682
Telephone	9,338	9,919	10,248	10,239	10,195
Travel	10,319	8,031	6,475	3,957	9,113
Utilities	92,058	115,562	135,738	129,403	145,347
Wages and benefits	95,000	95,000	95,000	95,000	95,000
	1,206,612	1,283,281	1,308,091	1,292,619	1,306,427
Other income	3,450	1,788	4,569	2,341	5,580
Earnings before income taxes	85,353	78,527	175,349	176,442	348,538
Provision for income taxes	17,071	15,705	35,070	35,288	69,708
Net income	68,282	62,822	140,279	141,154	278,830
Retained earnings, beginning	0	28,282	51,104	151,383	252,537
Net income	68,282	62,822	140,279	141,154	278,830
Dividend	40,000	40,000	40,000	40,000	40,000
Retained earnings, end	$ 28,282	$ 51,104	$ 151,383	$ 252,537	$ 491,367

EXHIBIT III – NOTES FROM THE MEETING WITH KEVIN

Historical Financial Results – Saskatoon Operations

» The menu of dishes was created by a celebrity chef, who regularly visits the restaurant. The chef is paid a royalty fee of 3.5% of gross revenue.

» The original cost of the current assets are as follows:

Fixed assets (net)	
Land	165,000
Building	650,750
Computer and equipment	55,000
Furniture, fixtures, and equipment	105,000
Kitchen equipment	275,000

» The capital assets are amortized in the same manner as their capital cost allowance (CCA). The following CCA rates are used: Building, 10%; Computer equipment, 30%; Furniture, fixtures and equipment, 20%; and Kitchen equipment, 30%.

» Deferred revenue represents the value of gift cards sold, but not yet redeemed.

» The company initially obtained a $1-million loan, which was repaid with blended payments over a five-year period, with interest of 7%.

» Kevin has been paying himself an annual dividend of $40,000. He would like this dividend to continue into the future. In addition, Kevin draws an annual salary of $95,000, which is reflective of the fair market value of the services he provides.

Future Financial Results – Regina Operations

» The Regina location is expected to generate the same revenues, and net income, as the Saskatoon operation.

Section 3: Intermediate Accounting I Cases

Alexander Properties

Contributed by
Sara Stonehouse CA
Assistant Professor, University of Guelph

INTRODUCTION

On January 1, 2014, Alexander Properties (AP), a private enterprise, adopted International Financial Reporting Standards (IFRS). Brian McParland, the company's Chief Financial Officer, was responsible for all financial reporting issues upon convergence. As he read through the new standards, he often saw the current Canadian GAAP accounting methods as an option for reporting under IFRS. In any instances where the Canadian GAAP method was still an option, he instructed the company's controller, Fran Bouchard, to take the strategy "if it isn't broken, don't fix it."

It is now January 5, 2015, and the management team at AP is excited for some big expansion plans that are set to start this fiscal year and continue for the next five years. In order to finance the large expansion plan, management has decided to take the company public within the next couple of years. As such, there is a significant focus on maintaining a strong net income and key financial ratios such as return on equity and return on assets.

When IFRS was adopted at the beginning of 2014, Brian did not see the benefit of recording the investment properties at their fair value. At that time, the main user of the financial statements was the bank. The bank was not concerned with the fair values of the properties. As the company contemplates the upcoming IPO, Brian is starting to wonder if it would make more sense for the company to use fair value accounting to account for its investment properties.

COMPANY BACKGROUND

Founded in 1990, Alexander Properties is well known for owning and operating commercial real estate. The company owns and operates several properties in large metropolitan areas including downtown Toronto, Montreal, Vancouver, and Ottawa. AP is headquartered in Toronto. Most recently, the company acquired two premium properties in New York City.

Alexander Properties operates as a private company but decided to adopt IFRS as opposed to Accounting Standards for Private Entities (ASPE) as it always viewed becoming a public company as a viable option for obtaining financing. Over the past five years, the company has experienced significant growth as a result of the purchase of seven new properties.

The company's accounting department is managed by the controller, Fran Bouchard. Fran has a great understanding of the business and the relevant accounting as she has been the controller for almost 15 years. In light of the decision to take the company public, it has become a priority of Fran to evaluate the balance sheet and look for areas that could be improved. The most significant asset on the balance sheet of the company is its investment properties. The company currently follows the cost method to account for these properties. By following this method of accounting, the true value of the asset is not reflected on the balance sheet. At this point, Fran is not sure if there are fair value options under IFRS with respect to investment property.

Earlier that week, Brian McParland had asked Fran to present a summary of her findings to the management team in a meeting at the end of the month. Brian was responsible for the notion "if it isn't broken, don't fix it." He stressed that if she thought a method of accounting should be changed, he wanted a detailed explanation of why the change makes sense for Alexander Properties. His concern was not related to any transitional issues, but focused on the long-term impact of any accounting change. Specifically, Brian wants to know what the impact would be on the current year net income, return on equity, and return on assets if any new accounting changes were adopted. He wants to know what the differences are between the revaluation model and the fair value model. The 2014 financial statements can be found in Exhibit I. Although Brian is concerned about these issues, he said to Fran "if worse comes to worse, we can just try out the fair value model, and if we don't like it, will just switch back." In addition, Brian was concerned about what would happen if AP decided to value the investment properties at their fair value if the company decided to become a public company in the United States.

STRATEGY

As the economy weakened during 2008 and 2009, Alexander was able to show modest growth. AP is built on a strong foundation and therefore did not endure significant losses during this time. Since the company's inception in 1990, fostering long-term relationships with tenants has been a priority. When the financial crisis was at its peak, 70% of AP's tenants were occupying office space for five or more years. In order to foster these long-term tenant relationships AP provides competitive prices in premium locations of the city. The companies AP serves have a desire and a need to be in the heart of the city.

At the end of 2009, AP purchased two premium properties in New York City at a discounted price. Although the properties required a significant amount of upgrading, AP was able to get them up and running in a very short period of time. Currently both locations have a combined vacancy of 15%. When AP purchased the properties, management had forecasted both locations would remain 40% vacant until at least the end of 2012.

As the two properties in New York City have been very successful, AP is planning on expanding further into the United States. AP has considered purchasing properties in Chicago and Atlanta. In order to facilitate this growth plan, the company is planning to go public either on the Toronto Stock Exchange or the New York Stock Exchange.

THE INVESTMENT PROPERTIES

The company owns and operates 10 properties. In December 2014, the company had a real estate company value the properties to comply with the new IFRS standards. The fair values of the 10 properties can be found in the accompanying notes to the financial statements in Exhibit II.

Required

Prepare a report for Brian to assess whether it is optimal for the company to use fair value accounting to account for their investment properties.

EXHIBIT I – SIMPLIFIED FINANCIAL STATEMENTS

ALEXANDER PROPERTIES
Statement of Income
December 31, 2014
In Thousands of Dollars

	2014
Rental revenue	31,711
Other property revenue	2,114
Total revenue	33,825
Property operating costs	10,809
Gross margin	23,016
Other expenses	1,350
Net income	**21,666**

Note: Depreciation expense for the year totalled $6,000

ALEXANDER PROPERTIES
Statement of Financial Position
December 31, 2014
In Thousands of Dollars

Assets		*Liabilities*	
Non-current assets		*Non-current liabilities*	
Investment property	12,980	Mortgages and loans	1,222
Loan receivable	1,407	Deferred tax liability	222
Investments	7,600	**Total non-current liabilities**	**1,444**
Total non-current assets	**21,987**	*Current liabilities*	
Current assets		Accounts payable	22,990
Deferred tax assets	850	Interest payable	500
Receivables	100,900	**Total current liabilities**	**23,490**
Cash and equivalents	110,980	**Total liabilities**	**24,934**
Total current assets	**212,730**		
Total assets	**234,717**	*Shareholders' equity*	
		Common shares	120,000
		Retained earnings	89,783
		Total equity	**209,783**
		Total liabilities and equity	**234,717**

EXHIBIT II – INVESTMENT PROPERTY ANALYSIS

(In Thousands of Dollars)

Location	Purchase Date	Net Book Value	Fair Value December 31, 2014	Fair Value December 31, 2013
Toronto	February 10, 1990	$1,880	$2,940	$2,800
Toronto	February 10, 1990	$ 800	$1,281	$1,220
Vancouver	February 17, 1992	$1,560	$2,016	$1,920
Montreal	March 27, 1993	$ 520	$1,181	$1,125
Montreal	April 21, 1998	$1,580	$1,680	$1,600
Toronto	April 25, 1999	$2,000	$1,100	$1,000
Vancouver	November 23, 2003	$ 880	$1,947	$1,770
Montreal	December 17, 2003	$1,110	$2,200	$2,000
New York	December 15, 2009	$1,650	$1,815	$1,650
New York	December 15, 2009	$1,000	$1,199	$1,090

Accounting Standards Overload?

As you return to classes this fall, you stop to reflect on an eventful and productive summer. You were able to gain valuable work experience through your summer placement, you completed a summer course, and you also had some time to rest and relax!

While walking to the bookstore, you bump into an old high school friend, Patricia, who is completing an engineering degree. She tells you that she too had a very busy and productive summer as her time was mostly occupied by her new start-up business. Patricia was able to develop a complete prototype of her new LCD touch screen design, and is in discussion with different companies regarding commercialization. In addition, Patricia met a few venture capitalists at a summer conference who displayed an interest in her prototype.

Patricia must now prepare a set of financial statements in order to apply for a bank loan. The bank loan is important to finance the company's immediate growth, and market the prototype. Patricia knows that you are an accounting major, and has asked you to join her for coffee at the university coffee house so that she can ask you a few questions. The following is a transcript of the discussion that took place:

You: Well, it sounds like you have been busy this past summer!

Patricia: Yes, time has just been flying by, but it has been fun so far! My next step is to now prepare a set of financial statements. My first question is, how are financial statements used?

You: Financial statements are important. They enable the user to assess…

(…before you could finish, Patricia interrupts you)

Patricia: Oh, Oh, and also, I have done a bit of research on preparing the statements, and I realized that there are different sets of standards. However, I am unsure of why there are different standards, and how a company should select between these standards.

You: Well, I can help you with that as well. The different standards…

(…before you could finish, Patricia interrupts you)

Patricia: And, not only that, but each set of standards is so long. It is daunting to look at the sheer size of the standards. What holds all these standards together? Is there an overriding theory or set of principles and characteristics? I heard that there is something called a conceptual framework. What's included in this framework, and what is its purpose?

You: Yes, there is a conceptual framework. It actually ties back into your first question as it provides a general…

Just as you are about to provide an answer, another old friend, who is passing by, stops and sits down to chat. Knowing that there are too many interruptions to provide Patricia with the answers she needs, you promise to email her a brief report that addresses the three questions that she raised.

Required

Prepare the brief report for Patricia.

Body and Soul Fitness Centre

The Body and Soul Fitness Centre (BSFC) is a newly established business that offers yoga classes and yoga clothing and accessories. The BSFC operates out of Saskatoon, Saskatchewan, and is owned by Carol Szabados, a former yoga teacher for a large gym franchise. Carol decided to start her own yoga centre in order to provide a larger variety of customized yoga classes to small groups, including beginner, intermediate and advanced classes. The BSFC also has a small storefront that is used to sell yoga clothing, along with other accessories, such as headbands, water bottles, and yoga mats.

In order to help finance operations, BSFC obtained a working capital loan from the small business department of a local credit union. The loan is a revolving line of credit that is secured by the company's inventory and accounts receivable. The loan is not to exceed a maximum of 50% of inventory and 75% of accounts receivable as at the company's year end (March 31, 2014). The BSFC must present reviewed financial statements, prepared in accordance with ASPE, to the credit union within 60 days of its year end.

It is now February 2014, and Carol is starting to get nervous about the preparation of the financial statements. Carol has minimal exposure to accounting duties; therefore, she hired a local bookkeeper to help her select an appropriate fiscal year end, set up an accounting software package, and design processes and documents to be used in day-to-day functions.

Carol has contacted Lebeau and Liang LLP in regards to conducting a review of the BSFC's financial statements. You are the senior accountant in charge of the review, and recently sat down with Carol to discuss the engagement.

Carol feels confident that all of her routine transactions have been posted correctly, but is unsure of some of the more complicated issues that arose during the year. Carol discusses with you the following unresolved issues:

1. BSFC was able to obtain a large corporate client, Haschuk and Roney, Barristers and Solicitors, LLP. On July 1, 2013, BSFC and the law firm agreed that the employees of the law firm would have unlimited access to the yoga classes for a yearly fee of $50,000, with 50% payable upfront. The fee is non-refundable, non-cancellable, and not dependent on the number of classes actually participated in by the law firm employees. Carol credited revenue for $50,000 when the contract was signed, and debited both cash and accounts receivable for $25,000 each. This large contract helped with cash flows, and is a major reason why BSFC has a current cash balance of $10,000.

2. Mid-way through the year, BSFC began selling energy bars and drinks in its storefront. BSFC reached an exclusive agreement to be the sole distributor of Excel Energy Plus bars in Saskatoon. BSFC was required to purchase 5,000 bars at the onset of the contract, at a cost of $2.50 per bar. On March 15, an ingredient included in the bars was allegedly linked to various illnesses. Currently, the Food and Drug Administration in the U.S. is investigating the allegations, and the outcome is uncertain. Canadian officials have not yet commented on the situation. BSFC sold 1,340 bars during the year.

3. The aged accounts receivable balance is as follows:

		Balance	Current	30 - 60 days	61 - 90 days	over 90 days
1	Haschuk and Roney, LLP	25,000				25,000
2	Yvette Seguin	200		200		
3	Jane Collie	45	45			
4	Nurses' association	4,125	4,125			
5	Arthur Smith	75			75	
6	Ian Waruszynski	150				150
7	Fresh Grocery Ltd.	850		850		
8	Timber Forest Products	1,650			1,650	
9	BioMed Ltd.	950		950		
10	Precious Metal Miners	1,275			1,275	
		34,320	4,170	2,000	3,000	25,150

BSFC reached an agreement with a local nurses' association to provide 55 pairs of yoga pants and shirts for an upcoming walk-a-thon in May 2013. The shirt and pants were customized with an embroidery of each nurse's name. BSFC charged the nurses' association a special promotion price of $75 per combo and delivered the goods mid-March. In late March, the nurses' association contacted BSFC stating that the goods received are not the same as the goods ordered. The nurses' association has asked for a 40% discount on the goods, or else it plans to return goods and cancel its order.

Receivables 7 to 10 are a result of a promotion held by BSFC in order to attract more corporate clients. Based on her experience with a larger gym franchise, Carol states that 10% of receivables past 60 days are typically uncollectible. However, she is very confident that the receivable from Haschuk and Roney, LLP will be collected.

Even though a violation of the covenant can result in the credit facility becoming cancelled with the outstanding balance due immediately, Carol states that she is not too concerned because her accounts receivable and inventory are $34,320 and $96,550, respectively, while her loan is only $65,000. However, she would like you to prepare a report, to go along with the review engagement, which discusses the appropriate accounting treatment of the above noted accounting issues.

Required

It is now March 30, 2014. Prepare the report for Carol, and provide any other recommendations relevant to the bank loan.

Fantasyfootball.net

Fantasyfootball.net (FFN) is a company whose primary activities are hosting a real-time, online fantasy football website and writing and publishing an annual magazine that discusses fantasy football strategies, predictions, and articles. FFN has an August 31 year end. This year end was selected as the main football season begins in September.

FFN is a privately held company, owned by Danny and Manny, two friends who started the business to build on their affinity of fantasy football and capture a portion of the $800-million industry. Danny holds a computer science degree, and Manny holds an Honours Bachelor of Commerce degree and is a professional accountant. By providing faster service, along with more statistics, projections, and game play options, Danny and Manny felt that they could offer a unique service that differentiates their website from all of the competitors. In addition, FFN is seeking to expand its services by offering fantasy coverage of American college and Canadian professional football, to go along with American professional football.

Given the significant growth in the industry, FFN has recently received many offers to sell the business. Danny and Manny are unsure about selling their business as they enjoy their jobs, and believe that there will be much room for future business growth. However, the owners also know that fantasy football could be just another fad that is currently at its peak. In addition, the rate of change in the on-line gaming industry could lead to a possible alternative platform. Therefore, the owners feel it is prudent to at least consider the offers to sell.

A general review of the purchase offers suggests that fantasy football companies generally sell for an average of 2 times revenues and 4 times net earnings. The owners review the internal financial statements for 2014, which report revenues of $975,000 and earnings of $536,250. Danny quickly determines that FFN could be sold for $2,047,500 or just over $1 million for each owner. This is a considerable sum of money given that they have invested only five years with FFN. However, Manny states that the internal financial statements are only draft at this stage because he has yet to consider the impact of the following events:

1. FFN writes an annual fantasy football magazine. The magazine goes on sale in July, and is sold through the company's website and through various retailers. This year, FFN secured a large contract with Books, a large book and magazine retailer in Canada. The contract allow Books to return any unsold magazines at the end of October (history suggests that annual magazines no longer sell after October as they become outdated and lose their relevance). A total of 40,000 magazines were shipped to Books in July. Books will be required to pay FFN $3 per magazine if all 40,000 are sold, $3.50 per magazine if less than 40,000 but more than 20,000 magazines are sold, and $4 per magazine if less than 20,000 are sold. The magazines have a retail price of $6.99.

    The cost to develop the content and publish the magazine was incurred in the months of April to July. Accordingly, Manny recorded $120,000 in revenue when the magazines were shipped. Historically, FFN has sold 70% of its stock prior to August. Danny and Manny believe that the amount of foot traffic at Books should increase the percentage of magazines sold.

2. FFN revised the layout, graphics, and content of the annual magazine this year. The redesign resulted in an additional $45,000 in expenses in the current year, relative to the past three years, whereby the magazine maintained the same format as in prior years. Magazines normally go through a redesign phase every three to four years in order to provide readers with a fresh and current magazine. Manny has capitalized the $45,000 as an intangible asset (magazine design). The finite life asset will be amortized over its useful life.

3.   FFN earns the majority of its revenue from fees charged to use its website to host a fantasy football league. FFN charges users $20 per season (seasons runs from September to January). This year FFN offered two new promotions:

(a) Early Bird Registration: Users who register and pay for a season prior to August 31 would be eligible for a reduced $15 fee. The fee is non-refundable, and must be used for the upcoming fantasy football season. A total of 5,000 users took advantage of the early bird price for the upcoming season. Revenue was recorded as users registered.

(b) Three-Year Membership Fee Reduction: Users can register and pay for the next three seasons for a total price of $30. The fee is non-refundable, and must be used for the upcoming three fantasy football seasons. A total of 7,000 users registered for the three-year membership fee. Revenue was recorded as users registered for the three-year seasons' package.

4.   In addition to redesigning the annual magazine, FFN also redesigned its website. The redesign resulted in some general changes, along with significant upgrades to the functionality of the website. The total cost of the website redesign was $95,000, of which $57,000 was a result of programming costs for the upgrades and advertising. Manny has capitalized all $95,000 in costs to the website intangible asset.

Given the nature of the company's operations, the vast majority of all costs are fixed overhead costs related to staff support, server maintenance, hardware maintenance, and website design. Any variable costs are immaterial.

Required

It is now September 2, 2014. Assume the role of Manny and determine the revised revenue and net earnings amounts in accordance with ASPE.

Forestry Limited (FL)

Contributed by
Irene Wiecek, FCA
Senior Lecturer in Accounting, University of Toronto
Director, CA Rotman Centre for Innovation in Accounting Education
Associate Director, Master of Management & Professional Accounting,
University of Toronto, Mississauga

Forestry Limited (FL) is a private company incorporated in Canada. Its head office is in Toronto but its primary operations are in China and include owning and managing tree plantations, sales of trees and logs, and manufacturing of wood products. In addition to the above, the company also holds tree-cutting rights for several large areas of government-owned forest. The company is currently at the centre of a major media debate. Another company has accused them of grossly overstating their estimated land and forest holdings. FL is denying all charges and maintains that it had qualified consultants estimate the value of the holdings. Due to an economic recession, sales are down this year.

In order to maximize the quality and quantity of trees harvested from the plantations, the company must manage the forest, including feeding the trees, using herbicides where necessary, managing water supply to trees, and thinning out trees so that the remaining trees have sufficient light and space to grow. In order to manage the water supply, the company builds terraces on the land on which the trees are standing. This helps hold the water but is very labour intensive and costly as it must be done by hand. All the materials needed must be trucked in and then carried to the worksite for installation. The trees are less susceptible to damage from bugs and/or other insects when they are well watered. It has been a very dry year and 25% of the forests are suffering from drought and insect infestation. FL is hopeful that with additional care, it can reverse any potential damage from this so that the value of the wood is not affected.

FL has just purchased the rights to cut down trees in a large forest in Northern China. The agreement allows it to harvest the trees for a five-year period. Although not written in the contract, it is understood that they will replant the area when finished. In order to access the trees, the company has had to build a major road into the forest. After the harvest is completed, the road will not be used by FL but the government has indicated that it would like to consider buying the road. The acquisition was financed by the issuance of non–interest-bearing convertible debt to an institutional investor. Under the terms of the debt, FL must maintain a debt to equity ratio of no greater than 2:1.

On December 31 (year end), the company signed an agreement to buy a plantation in New Zealand for $20 million from NZL. Immediately thereafter, FL agreed to sell the property to Gray Trees Limited (GL) for $22 million. GL had been unsuccessful in acquiring the plantation directly and had enlisted FL to negotiate on their behalf. In the December 31 financial statements, FL has booked the transaction as two separate transactions - a purchase and sale (resulting in revenues for the current year showing a significant increase). The deal with GL closes on January 1 and GL will pay cash of $22 million to FL at that time. The $20-million payment to NZL is due January 1. GL is an established company that deals with FL all the time. GL is very profitable.

On December 15, FL signed an agreement with Logs Limited (LL) under which FL will harvest timber from a forest owned by LL and "sell" the logs back to LL. The agreement is worded such that FL "buys" the cutting rights for $7 million and then sells the cut logs for $14 million (market price). No money will change hands until the job is done, at which point, LL will pay FL the net amount of $7 million upon delivery of the logs. The harvesting was completed by year end and FL booked $14 million as revenues.

FL is not sure whether it should follow IFRS or ASPE.

Required

Adopt the role of the company's auditors and discuss the financial reporting issues.

Global Logistics

Global Logistics is a newly formed private company that manufactures and sells general and specialized golf carts with global positioning computers built in. The computers allow the golf courses to provide information to golfers on hole location and distance. It also communicates with golfers by providing them with information on how fast they are playing, when to speed up, and if they have gone off of the required golf path. It also allows golfers to order food at the beginning of the ninth hole and get picked up quickly on the tenth hole. Golf courses find these computers provide an advantage as they keep the speed of play going and also tend to increase food revenues by encouraging golfers at the ninth hole.

This is the first year of operations for Global and you are its manager of accounting, having recently being hired after completing the requirements of your accounting designation. The controller of Global has left you in charge of establishing the accounting policies over inventory. In anticipation of the upcoming year end, you have been asked to prepare a memo to the controller that she can then use to discuss with the founder of Global regarding the proper financial accounting and presentation of the inventory-related items. The controller would like you to identify any potential financial disclosure requirements in addition to accounting policies. The inventory details follow in Exhibit I.

Required

Prepare the report.

EXHIBIT I – INVENTORY DETAILS

» A contract was signed between Global and Golf Carts of America (GCA). The contract called for GCA to manufacture unpainted golf carts for Global at a cost of $350 per cart. Shipping for each golf cart amounts to $20 and is payable by Global.

» The computerized component was developed by Global and is manufactured in its plant. Parts include the screen, computer module, and battery pack. Labour charges are required to manufacture the component and paint the golf cart. Global has a policy of keeping several weeks' supply of parts on hand at all times to ensure there is no shortage.

» Early in the year, Global manufactured 10,000 GC100 computer modules at a total manufacturing cost of $150 each. Due to very quick changes in technology, the GC100 component is already outdated and has been replaced by the GC200. Global still has 2,000 GC100 modules in inventory. The production manager believes that Global could sell the components to a third party that would disassemble and recycle the parts. The amount the third party would give Global is $110 per unit with Global paying shipping costs of $5 per unit. The founder has not yet agreed to this arrangement.

» Global sells two different types of golf carts. The first is its standard cart that includes the golf cart above and the computerized module. The colour is a standard green colour. The second golf cart includes advanced features. In addition to the cart and module, this model also includes a small on-board cooler and front glass protector. The second model is expected to be a big seller within the private golf course industry.

Gunness Industries

Gunness Industries (GI) was established in 1980 as a manufacturer of canoes and kayaks. It has quickly become a respected company and well known for its creation of highly durable canoes and kayaks. In 1990, GI went public and is following IFRS for financial reporting purposes and has a December 31 year end. Ted, GI's controller, has been with GI for 10 years and oversees the financial functions and the year end audit functions. GI's auditors, Bomanji, Dagwood LLP (BD), have completed the audited financial statements for the last eight years. GI has typically had a very good report with the firm. You, CA, are a newly minted senior staff accountant and this is your first time on the audit engagement and your first time as a senior on an audit.

During the past fiscal year, GI has undertaken some innovative approaches to its business. This has been spearheaded by GI's founder and major shareholder, Patrick Pilek. While canoeing and kayaking still remains a popular pastime in Canada, the current economic recession has resulted in some customers delaying replacement of their recreational watercraft. As a result, Patrick has looked at new ways to lower costs and this has led to some accounting events that are not a normal occurrence for GI.

In is now January 3 and in anticipation of the upcoming audit, Ted has asked your firm to provide some alternatives and recommendations on how to deal with some of the year's events. GI has always prided itself on providing the most transparent financial presentation possible while maximizing net income under GAAP.

Exhibit I summarizes the accounting issues that GI is requesting guidance on. Your partner would like you to provide a draft report to Ted and Patrick that fully analyzes the alternatives available.

Required

Provide the report.

EXHIBIT I – SUMMARY OF GI'S ACCOUNTING ISSUES

» GI's kayaks are manufactured with layers of fibreglass and Kevlar cloth. Patrick researched ways of reducing the cost of manufacturing through the use of an advanced, computerized machine. The machine was created, on paper, by Patrick, and built by a company that designs and manufactures specialized equipment for businesses. The machine was built for a cost of $885,000 with installation costs totaling $10,500. Installation occurred in November. It is expected to last 10 years and substantially reduce operating costs. It is not clear yet if this new machine will reduce the number of employees at GI as the highly computerized equipment may replace some of the work currently being done. It will improve the quality of the kayaks even further and create a competitive advantage within the marketplace.

» In order to help finance the cost of the new equipment, Ted researched and applied for a number of government grants that were put in place to stimulate the economy. While he didn't expect to necessarily receive all of the grants, he was pleasantly surprised that GI was awarded two different grants. A summary of each follows:

  • Grant #1: The Government of Canada provided GI with a $300,000 capital grant to offset the cost of the new equipment. The terms of the grant called for the construction of new equipment that would allow Canadian companies to continue to be competitive throughout the world. Payment would be made upon completion of, and installation of, the equipment. The government required proof via invoices and a letter from the manufacturer of the equipment. GI has completed all the documents and mailed the information on December 15. GI was told to expect eight to 12 weeks for payment.

  • Grant #2: The Government of Quebec agreed to provide a $150,000 grant to offset labour costs for medium sized manufacturing firms. The terms of the grant were that GI would maintain a labour force of a minimum of 25 employees as calculated on a monthly weighted average throughout each of the next three years. The entire $150,000 (assume to be divided equally between the three years) was received on December 1. Should GI not achieve the labour targets in any given year, they will be required to repay that year's portion only. According to labour data received by Ted, the required minimum of 25 employees was achieved this year.

» In addition to grants received this year, Ted informs you that there were some issues with a $60,000 grant received three years ago. The grant was to offset the hiring of recent university graduates under a federal government hiring program. The grant required GI to maintain a university graduate in its employment for each of three years with $20,000 each year being used to offset labour costs. Should the university graduate leave the employment of GI at any time within the three year period, the entire amount would be repayable to the government. The entire $60,000 was received in cash and initially recorded as deferred revenue; $20,000 was recognized in year 1 as revenue and a further $20,000 recognized in year 2. When you examine the audit file, you note that the partner agreed with this accounting as there was strong evidence that the graduate would remain within GI's employment for substantially longer than three years. This year, however, the graduate decided to leave GI in order to sail around the world. The government has sent notification that it will be seeking repayment of the $60,000 as a result of this.

Kentuckyville Slugger

Kentuckyville Slugger (KS) is a manufacturer of baseball and softball accessories. The company was established by Sammy Sousa in 1913, and produced only wooden baseball bats. KS has evolved over the past hundred years to offer a wide variety of products, including aluminum bats, batting gloves, cleats, and fielding gloves. KS's products are sold in Canada, the United States, and Mexico. Since inception, the company has continued to be a family-run, closely held business with its manufacturing plant located in Red Deer, Alberta.

Recently, the company has been finding it difficult to compete in the global marketplace due to the rising Canadian dollar, the lower wage costs in Asia, and a general decrease in consumer discretionary spending following the global credit crisis. The recent competitive pressures have made it difficult for KS to reinvest in its capital assets in order to become more efficient.

The current CEO, Michael Sousa, does not want to relocate as the company is a long-standing member of the Red Deer community, providing many citizens with well-paying jobs. However, the competitive landscape is making it difficult to continue the status quo.

Michael has recently come across a new government grant program that is part of an initiative to improve the productivity of Canadian companies and promote employment. The program provides eligible manufacturing companies with the opportunity to receive a forgivable loan to upgrade their capital assets in the interest of efficiency. The following criteria are used to assess eligibility:

» The grant must be used to invest in capital assets that will improve productivity, as measured by output per employee hour.

» The grant must promote employment in the manufacturing sector in Canada.

» The company must display a financial need for the application.

If obtained, the grant would allow KS to continue to operate in Red Deer with the same workforce and increase its output by at least 20%. Audited financial statements must be included with the grant application.

Brandon Sousa, CA, is the controller of KS. Recently, Brandon has begun preparing the December 31, 2014 year-end financial statements to provide to the external auditors. Brandon recently met with Michael in order to discuss certain transactions that have yet to be recorded in the books of account. Michael would like Brandon to prepare a report that discusses the appropriate accounting treatment of these transactions. The notes from the meeting can be found in Exhibit I.

Required

Assume the role of Brandon and prepare the report. The financial statements are prepared in accordance with ASPE.

EXHIBIT I – NOTES FROM MEETING WITH MICHAEL

» KS entered into a sales agreement with the Canadian Hardball Association (CHA) to provide 5,000 hardball bats (at a price of $50 per bat) for an upcoming international baseball tournament that will be held in Canada. The bats were shipped to the CHA during the month of November 2014. As per the agreement, the CHA has until February 2015 to inspect the bats in order to determine if they meet international safety and performance standards.

» KS has manufactured bats for similar tournaments in the past and has never had an issue meeting the safety and performance standards. Michael suggests not recording any revenue in the current year because the CHA has the right to accept or reject the quality of the bat.

» KS delivered 2,500 soft-spike cleats to The Shoe Store for $100,000 in December. The cleats were sold during the holiday season. The cleats can be returned to KS within one year of the purchase date in the case of a manufacturer defect. Past history suggests that 5% of the cleats are returned within the one-year return period. Michael suggests that the revenue should be recorded once the right of return period lapses.

» During the year, KS entered into a sales agreement with SportStore (SS) whereby KS designed and manufactured an aluminum bat that is to be sold exclusively through SS's retail stores across Canada. The exclusive agreement is for a two-year period, at which point the bat can be sold through other retailers. During the agreement period, SS must purchase a minimum of 100,000 bats from KS at a price of $55 per bat. During the year, SS purchased 45,000 bats.

» KS incurred $155,000 in design and development costs during the year in developing the bat. KS incurs $25 in costs to manufacture the bat. Michael suggests that the $155,000 design costs be expensed in the current year.

» KS sold on credit 2,500 KSX baseball gloves for $50,000 to Q-Mart in November 2014. Q-Mart is a large public company, with retail stores across Canada and the U.S. Around year end, analysts have begun reporting that Q-Mart is having serious financial difficulties and may file for bankruptcy if its lenders do not restructure its debt. Q-Mart's share price has plummeted in recent weeks. Michael suggests writing off the $50,000 account receivable.

» During the year, KS acquired a new storage warehouse in Red Deer. The warehouse was purchased for $250,000. KS then incurred $10,000 in costs to install an HVAC system, and $7,500 to replace the roof shingles. Michael suggests expensing the additional costs ($17,500) as repairs and maintenance.

Old Bay Manufacturing

Old Bay Manufacturing (OBM) is a medium sized Canadian company that is publicly traded. Located in Nova Scotia, OBM manufactures large steel components built to the specifications of its customers. In the past, OBM has manufactured steel beams for the fishing industry and specialized steel buckets for the mining industry. OBM's clients include Canadian and American companies, with some companies in the United Kingdom. In more recent years, OBM has begun to expand its client base to customers with companies near the Mediterranean and Aegean Seas. OBM's investors have always felt confident about OBM's success. With some current expansion programs on the horizon, OBM is hoping to take advantage of its current investors' satisfaction and is contemplating issuing more shares to the public.

A typical OBM sale proceeds as follows:

» Clients will generally contact OBM's sales office located just outside of Halifax. They have several repeat clients, and new clients generally find them due to their stellar reputation for quality products and support after the sale.

» Once a general understanding of the client's needs is understood, OBM will determine if a site visit is required. Typically if the order is a repeat order or the requirements are standard (for example a standard-sized steel beam), no site visit is required and a sales quote is prepared.

» If a site visit is required, OBM charges the client for the travel costs and the designer's time. While this may differ depending on the region being travelled to, they have developed a standard fee to simplify the process. The standard fee is $10,000 and is non-refundable and payable in advance. Once the plans have been accepted by the client, OBM requires a deposit of 50% of the quote prior to beginning manufacturing, which can take between eight weeks and two years.

» The balance of the payment is required after OBM has delivered the goods to the client. The sales office will invoice the client with payment terms of 30 days. Typically, uncollectible amounts are minimal given the project commitment by the clients.

» In addition to custom orders, OBM also manufactures and sells standard steel beams and products. Clients place orders for the products by calling the sales office. If a client has ordered with OBM before and their credit is satisfactory, the order is placed and delivered. A sales invoice follows, requiring payment in 30 days. If it is a new client, a credit check is performed first. If a client's credit is satisfactory, they will be invoiced with the same payment terms. If there are concerns, the client is required to pay in advance.

OBM records any site visit fees initially as unearned revenue. Once the site visit, drawings, and quote has been completed, OBM records the revenue and the related expenses. If the client decides to go ahead with the project, OBM collects the 50% deposit and records it as unearned revenue.

At year end, OBM assesses the completion of each project. Typically, although each is customized, they have sufficient information to comfortably know the percentage of completion and can reliably measure the costs to date. The related revenues, expenses, and profit are recorded based upon these assessments.

You are the junior accountant, recently employed by OBM, and you are assisting in the preparation of December 31 year-end details prior to the auditors visiting. It is now February 1 and OBM has been faced with two unusual issues (Exhibit I) that you and your manager are trying to resolve. Your manager has stressed that the senior personnel is interested in maintaining high revenues and profits in anticipation of the release of more common shares. You have been asked to discuss the issues that have arisen, by preparing a memo to your manager addressing the alternatives and providing recommendations. While your goal is to meet the objectives of senior management, your manager stresses the need to follow IFRS.

Required

Prepare the memo.

EXHIBIT I – ISSUES FACING OBM

CHEEMA CORPORATION

Cheema Corporation came to OBM early in the year requesting some specialized steel buckets used at its fisheries plant located near the Aegean Sea. The initial site visit fee of $10,000 was paid immediately by Cheema and when a credit history was completed, no issues arose that would suggest there would be collection challenges. Cheema accepted the quote of $850,000 and paid half of the fee upfront, as required. The project was completed and delivered via ship on December 15. An invoice was prepared on December 15 and sent to the client. Unfortunately, right at the same time that the project was completed, there was significant political unrest that had thrown Cheema's country into turmoil. This political crisis has resulted in the inability for any monies to flow in and out of the country. The most current information suggests that there is no end in sight for a resolution. While the invoice was delivered to Cheema, no journal entry for the balance of the contract has yet to be recorded as there are differing views among OBM management as to how the transaction should be recorded. The CFO would like the revenue recorded, suggesting that the crisis is temporary and that Cheema has every intention of paying. The assistant controller is suggesting that revenue should be recorded with a corresponding allowance for doubtful accounts to recognize the potential bad debt. Your manager is unsure if revenue can be recorded at all given the circumstances.

DOCKSIDE VILLAS

Dockside Villas in Florida came to OBM last year looking for a sophisticated steel platform that could safely have luxury personal boats dock and then be removed. Once passengers had safely disembarked, the boat is lifted with a hydraulic system and moved out of the way and stored above the water. This allows Dockside Villas to store more boats in its marina. The total cost of the project was $1,320,000 and was unique in that OBM was required to install the equipment. Most clients installed their own equipment, but as part of the contract, OBM agreed to install the docking system using subcontractors. The system was built and delivered to the Dockside Villas location on October 20 and installation was expected to be completed by December 20. Due to some severe weather and labour issues, installation has been delayed significantly and is not expected to be completed until late January. The controller is recommending that the revenue be recognized at year end for this contract as the project has been manufactured and delivered to the client.

Senior Frog's Wines Inc.

Contributed by
Stephanie McGarry CA
Guest Lecturer, Lakehead University

Niagara-on-the-Lake (NOTL) is a small town in Southern Ontario, which is situated on the south shore of Lake Ontario. NOTL is home to a wealth of owner-managed and large commercial businesses, historical sites, and a theatre. This old town is known for the surrounding shipping yards and small shops but mainly for the production of wine.

Senior Frog's Wines Inc (SF) manufactures a number of different wines, including ice wines, dessert wines, and red and white wines. SF has been manufacturing wines for the past 100 years in NOTL and distributes its wines all across Canada. The senior management team of SF is responsible for the preparation of the financial statements and the presentation of the financial results to the 200 private shareholders of SF.

As the auditor of SF, you are responsible for issuing an unmodified audit opinion and are required to ensure SF's financial statements are in accordance with Accounting Standards for Private Enterprises (ASPE).

Audit evidence obtained for December 31, 2014 year end:

» During the month of February, it was noticed by one of the staff members that the holding unit for a chemical solution used to clean the wine bottles before they are filled has been leaking. SF is not sure how long this has been occurring as production is steady and the supplier fills up the tank each week.

» Upon further investigation, it was found that the cleaning solution machine has not been working. As a result, sterilization of the bottles has not occurred for some time and the chemicals have been leaking into the fields where the grape vines grow. The leak was fixed in March 2014 and the sterilization process is now working.

» In January 2014, the Liquor Control Board of Ontario informed SF that a significant amount of customers had brought the wine back showing unknown particles in the bottles and they reported feeling ill after consumption. Potential claims are unknown at this time (Exhibit I).

» Since SF's incorporation over 100 years ago, the market has shifted and sales for dessert and ice wines have fallen significantly. These wines made up over 35% of SF's total sales. As a result, SF hired a marketing guru named Charlie van Baaren to research market needs, and Charlie suggested focusing more on the dry, sweet, and blush wines. SF's decision was to discontinue selling ice and dessert wines (Exhibit II).

» Since SF will no longer be manufacturing some of its previous key wines they no longer need the equipment associated with their production (Exhibit II).

Required

Based on your review of the financial statements and the information obtained during your audit, explain to the senior management team the accounting issues you have identified, and the appropriate treatment in accordance with ASPE.

EXHIBIT I – POTENTIAL CLAIMS

» Legal letters were returned to the auditor and potential claims were listed. Financial amounts for the claims were not recorded on the legal letter, but further discussion with legal counsel shows that the claims will be likely to occur at a 35%-50% chance of legal progression.

» Additional legal letters have come back from the town of NOTL suggesting the clean-up of the chemical leak needs to be done immediately or additional legal advice will be sought. Estimated costs for this clean-up will be about $650,000 to $700,000, with an expectation that it will be more towards the higher end.

EXHIBIT II – DECISION TO DISCONTINUE MAKING ICE AND DESSERT WINES

» Sales and cash flows for the past three years related to dessert and ice wines is as follows:

2012	2013	2014
• $400,000 – Sales	• $290,000 – Sales	• $165,000 – Sales
• $365,000 – Cash flow	• $175,000 – Cash flow	• $38,000 – Cash flow

» Manufacturing asset costs, accumulated depreciation, and net book value (NBV) with respect to these two discontinued operations are as follows (purchased in 2012, no major repairs, 30-year useful life):

Year	2012	2013	2014
Cost	$750,000	$750,000	$750,000
Accumulated Depreciation	(25,000)	(50,000)	(75,000)
NBV	$725,000	$700,000	$675,000

» According to the Board of Director minutes, while management of SF intends to sell the machinery as it is only three years old and still has considerable life, they may continue to produce some ice and dessert wines until a buyer is found.

» Management is responsible for these decisions, assets can be ready within 30 days' notice, and the marketing department has begun the process of advertising on local websites in order to sell the equipment.

» Based on the area in which SF is located, there are many wine manufacturers and a sale should occur in the short term. (Date the sale went up was January 20, 2014)

» SF is asking $450,000 for the equipment.

» It will take approximately one month to disassemble the equipment.

» The wine equipment was posted on many websites in January 2014. SF has had a number of interested buyers but one in particular has expressed some strong interest. A new company wanting to produce ice and dessert wines is interested, but is unable to purchase the equipment immediately as it won't be opening up until February 2014. It is, however, willing to place a 25% deposit on the equipment immediately.

Star Gazer Ltd.

Star Gazer Ltd. (SGL) is a manufacturer of telescopes and binoculars, offering products to amateurs and professionals. The company has experienced significant growth in the past five years due to an increase in the popularity of star gazing, combined with an effective branding campaign and enhanced distribution network.

The company has applied to the Bank of Winnipeg for a $1-million long-term loan in order to finance further expansion plans. Specifically, the funds would be used to purchase additional capital assets.

SGL's application and financial statements have been provided to Peter Sparks, a newly hired junior analyst with the Bank of Winnipeg. Peter has been asked by his supervisor, Maria Simms, to conduct a preliminary review of SGL's financial statements and determine whether SGL should proceed further into a more detailed analysis. Maria has asked Peter to document his recommendation and supporting analysis in a report that will be maintained in SGL's file.

Maria: "SGL has provided us with a copy of their most recent balance sheet and income statement (Exhibit I). I know that this may not be enough to make the final decision, but it should be more than enough for you to get started."

Peter: "Yes, I can obtain much information from these two statements."

Maria: "Okay, that's great. I took a quick look at the balance sheet and am wondering what has caused the change in cash. Cash is needed to pay back the loan. Although I haven't done any rigorous analysis, it is a bit concerning to see the cash decline by such a large amount."

Peter: "I can definitely look into the decrease in cash."

Maria: "It may also be useful to give some thought to what the balance sheet may look like if the loan is approved. Historical statements are fine, but they will not be able to provide you with this information. Additional information on the use of the loan is provided in Exhibit II."

Peter: "That is a great point. I will take this into consideration."

Maria: "Alright. Let me know if I can be of any further assistance. I look forward to reading your report. If you recommend to proceed with future due diligence, can you prepare a list of additional information that would be useful in making our final decision?"

Peter: "Yes, I can most certainly do that. I will get started right away."

Peter is excited about his first assignment, and wants to impress Maria. Peter begins to conduct some preliminary research by searching the bank's database for industry comparables. Peter has located various industry ratios that can be used as a benchmark (Exhibit III).

Required

Assume the role of Peter and prepare the report.

EXHIBIT I – FINANCIAL STATEMENTS

STAR GAZER LTD.

BALANCE SHEET

As at December 31	2015	2014	2013
Assets			
Current			
Cash	381 139	$ 235,359	$ 134,550
Marketable securities	0	145,780	457,206
Accounts receivable	312 830	223,450	174,930
Inventory	596 078	425,770	355,790
Prepaid expenses	24 500	17,500	19,500
	1 314 547	1,047,859	1,141,976
Property and equipment, net	3 690 283	2,756,950	2,492,655
	5 004 830	3,804,809	3,634,631
Liabilities and shareholders' equity			
Current			
Accounts payable	412 027	294,305	95,700
Accrued and other liabilities	229 014	237,595	244,760
Current portion of long-term debt	500 000	375,900	345,900
	1 141 041	907,800	686,360
Long-term debt	2 260 330 1 780 330	1,280,330	1,601,500
Common shares (50,000 outstanding)	595 817	595,817	595,817
Retained earnings	1 487 642	1,020,862	750,953
	2 083 459	1,616,679	1,346,771
		$3,804,809	$3,634,631

Net income 2015 → 466 780

EXHIBIT I CONTINUED – FINANCIAL STATEMENTS

STAR GAZER LTD.

INCOME STATEMENT

For the year ended December 31	2014	2013
Sales	$2,975,990	$2,575,990
Cost of sales	1,368,955	1,184,955
Gross profit	1,607,035	1,391,035
Expenses		
Amortization	155,490	125,490
General and administrative	134,500	102,800
Marketing and sales	175,680	155,600
Interest expense	76,820	96,090
Office expense	295,980	255,000
Wages and benefits, administration	315,000	315,000
Total operating expenses	1,153,470	1,049,980
Operating income	453,565	341,055
Gain (losses) on marketable securities	25,475	9,800
Impairment loss on capital assets	0	0
Income (loss) before taxes	479,040	350,855
Provision for (benefit from) income taxes	134,131	98,239
Net income	344,909	252,615
Opening balance—retained earnings	750,953	573,338
Net income	344,909	252,615
Dividends	75,000	75,000
Closing balance—retained earnings	$1,020,862	$750,953

EXHIBIT II – INFORMATION ABOUT THE USE OF THE LOAN

» The loan will be used to purchase $1 million in additional capital assets. The additional assets will result in an increase in revenues of 20%.

» The loan will bear interest at 6%. Principal payments of $200,000 per annum will be required.

» The company will withhold any dividend payment during the foreseeable future in order to support the debt to equity ratio.

» The capital assets are expected to have a useful life of 15 years with no residual value.

» All other fixed expenses are expected to remain consistent.

» The existing loan will require a principal payment of approximately $375,900 during the upcoming fiscal year. The payment for the following fiscal year is expected to be $300,000.

» Accounts receivable, inventory, prepaid expense, and accounts payable will all increase by 40% as a result of the increased sales.

» The marketable securities will be converted to cash at the beginning of the year.

EXHIBIT III – INDUSTRY BENCHMARK RATIOS

	Ratio	Industry Average
	Profitability	2014
1	Return on equity	15.0%
2	Return on assets	8.0%
3	Financial leverage percentage	7.0%
4	Earnings per share	$4.40
5	Quality of income	75.0%
6	Profit margin	10.0%
7	Fixed asset turnover	2.00
	Tests of liquidity	
8	Cash ratio	7.0%
9	Current ratio	1.00
10	Quick ratio	0.75
11	Receivable turnover	13.00
12	Average days in accounts receivable	28.08
13	Payable turnover	19.00
14	Average days in accounts payable	19.21
15	Inventory turnover	6.50
16	Average days in inventory	56.15
	Solvency and equity position	
17	Times interest earned	5.40
18	Cash coverage	6.30
19	Debt to equity ratio	1.35
	Miscellaneous	
20	Book value per share	$29.00

Zenith Security Ltd.

Zenith Security Ltd. (ZSL) is a home and commercial security company. The company was established in 1968 by Paolo Santiago, its sole shareholder, to provide security services in Halifax. Since its inception, ZSL has grown to provide its services across all major cities in Atlantic Canada.

In order to continue growing the company, Mr. Santiago has decided to expand into Ontario and Quebec. In order to facilitate the expansion, ZSL is planning to become a franchiser whereby local entrepreneurs can purchase an exclusive right to be the Zenith Security provider in their community. This is a significant change in strategy as ZSL currently owns and operates all of the locations in Atlantic Canada.

In order to help facilitate the strategic shift, Mr. Santiago hired Jason Armand early in the fiscal year as the new manager of the Ontario and Quebec region. Jason is familiar with the franchisee-franchisor relationship as he was formerly employed at a large pizza restaurant chain.

Mr. Santiago is very happy with the performance of Jason thus far as 15 franchises have been opened throughout Ontario and Quebec during the year, along with 5 locations opened and operated by ZSL. Mr. Santiago will have no problem signing Jason's bonus cheque, which is calculated as 5% of the operating income generated from the Ontario and Quebec markets.

You are the Controller of ZSL and recently began preparing for the December 31, 2014 year-end audit. The year-end audit will require more work this year because of the company's expansion, specifically the new franchisor transactions. As you prepare for the audit, you review the preliminary income statement, as prepared by Jason, for the Ontario and Quebec segments (Exhibit I), along with information regarding various transactions that occurred during the year (Exhibit II). ZSL prepares its financial statements in accordance with ASPE.

Required

Prepare a report that discusses the appropriate accounting treatments for the Ontario and Quebec markets. As the report will be used as part of Mr. Santiago's evaluation of Jason's performance, be sure to discuss various alternative accounting treatments.

EXHIBIT I – SEGMENTED INCOME STATEMENT

	Ontario	Quebec	Total
Revenues			
Initial franchise fee—promotional rate	$ 225,000	$ 450,000	$ 675,000
Initial franchise fee—regular rate	1,350,000	1,350,000	2,700,000
Continuing franchise fee	20,000	20,000	40,000
Security services	165,000	137,500	302,500
	1,760,000	1,957,500	3,717,500
Expenses			
Advertising and promotion	113,500	128,750	242,250
General and administrative	98,700	101,240	199,940
Office expense	97,750	106,790	204,540
Professional fees	37,620	38,980	76,600
Supplies and material	97,890	102,810	200,700
Wages and benefits	394,550	425,780	820,330
	840,010	904,350	1,744,360
Income from operations, pre-tax	$919,990	$1,053,150	$1,973,140
Bonus	$ 91,999	$ 105,315	$ 197,314

EXHIBIT II – ADDITIONAL INFORMATION REGARDING THE ONTARIO AND QUEBEC OPERATIONS

» Before the franchise agreement is signed, there is a period of discussion whereby the general feasibility of the new location is assessed. Market research is conducted and the prospective franchisee's financial strength is examined. ZSL incurs all of the costs during this stage. During the year, ZSL franchised 7 locations in Ontario and 8 locations in Quebec. The franchise agreements were signed during the following months:

	Jan.	Feb.	Mar.	Apr.	May	June	July	Aug.	Sep.	Oct.	Nov.	Dec.	Total
Ontario	0	0	0	0	1	1	2	1	2	0	0	0	7
Quebec	0	0	0	1	1	1	2	1	1	1	0	0	8

» As is standard in the franchisee industry, ZSL developed a policy to charge an initial franchise fee and a continuing franchise fee. The initial fee of $225,000 is paid through the following, non-refundable payments:

  • The franchisee must pay a down payment of $25,000 when the franchise agreement is signed. Once signed, ZSL will provide significant assistance to help the franchisee commence operations (e.g., help select an appropriate location, train employees, develop policies and procedures, provide legal and management assistance); however, the franchise is responsible to pay for all of the direct costs of establishing the new location.

  • A second payment of $50,000 is due once the franchisee commences operations. It takes approximately six months from signing the franchise agreement to commencing operations. ZSL's involvement with the franchisee largely ends when the new location commences operations. Five of the seven locations Ontario are open and six of the eight locations in Quebec are open.

- The final payment of $150,000 is due within one year of operations commencing. ZSL does not have any experience to assess the likelihood of a franchisee surviving its first year.

- Each franchisee is required to pay $2,500 per month in a continuing franchise fee for ZSL. The continuing franchise fee covers various shared costs, such as regional advertising, software and hardware upgrades, and ad hoc support.

» Jason encouraged initial growth by providing a promotional agreement with the first three franchisers. These franchisers were charged an initial franchise fee of $225,000, due upon opening, with no continuing fee for the first three years. All three franchises are open and paid their initial fee. These franchises have been opened for a combined 10 months during the fiscal year.

» The following are number of months the franchisees were required to pay monthly franchise fees:

	Jan.	Feb.	Mar.	Apr.	May	June	July	Aug.	Sep.	Oct.	Nov.	Dec.	Total
Ontario	0	0	0	0	0	0	0	0	0	1	3	4	8
Quebec	0	0	0	0	0	0	0	0	0	1	3	4	8

No continuing franchise fees were collected from the franchises that opened in April and May.

» During the year, ZDL opened and operates two stores in Ontario (Toronto and Ottawa), and one store in Quebec (Montreal). The locations were opened late in the fiscal year, but were still able to generate sales during November and December. The Ontario locations sold 30 security systems, while the Quebec locations sold 25 security systems.

The security systems during the year were sold for the promotional price of $5,500, which includes the hardware, installation, and a two-year monitoring contract. The promotional price was issued with the hopes of attracting new business as ZSL penetrates into the new markets. The normal retail price of the hardware alone is $6,000, with an additional $500 for installation. Customers can opt out of the two-year monitoring contract, which will reduce the price by $750. In addition, customers that already have the hardware can purchase the monitoring services for $1,250.

» Jason undertook a large marketing campaign in November and December 2014 with the intention of attracting new franchises and increasing awareness of ZSL's service offering. The advertising blitz is going to run into January 2015. Jason believes that the benefits of the marketing program will be realized in the next year. Accordingly, he capitalized $250,000 in marketing costs as at year end in order to match the costs to sales in future periods.

Antique Automotive Restoration

Greg Schwartz is an automotive enthusiast. He has over 25 years experience working as a mechanic for the dealership of a large car manufacturer in Oakville. Greg also gained experience doing minor body work and painting.

Recently, Greg decided to retire from the car dealership and pursue his interest of restoring classic American muscle cars. Accordingly, Greg started Antique Automotive Restoration (AAR). Greg leased an industrial building, and converted it into a repair and body shop. The building's land has a small parking lot that is used to showcase the restored vehicles that are for sale.

Generally, Greg selects the classic muscle cars that AAR will restore and then places them for sale to the general public in the lot. Greg also posts his vehicles to various Internet sales sites, frequents car shows, and uses the classifieds of local newspapers to market his inventory. AAR also takes custom jobs, whereby an individual can request the car to be restored.

AAR has a December 31, 2014 year end, and just completed its first year of operations. Greg had a friend help him compile financial statements for the year end (draft financial statements can be found in Exhibit I). AAR's bank requires the preparation of annual audited financial statements in accordance with IFRS (details of the loan agreement can be found in Exhibit II) and the auditors are scheduled to commence year-end work on January 18.

Realizing that AAR needs accounting assistance, Greg has hired you, CMA, as a consultant on December 24, 2014. Your first task is to review the draft financial statements and provide any recommendations to comply with IFRS. In addition, Greg required some assistance preparing a statement of cash flow. Greg has provided you with a file for review, which outlines all of the significant transactions that have taken place during the year (Exhibit III).

Aside from the year-end statements, Greg would also like to know whether he will be able to pay any dividends in the current year. He has drawn a minimal salary, and is hoping to supplement his income by paying a $35,000 dividend with the current cash balance.

Finally, Greg has asked you to provide some advice regarding the additional controls or procedures that could be implemented to improve the day to day operations of the company.

Required

Greg has asked you to prepare a report that discusses all of the material accounting issues (i.e., identify the issues, discuss the implications, offer alternative treatments, and provide a recommendation). Revised financial statements should be included in the report. The report should also address Greg's other concerns. Provide journal entries, where appropriate.

EXHIBIT I – DRAFT FINANCIAL STATEMENTS

BALANCE SHEET

As at December 31 (unaudited)	2014
Assets	
Current	
Cash	$ 35,449
Accounts receivable	45,000
Inventory	95,775
Prepaid insurance	1,775
	177,999
Capital assets	287,250
	$465,249
Liabilities and shareholders' equity	
Current	
Accounts payable and accruals	$ 8,455
Income taxes payable	17,334
	25,789
Long-term bank loan	277,240
Common shares	74,500
Retained earnings	87,721
	162,220
	$465,249

INCOME STATEMENT

For the year ended December 31 (unaudited)	2014
Sales	$320,000
Cost of sales	128,000
Gross profit	192,000
Expenses	
Advertising and promotion	2,000
Amortization	22,750
Bad debt	0
Insurance	1,500
Interest	16,920
Legal and accounting	2,500
Lease expense	30,000
Office and general expenses	2,775
Repairs and maintenance	750
Utilities	11,000
Wages and benefits	22,500
	112,695
Operating income	79,305
Other service income	25,750
Income before taxes	105,055
Provision for income taxes (16.5%)	17,334
Net income	87,721
Opening balance—retained earnings	0
Net income	87,721
Dividends	0
Closing balance—retained earnings	$ 87,721

EXHIBIT II – BANK LOAN AGREEMENT

The Bank of Toronto has provided a $300,000 loan to help finance working capital and capital assets. The following are the terms and conditions of the loan.

» **Security:** The bank secures their loan with a first claim against inventory and accounts receivable.

» **Repayment:** The loan is to be repaid over a 10-year period, with blended monthly payments.

» **Interest rate:** The rate of interest is 6%, effective annual rate (EAR).

» **Covenants:** AAR must comply with the following covenants:

  • The current ratio must not be below 2:1.

  • The debt to equity ratio must not exceed 3:1. Debt is defined as both current and long-term liabilities.

A violation of either covenant will result in the loan becoming payable upon demand.

» **Financial statements:** Audited financial statements are to be presented no later than 60 days after year end. Financial statements can be prepared with IFRS.

EXHIBIT III – NOTES OF SIGNIFICANT TRANSACTIONS

» During the first year of operations, AAR made the following sales:

1.	1972 Chevy Camaro, Z28	$45,000	5.	1974 Dodge Dart	$33,000
2.	1978 Chevy Corvette Coupe, 25th Anniversary	$33,000	6.	1970 Buick GSX	$40,000
			7.	1970 Chevelle 454 SS	$37,000
3.	1969 Pontiac GTO	$38,000	8.	1970 Plymouth Hemi 'Cuda	$39,000
4.	1967 Ford Shelby Mustang	$55,000			

» AAR is so confident in its workmanship that it offers a 10-year bumper-to-bumper warranty with all car sales. The warranty covers all defects and breakdowns that are not directly related to regular wear and tear. Greg is unsure of how much the warranty will cost to service, but is confident that his vehicles will stand the test of time. Based on his experience, Greg estimates the probability of a vehicle making a warranty claim during the 10 years of coverage are as follows:

Year 1	2	3	4	5	6	7	8	9	10
1%	2%	2%	5%	5%	10%	12%	15%	18%	20%

The average retail value per claim is $1,250. The average cost of parts and service at AAR is about 60% of that of a dealership.

» AAR sold the 1972 Chevy Camaro to wealthy telecom CEO during the year. Shortly after delivery of the vehicle, Greg found out that the CEO resigned from the company due to various accounting irregularities and restatements. Greg has been in contact with the customer and knows that he is happy with the car, and fully intends to pay once things settle down.

» AAR entered into a lease agreement on January 1 for the land and building that is used as the repair and body shop. AAR is required to make monthly payments of $2,500, commencing January 31, for a 10-year period (at which point, Greg expects to be fully retired and live off of his pension). The following additional information is available regarding the lease:

- The rate implicit in the lease is 7%.
- The building and land have fair values of $170,000 and $250,000 respectively.
- The building has a useful life of approximately 13 years.
- The lease payments were set to provide the lessor with a return of 75% related to the building and 25% related to the land.
- There is no bargain purchase option, or renewal option, at the end of the lease.

» The capital asset breakdown is as follows:

Capital Assets	Cost	Accumulated Amortization	NBV
Machinery and equipment	$250,000	$15,500	$234,500
Leasehold improvements	10,000	1,000	9,000
Office equipment	25,000	3,125	21,875
Vehicles	25,000	3,125	21,875
	$310,000	$22,750	$287,250

The leasehold improvements include changes to the building and land (e.g., paving). The machinery and equipment is expected to have a residual value of $95,000 after their 10-year useful life. Both the office equipment and vehicle are expected have useful lives of 8 years, with no residual values.

» The income taxes presented in the financial statements are based on the pre-tax income times the tax rate of 16.5%. No adjustments have been made to calculate taxes in accordance with the Income Tax Act. The following are the CCA rates relevant to the capital assets of AAR:

  1. Machinery and equipment: 30%

  2. Leasehold improvements: 10 years, straight-line

  3. Office equipment: 20%

  4. Vehicles: 30%

» The inventory balance includes a 1971 Corvette Coupe. The car was a custom order for a doctor. Due to financial problems, the doctor was unable to purchase the vehicle, at which point AAR repossessed the vehicle. The vehicle is included in inventory at its cost of $35,000. The vehicle will require minor moderations, costing up to $5,000, to make it ready for resale at a price of $35,000.

Apartment HoldCo.

Mitch Poirier is considering an investment in a multiple-unit, residential building. The building has 30 units, which are all currently rented to tenants. Further details on the apartment building are provided in Exhibit I. If Mitch decides to proceed with the investment, he will purchase the apartment through a newly formed holding company (HoldCo.).

The apartment building, and required initial working capital, will require an investment of $1 million ($900,000 for the building and $100,000 for working capital). Mitch is contemplating various alternatives by which the apartment could be financed. The following four options are available:

1. Borrow $950,000 from the Bank of Calgary, with the remaining $50,000 being financed through personal equity. The loan would be repaid on a monthly basis over a 20-year term with an effective annual interest rate of 6%. The bank would require that the debt to equity ratio not exceed 3.75:1.

2. Borrow $750,000 in the form of an interest-only note from a local, wealthy businessperson, with the rest coming from personal equity. The loan would require annual interest payments, but no principal payments until the end of the 15-year term. Interest is payable at a rate of 7% per annum. The loan covenant stipulates that the debt to equity ratio not exceed 2.75:1.

3. Borrow $600,000 from the Bank of Edmonton, on a 15-year loan with an effective interest rate of 5%. The bank would require a debt to equity ratio of 5:1. An additional $300,000 could be obtained from issuing preferred shares to Joe Poirier, Mitch's brother. The preferred shares would be cumulative, with a 6% dividend yield. Mitch would finance the remaining $100,000 through common equity.

4. Allow Joe to become a shareholder, whereby both Mitch and Joe would invest $500,000 in common share, equity financing. In this scenario, there would be no long-term debt taken by the HoldCo.

Mitch has contacted you, CA, in order to provide assistance regarding the possible financing alternatives. Mitch would like you to assess the impact of four alternatives on the return on common-equity, debt-to-equity ratio, and ability to pay dividends at the end of the first year, fifth year, and tenth year. Mitch will not proceed with the investment if the debt to equity covenant is likely to be violated, or the return on equity is below 10%. In addition, he would like to be able to draw out dividends of at least $20,000.

Required

Prepare a report that addresses the concerns of Mitch Poirier by assessing the four financing alternatives and recommending a source of financing. A pro forma balance sheet under each alternative for the future periods should be included in your report.

EXHIBIT I – DETAILS REGARDING THE OPERATIONS OF THE APARTMENT BUILDING

» The apartment building has a total of 30 units, all of which are currently rented to tenants. The average rent of a unit is $550 per month.

» Historical financial statements reveal the following operating expenditures (they do not include any financing expenses):

	Last Year	Two Years Ago	Three Years Ago	Four Years Ago
Advertising	$ 1,500	$ 1,250	$ 2,250	$ 1,760
Amortization	23,333	23,333	23,333	23,333
Bad debt expense	0	550	0	0
Insurance	4,450	4,450	4,250	4,250
Office	5,500	5,700	6,700	4,200
Professional fees	2,500	2,250	2,250	2,000
Property management fees	30,000	30,000	30,000	30,000
Repairs and maintenance	23,550	45,375	17,075	17,500
Wages and benefits	5,575	5,275	4,775	5,735
Total operating expenses	$96,408	$118,183	$90,633	$88,778

» Historically turnover is about one tenant per year. When someone leaves, it normally takes about three months to replace the tenant, during which the unit is vacant.

» The nature of the business is such that most revenues and expenses are paid for on a cash basis. Accordingly, there are very few accounts receivable or accounts payable at year end. Therefore, Mitch has said that it is safe to assume that all revenues are received when earned and all expenses paid when incurred.

» The building is expected to have a useful life of 30 years, with a residual value of $100,000.

» The working capital should not decrease below $100,000. This amount is required in order to pay for emergency repairs, and so on.

» Assume that Apartment HoldCo. has a tax rate of 30%.

Auto Parts Inc.

Today is November 1, 2014. You, CMA, have just been hired by Auto Parts Inc. (API) as an accountant to provide financial expertise during its current expansion. API was founded in 1995 by John Blackman (sole shareholder) and API has remained a private corporation ever since. From its humble beginnings, API has grown substantially. API's operations focus on the production of both standard and unique car parts. API always strives to use modern technology to produce quality car parts. When API commenced, they produced car parts for Canadian automotive companies that were seeking to outsource their production. Soon after, as word spread on the quality of its parts, API's products were being sought after by companies outside of Canada. In addition, API began selling its products to individuals who were looking for unique car parts to restore older cars.

As a car buff, you are very excited about the position as it allows you to apply your accounting knowledge in an industry that interests you. On your first day, you met with API's CFO, Jeff Ahmad. Jeff begins by explaining how excited he is that you have joined API's team and he looks forward to the expertise that you will bring to API's accounting department.

Jeff continues by explaining that as API has grown, so has its dependency on external financing. Just this year, API had purchased additional equipment to handle its recent growth. API has had a long-standing relationship with its bank. However, given the recent credit crisis, the bank has changed its policies on all loans. Jeff has provided you with a copy of API's balance sheet (see Exhibit I) as at October 31, 2014, which is API's fiscal year-end date.

After the meeting, Jeff asks you to analyze the new accounting issues surrounding API and to provide recommendations on their resolution. He concludes by reminding you that the bank is eager to see the year-end financial statements. As you make your way back to your desk, you begin by reviewing a file outlining important transactions undertaken by API. You note the following issues:

1. On November 1, 2013 (the beginning of the fiscal year), API acquired a portion of its equipment through a lease agreement with Lessor Corp. The lease contract has the following terms and conditions:

   - API agrees to lease equipment from Lessor Corp. with a fair market value of $900,000;

   - The term of the lease is for seven years, with annual rental payments of $145,000 due at the beginning of each year. API knows the implicit interest rate on the lease agreement is 5%. However, API knows that it could borrow at an incremental rate of 6%, if it were to negotiate with its bank.

   - There is no residual value.

   - API will cover the executory costs associated with the lease. The executor costs will be approximately $10,000 per annum and are included as part of the $145,000 rental payment.

   - The lease offers a bargain purchase option to purchase the equipment for $50,000 at the end of the seventh year. At the end of year seven, the fair market value of the asset is expected to be $70,000.

   - The first payment was made on November 1, 2013, with annual payments thereafter.

   You remember from auditing a client in the past, that equipment such as this usually has an economic life of nine years. API has classified this lease as an operating lease. You remember from your discussion with Jeff that he was unsure of the benefits of leasing versus buying an asset. This information is important for Jeff for any future capital budgeting decisions.

2. After reviewing the balance sheet, you notice that there are preferred shares valued at $100,000, which equals a total of 1,000 shares outstanding. The preferred shares are redeemable and have a 5% annual dividend. The dividend will double every three years up to a maximum 20% dividend yield. The preferred shares become convertible into common shares if API does not pay the specified dividend on the preferred shares.

3. The file also contained a letter from API's lawyer (Stonechild, Pilla, and Partners). The letter from the lawyers explained a current lawsuit undertaken against API. Apparently a customer had asked for 50,000 parts to be produced and delivered no later than July 15, 2014. However, due to major downtime in July, API could not produce the parts as scheduled. In turn the customer was late in delivering its vehicles to its distributors and had to pay a penalty equivalent of $600,000. This customer is now suing API for retribution for these costs. The letter goes on to state that retribution will be inevitable; however, it is believed that a settlement between $350,000 to $550,000 can be reached.

4. On November 1, 2013, an additional $500,000 of long-term loan was taken out to help finance the purchase of certain manufacturing equipment for $600,000. (Note: the additional $100,000 was paid for with cash.) The loan is repayable at $100,000 per annum. Given this new loan and API's revised debt load, API must now maintain a maximum debt to equity ratio of 3:1 and its financial statements must comply with ASPE. If API breaches the covenant, the bank has the ability to call for the loan in full.

    The manufacturing equipment that was purchased during the year will be amortized over 10 years. It is classified as class 39 and has a CCA rate of 25%. API is taxed at the highest possible rate of 45%, and the half-year rule applies. Jeff explained that API has not taken any consideration for potential tax consequences on the equipment purchase. (Note: for simplicity, assume that all other future tax considerations have been properly addressed.)

After reviewing this information, you realize that you have much to contemplate as to how these issues should be dealt with.

Required

Provide a report to Jeff outlining your recommendation on the accounting issues and note other important issues.

EXHIBIT I — API'S FINANCIAL POSITION

AUTO PARTS INC.
STATEMENT OF FINANCIAL POSITION
AS AT OCTOBER 31

Assets

Current assets

	2014	2013
Cash	$ 35,000	$ 20,000
Accounts receivable	13,000	10,000
Inventory	20,000	12,000
Prepaids	3,000	3,000
Total current assets	71,000	45,000
Property, plant, and equipment (net)	2,800,000	2,200,000
Total assets	**2,871,000**	**2,245,000**

Liabilities

Current liabilities

Accounts payable	25,000	20,000
Notes payable	13,000	25,000
Current portion of long-term debt	150,000	50,000
	188,000	95,000
Long - term debt	1,900,000	1,450,000
Total liabilities	**2,088,000**	**1,545,000**

Shareholders' equity

Share capital	100	100
Preferred shares	100,000	100,000
Retained earnings	682,900	599,900
Total equity	**783,000**	**700,000**
Total liabilities and shareholders' equity	**$2,871,000**	**$2,245,000**
Debt to equity	**2.67**	**2.21**

Car-Tunes Ltd.

Car-Tunes Ltd. is a young company that recently completed its initial public offering. The company designs and develops leading edge car stereo equipment, including MP4 compatible decks, speakers, amplifiers, and subwoofers.

The company is investing heavily in research and development. In order to reduce strain on cash, the management team is compensated mostly through share-based compensation in the current year. In addition, the company has raised cash through the issuance of common shares in the open market, and by offering various complex financial instruments. Management believes that all cash should be diverted towards the research and development process in order for the company to become the leader in automotive stereo equipment.

In addition to the stock options, management receives a bonus of 5% of net income if diluted EPS is greater than $0.10. The bonus is the only cash compensation that management receives at this stage of the company's life cycle. Management is excited because this year's draft income statement (Exhibit I) shows diluted EPS in excess of $0.10, and therefore, a bonus will be paid.

Lebeau and Liang LLP has been the auditor of Car-Tunes since the company's inception. You are a senior accountant with the firm, and have been assigned the year-end audit for Car-Tunes. The partner has just met with the company's management, and discussed various accounting issues. She has asked you to prepare a report to be provided to the client that addresses all of the accounting issues, along with any other issues that you feel are important. The partner's notes from the meeting can be found in Exhibit II. In addition, the company's current and future tax expenses must be calculated. Tax-related details can be found in Exhibit III.

Required

Prepare a report for the partner. IFRS is the appropriate accounting standards for Car-Tunes.

EXHIBIT I – DRAFT INCOME STATEMENT

Car-Tunes Ltd.
As at December 31, 2014

REVENUE	$44,500,740
Cost of goods sold	23,540,891
Gross margin	20,959,849
EXPENSES	
Advertising and promotion	$ 1,575,000
Amortization	1,276,758
Bad debt	87,500
Insurance	85,000
Interest on convertible bonds	80,000
Legal fees	225,500
Accounting and consulting fees	175,000
Office and general expenses	750,850
Rent	325,000
Repairs and maintenance	450,755
Research and development	11,345,000
Travel	133,750
Utilities	333,565
Wages and benefits	325,000
	$17,168,678
Earnings for the year before income taxes	$ 3,791,170
Income tax expense	1,137,351
Earnings for the year	$ 2,653,819
Earnings per share—basic	$0.13
Earnings per share—diluted	$0.11
Weighted average shares outstanding—basic	20,550,750*
Weighted average shares outstanding—diluted	23,630,750*

* Note that these values have been calculated and verified by the manager on the file, and are deemed to be correct.

EXHIBIT II – NOTES FROM THE PARTNER'S MEETING WITH CAR-TUNES LTD.'S MANAGEMENT

1. At the beginning of the year, the Board of Directors approved a compensatory stock option plan that grants options to the company's four executives to purchase 100,000 shares each of the company's common shares. The options can be exercised any time within the next five years at a strike price of $1 per share. The Board expects that the period of benefit/service for these options is two years. The fair value of the options, as determined using an option pricing model, is $1,550,000.

2. The company issued 500,000 preferred shares for $4 per share to an investment bank in June 2014. Each preferred share is convertible for a fixed number of common shares (6 common shares), and has a mandatory 7% annual dividend that must be paid on December 31 of each fiscal year. The shares must be redeemed by the company for cash if the market price of the common shares exceeds $4 per share. Currently, the common shares are in a trading range around $1.25 per share. The Board declared and paid the mandatory cash dividend on December 31.

3. At the beginning of the current year, the company issued $2.5 million convertible bonds, of which $2 million was allocated to debt. The bonds' market yield is 4% annually, pay interest semi-annually, mature in five years, and can be converted into common shares at the ratio of 1,500 shares per $1,000 bond.

4. Given the volatility of commodity prices, Car-Tunes entered into a forward contract with the Bank of Vancouver. On July 1, Car-Tunes locked the price of 5 million kg of aluminum at $1.25/kg. Aluminum is important to the company's operation because it is used to create a cabinet that houses all of the components in the CD player deck. Upon its inception, Car-Tunes did not have to put forth any cash. All cash transfers will take place on settlements in two years. As at December 31, the price of aluminum is trading on the Chicago Board of Trade at $1.15/kg.

EXHIBIT III – TAX-RELATED DETAILS

5. The company's tax rate is 30%. The income statement tax amount is calculated with the taxes payable method.

6. The office and general expense account contains $85,000 in meals and entertainment.

7. The are $175,000 in non-deductible expenses included in the consulting, legal, and professional fee line items on the income statement.

8. The UCC and NBV for the capital assets are as follows:

	NBV		UCC	
	2014	2013	2014	2013
Land	$ 1,250,000	$ 1,250,000	$ 1,250,000	$ 1,250,000
Buildings	4,500,750	4,650,775	2,767,211	3,255,543
Furniture and fixtures	650,000	693,333	412,533	485,333
Machinery and equipment	12,567,000	13,404,800	7,975,856	9,383,360
Leasehold improvements	2,456,000	2,701,600	1,607,452	1,891,120
	$ 21,423,750	$22,700,508	$14,013,052	$16,265,356

9. There were no capital asset additions or dispositions during the year.

CopyCat Technologies Inc. (CCTi)

You, Kevan Sturges, are an accountant employed at Enright & Co. Reena Siddiqui, a partner in your firm, leaves you the following voicemail message:

"Kevan, the scheduling manager tells me you have some time available. We have recently been advised that management of CopyCat Technologies Inc. (CCTi) has received an offer from Ventura Capital Partners (VCP) to sell 100% of all issued and outstanding common shares. I have a meeting with management in two weeks regarding this issue, and I haven't had much time to think about this engagement.

I have prepared some background information on the company for you to review including a general description of the client (Exhibit I), the company's most recent internal financial statements (Exhibit II), and the proposed share purchase agreement (Exhibit III). I also met with CCTi management earlier this month and made some notes from that meeting (Exhibit IV). They should all be in your inbox by now.

Can you please prepare a report that I can use for the upcoming meeting?

Thanks Kevan. I am glad that you have some time available!"

Required

As Kevan, prepare the report for Reena.

EXHIBIT I – BACKGROUND INFORMATION

CopyCat Technology Inc. (CCTi) duplicates videotapes, DVDs, and CDs from masters provided by its clients. The company started operations in 2000 in the basement of the home of part owner Rico Parthurs. Sales increased quickly, and within one year of commencing operations the company moved into a rented premise in downtown Toronto. The market that CCTi currently serves is mainly large companies that require training programs, corporate messages, and so on.

The company is owned equally by Rico Parthurs, Richard Composer, and Patrizia Mancinelli. Rico started the venture and has always managed the sales function. In order to keep the company growing, he brought in Richard and Art as equal shareholders. Rich and Patrizia each paid $30,000 for one third of Rico's shares.

Richard is a good administrator and handles the accounting functions for the company. Rico's skills are mainly in sales. Patrizia looks after the production end and stays abreast of changes in technology.

CCTi has an October 31 fiscal year end.

EXHIBIT II – INTERNAL FINANCIAL STATEMENTS

BALANCE SHEET

As at October 31 (unaudited)	2014	2013
Assets		
Current		
Cash	$ 151,764	$ 160,502
Accounts receivable	334,894	411,760
Inventory	86,800	124,200
Prepaid insurance	4,720	2,060
	578,178	698,522
Capital (note 1)	661,897	417,158
Future income tax asset (note 2)	35,000	35,000
Long-term note receivable	20,000	—
	$1,295,075	$1,150,680
Liabilities and shareholders' equity		
Current		
Accounts payable	$ 158,318	$ 130,176
Bank loan—current portion	41,998	72,000
Income taxes payable	44,609	92,920
	244,925	295,096
Long-term bank loan (note 3)	35,334	77,334
Due to shareholders	58,100	53,100
Common shares	1,200	1,200
Preferred shares	20,000	20,000
Contributed surplus	4,000	0
Retained earnings	931,516	703,950
	956,716	725,150
	$1,295,075	$1,150,680

EXHIBIT II – INTERNAL FINANCIAL STATEMENTS (CONTINUED)

INCOME STATEMENT

For the years ended October 31 (unaudited)	2014	2013
Sales	$2,531,760	$2,221,720
Cost of sales		
Opening inventory	124,400	26,860
Purchases—materials	1,018,972	959,138
—wages	289,663	219,416
Total	1,433,035	1,205,414
Closing inventory	(86,800)	(124,400)
	1,346,235	1,081,014
Gross profit	1,185,525	1,140,706
Expenses		
Commissions	199,372	174,957
Amortization	127,684	104,796
Management salaries and benefits	110,448	110,040
Management fees	109,600	112,600
Rent	75,840	74,020
Office and general expenses	48,723	46,877
Advertising and promotion	37,585	31,284
Repairs and maintenance	27,173	24,686
Automobile and travel	26,326	22,782
Bad debt	15,596	21,188
Interest	16,864	39,320
Computer system installation	13,760	0
Telephone	13,458	10,510
Insurance	10,864	10,214
Legal and accounting	8,083	3,414
Lease expense	18,143	0
	859,519	786,688
Operating income	326,006	354,018
Gain on sale of equipment	4,560	0
Income before taxes	330,566	354,018
Provision for income taxes	99,000	112,000
Net income	231,566	242,018
Opening balance—retained earnings	703,950	465,932
Dividend on preferred shares	(4,000)	(4,000)
Closing balance—retained earnings	$ 931,516	$ 703,950

EXHIBIT II – INTERNAL FINANCIAL STATEMENTS (CONTINUED)

NOTES TO THE FINANCIAL STATEMENTS

1. Capital assets

	Cost	Accumulated Amortization	2014 Net Book Value	2013 Net Book Value
Furniture and fixtures	$ 23,434	$ 12,418	$ 11,016	$ 13,770
Computer equipment	50,842	12,835	38,007	18,421
Leasehold improvements	19,404	19,404	0	2,842
Vehicle	40,352	27,985	12,367	17,667
Production equipment	931,074	330,567	600,507	364,458
	$1,065,106	$403,209	$661,897	$417,158

2. Future tax asset

A future tax asset has been recorded for non-capital losses carry-forward. The losses were incurred during a bad year in fiscal 2012. CCTi expects strong future profits to be able to generate taxable income to fully utilize the tax losses. The owners decided not to use the tax losses in the 2013 or 2014 fiscal years because they expect their marginal tax rate to increase significantly in the near future due to significant growth in income.

3. Bank loan

A small business bank loan and line of credit for $200,000 (presently unused) are secured by a general security agreement, a registered general assignment of book debts, and chattel mortgages on duplication equipment. Principal repayments on the small business loan are due as follows during the years ended October 31:

2015	$41,998
2016	20,034
2017	11,700
2018	3,600

Interest on the small business bank loan is paid at 10% on the outstanding monthly balances. Interest on the line of credit is calculated at prime $+1\frac{1}{2}\%$ on outstanding monthly balances.

EXHIBIT III – SHARE SALE AGREEMENT

Purchase Price Calculation

The final purchase price is to be determined based on an adjusted book value approach, whereby all assets and liabilities are adjusted to their fair values to determine the fair value of the equity. In addition, a premium for goodwill will be calculated based on a multiple of net income for the most recent fiscal year.

Therefore, the purchase price is calculated as follows:

$$\text{Purchase Price} = \text{Adjusted Equity Value} + (\text{Net Income} \times \text{Earnings Multiple})$$

Earnings Multiple

A goodwill multiple of between 1 and 2 is common for similar companies.

Net Income

Net income must be determined based on Generally Accepted Accounting Principles (IFRS).

Adjusted book value

All assets, liabilities, and equities must be recognized and measured in accordance with Generally Accepted Accounting Principles (IFRS).

EXHIBIT IV – NOTES FROM MEETING WITH RICHARD

New Lease Agreement

CCTi signed an agreement on November 1, 2013 to lease equipment from LeBlack Limited. The following information relates to the agreement:

1. The term of the non-cancellable lease is five years, at which time the asset is expected to have a residual value of $7,000, which is not guaranteed.
2. The asset's fair value, at November 1, 2013, is $80,000, with an economic life of seven years.
3. The asset will revert to LeBlack at the end of the lease term, at which time the asset is expected to have a residual value of $7,000, which is not guaranteed.
4. LeBlack Limited assumes direct responsibility for the executory costs.
5. The agreement requires equal annual rental payments of $18,143, beginning on November 1, 2013.
6. The lessor's implicit rate is 12% and is known to CCTi.

Richard has recorded this as an operating lease, and expensed the annual payment during the fiscal year.

EXHIBIT IV – NOTES FROM MEETING WITH RICHARD (CONTINUED)

Provision for income taxes

The provision for income taxes included in the financial statements is recorded based on the taxes payable in the current period (i.e. the amount payable based on taxable income). Management has done this because there are very few differences between taxable income and accounting income. The only significant difference is related to the depreciation of capital assets. A review of Schedule 8 of the Corporate T2 reveals undepreciated capital cost (UCC) balances of the following:

	Cost	UCC
Furniture and fixtures	$ 23,434	$ 10,518
Computer equipment	50,842	6,835
Leasehold improvements	19,404	19,404
Vehicle	40,352	29,985
Production equipment	931,074	289,567

The total capital cost allowance (CCA) taken in 2014 was $140,545. The average tax rate for CCTi is 31.16% on the current year's income.

Preferred shares

On November 1, 2013, CCTi issued 2,000 redeemable and retractable preferred shares at a value of $10 per share. The shares are redeemable by CCTi at any time after January 2018. The shares are retractable for the original $10 per share at the discretion of the holder at any time up to January 2018, after which the retractable feature expires. The preferred shares require the payment of a mandatory $2 per share during the retraction period, after which the dividends become non-cumulative and are paid at the discretion of the board only.

Long-term note receivable

On July 1, 2014, CCTi provided certain services to a preferred customer in exchange for a long-term note receivable. CCTi provided services in exchange for five payments of $4,000. CCTi provides its preferred customer with this offer to help stimulate the sale given the recent financial crisis. The first payment is due July 1, 2015.

Loyalty program points

During the most recent Board meeting, it was decided that CCTi will begin offering points under a loyalty program. CCTi will provide customers with 1 point for every $100 spent. The points can then be redeemed for a discount on future services. A total of 100 points will result in a $500 discount.

Post-retirement benefits

CCTi has just implemented and sponsored a defined benefit pension plan in fiscal 2014. No past service benefits have been granted.

The following additional information was obtained from an actuarial report that has been prepared as at the year end:

Service cost for 2014:	95,000
Discount or settlement rate:	9%
Actual return on plan assets for 2014:	0
Contribution (plan funding) in 2014:	87,000
Expected rate of return for 2014:	8%

The initial contribution of $87,000 was made on August 1, 2014. Currently, CCTi has expensed the contribution as part of the management salaries and benefits (on the income statement).

Dryden Natural Springs

Dryden Natural Springs (DNS) sells bottled water that comes from a fresh water spring in the town of Dryden, Ontario. DNS owns the land, and much of the surrounding area, where the fresh water spring is located. In addition, DNS has all of the equipment needed to extract the water from the spring and place it into bottles.

As a young, newly qualified professional accountant, you are looking to get out of public practice and become an active owner/manager of a small business. An opportunity has arisen to purchase all of the common shares of DNS, and you are contemplating this acquisition.

The significant competition in the bottled water market, combined with the relatively small operation of DNS and lack of brand equity suggests that there is currently no significant goodwill associated with DNS's earnings. Accordingly, the purchase price will be based on DNS's net book value, calculated in accordance with ASPE, with an adjustment for only the fair value of capital assets. Your intention is to use your business network, and social media marketing skills, to expand DNS's operations and increase profitability.

As part of your due diligence, you discovered the following information:

1. The long-term debt is a zero-bearing note payable to a local credit union. No payments must be made until the end of 10 years, at which point the principal and all accrued interest are due in full. DNS received $250,000 four years ago to this day, and interest accrues at 6% annually.

2. DNS implemented a new rewards program at the beginning of this year. DNS included a liner under the bottom of each cap. The liner includes the text: (1) free bottle of water; or (2) please try again. One in 10 bottles includes a free bottle of water. The promotion was a success. A total of 105,455 bottles were sold during the year, and 4,556 free bottle liners were redeemed. The cost of a bottle of water is $0.75 and the retail value is $1.50.

3. Capital assets are appraised at $485,000 by an independent, qualified third party.

4. The capital stock includes common shares and preferred shares. There are 500 preferred shares with a cost and redemption value of $10 and $12 per share, respectively, and a 6% mandatory, cumulative dividend yield. These shares will be retained by the current owners of DNS.

A copy of DNS's most recent internal balance sheet is presented in Exhibit I. DNS has never had an audit or review.

Required

Based on your review of the financial statements and the information obtained during due diligence, prepare your estimate of the purchase price. Be sure to fully discuss any proposed changes to the financial statements required to comply with ASPE.

EXHIBIT I – INTERNAL FINANCIAL STATEMENTS

BALANCE SHEET

As at Year End (unaudited)

Assets

Current

Cash	$ 17,555
Accounts receivable	55,780
Inventory	234,575
Prepaid insurance	2,335
	310,245
Capital assets	455,775
	$766,020

Liabilities and shareholders' equity

Current

Accounts payable and accruals	$256,775
Income taxes payable	33,455
	290,230
Long-term debt	$250,000
Capital stock	$55,000
Retained earnings	170,790
	225,790
	$766,020

Notes to Internal Balance Sheet

Inventory

Inventory is carried at the lower of cost and net realizable value.

Guarantee/Commitment

DNS has provided a guarantee on $50,000 of debt for a related company, Kenora Fresh Water Ltd (KFW). KFW has been experiencing financial difficulties, and there is a 10% chance that it may be insolvent within the next six months. KFW is currently working with its bank to refinance its debt, and avoid bankruptcy.

Contingencies

1. DNS is being sued by a former employee for wrongful dismissal. The employee is suing DNS for $40,000, and the case is currently in mediation. Legal counsel suggests that it is unlikely that $40,000 will be paid out, but there is a 50% chance of paying $20,000 and a 50% chance of paying $10,000. The case will likely settle at the end of next year.

2. DNS is suing a competitor for infringement regarding the use of its trademarked logo. Legal counsel suggests that it is very likely that DNS will be awarded a settlement of $25,000.

Eastjet Airlines

Eastjet Airlines (EA) is a regional airline that services most cities in the Maritimes and Eastern Canada. The company began in 2005 when three friends felt that the Maritimes was an underserviced market. Joe, Jack and John each own one-third of all the issued common shares and exercise equal control over the company.

After their start-up phase, management began to expand its routes. Currently, EA offers only short-haul flights to and from Halifax, Moncton, and Sydney. However, EA has planned an expansion of operations into Ontario as it received approval to fly into both Toronto's Pearson Airport, and the Thunder Bay International Airport. EA plans to offer its first flights into Ontario in early 2016.

In order to service the new routes into Ontario, EA purchased a new airplane for $1 million. EA obtained a 10-year mortgage from the Bank of Sydney in order to finance the acquisition of the plans. The terms and agreement of the mortgage can be found in Exhibit I.

Jack, who is responsible for the accounting functions, has always prepared the financial statements for internal reporting purposes. The balance sheet, as at December 31, 2014, is included in Exhibit II.

As a result of the new bank loan, the financial statements must now be audited. As a result, EA has hired Lebeau and Liang LLP (L&L), a Chartered Accountant, firm to complete the audit. You are the senior accountant at L&L, assigned to the audit.

You met with Jack as part of your auditing planning. Jack states "I understand that there is Part I (IFRS) and Part II (ASPE) GAAP in Canada. Currently, the bank has not disclosed which set of standards must be used to prepare the financial statements. Therefore, could you help me understand the significant differences between ASPE and IFRS, as they relate to our financial statements?" The notes from your meeting can be found in Exhibit III.

It is now January 10, 2015. The partner has asked you to prepare a report addressing the client's concerns, and to discuss the policy differences between ASPE and IFRS.

Required

Provide the report.

EXHIBIT I – MORTGAGE AGREEMENT WITH THE BANK OF SYDNEY

Total balance:	$1,000,000
Term:	10-year amortization, blended annual payments due on December 31.
Commencement date:	January 1, 2014
First payment:	Due December 31, 2014
Interest rate:	8% fixed over the 10-year period
Covenant:	EA shall maintain a debt to equity ratio that is no greater than 2:1.
Collateral:	Secured debt against the value of the aircrafts
Compliance:	Audited financial statements to be filed by January 31 of each year.

EXHIBIT II – INTERNAL FINANCIAL STATEMENTS

BALANCE SHEET

As at December 31 (unaudited)	2014	2013
Assets		
Current		
Cash	$ 151,764	$ 160,502
Accounts receivable	334,894	411,760
Inventory	86,800	159,400
Prepaid insurance	4,720	2,060
	578,178	733,722
Capital	661,897	417,158
Future income tax asset	35,000	35,000
Long-term note receivable	20,000	–
	$1,295,075	$1,150,880
Liabilities and shareholders' equity		
Current		
Accounts payable	$ 158,318	$ 130,176
Bank loan—current portion	41,998	72,000
Income taxes payable	44,609	92,920
	244,925	295,096
Bank loan—FirstBank of Canada	93,434	130,664
Common shares	900	900
Preferred shares	20,300	20,300
Contributed surplus[1]	4,000	0
Retained earnings	931,516	703,950
	956,716	725,150
	$1,295,075	$1,150,880

[1] Related to common share redemptions in the past.

EXHIBIT III – NOTES FROM YOUR DISCUSSION WITH EA MANAGEMENT

Purchase of Aircrafts and New Bank Debt

Jack informed you of the fact that the December 31, 2014 balance sheet does not include the acquisition of the new aircraft, or the new bank debt. Jack did not even record the journal entry for the first payment made on December 31, 2014.

Bank Loan with the FirstBank of Canada

The total outstanding balance of $93,434 is due in full on January 15, 2015. Jack has left the total balance as long-term as at the December 31 year end because on January 3, 2015, he was able to renegotiate the loan on a long-term basis. Jack has provided you with a copy of a non-cancellable agreement to refinance the debt as January 3, 2015.

Flight No. 877

On November 24, 2014, 26 passengers on Flight No. 877 were injured upon landing when the plane skidded off the runway. Fortunately, no one was injured seriously; however, personal injury suits were still filed on December 1, 2014, for damages totalling $50,000. Legal counsel has studied each suit and advised EA management that it is probable (about a 55% chance) that they will lose the lawsuit. The loss could range anywhere between $20,000 and $50,000. There is a 30% chance that EA will have to pay $20,000, a 25% chance that it will have to pay $50,000, and a 45% chance that EA will pay $35,000.

Cancellation of Common Shares

On September 15, the company reacquired and cancelled 9 shares (3 from each of Jack, Joe, and John). The redemption price was $1,035 per share. Jack was unsure of how to account for this transaction, and therefore did not make any entries as at year end for the redemption. Prior to the reacquisition, there were 900 shares outstanding.

Convertible Bonds

In order to obtain additional capital to finance the expansion, EA issued $500,000 in 8%, 10-year convertible bonds on January 1, 2014, for $500,000 cash. Each $1,000 bond includes the right to purchase 1 share for $750 during the life of the bond. The current market rate for similar non-convertible bonds is 9%. The fair value of the option using an option pricing model is $49,760.

Fresh Subs

Fresh Subs is a deli that sells fresh subs, soups, and salads. Fresh Subs was founded by Jenny and Jason, who are brother and sister, and began as a small, local deli in Calgary. Based on rave reviews of their subs, Jenny and Jason have decided to expand operations within Alberta. As part of the expansion plans, all of the assets were rolled over into a newly formed corporation that has a fiscal year end of December 31, 2014. The corporation issued 50,000 shares to each of Jenny and Jason for $3 per share. Upon incorporation, Fresh Subs also received a $250,000 loan from the First Bank of Calgary to help finance the expansion.

During their first year of operations, Jenny and Jason decided to hire Lebeau and Liang LLP (L&L) to help develop accounting policies that are consistent with ASPE for various new transactions. You, a senior accountant with L&L, have been assigned to the Fresh Sub file and met with Jenny and Jason to discuss the various new issues. Jenny and Jason have provided you with the following information regarding the new issues:

1. Fresh Subs recently implemented a new customer loyalty program. Each customer receives 1 Sub Club point for every large sub that they purchase. A customer receives a free large sub once they earn 10 Sub Club points. A large sub sells for an average of $5 and costs an average of $3 to produce. As of year end, a total of 23,500 Sub Club points have been issued. Jenny and Jason did not know how to account for this program and stated that they will record the expense of the free sub when a customer redeems their points.

2. To help finance their expansion across Alberta, Fresh Subs issued 10,000 preferred shares to a group of private investors for $10 per share. The preferred shares carry a 10% annual, cumulative dividend yield and are redeemable by Fresh Subs. The dividend rate was issued at such a high level because Fresh Sub does not have access to any other sources of capital in the current year. In five years, the dividend is expected to double. Given that they are preferred shares and not retractable, Jenny and Jason recorded these shares as equity.

3. Given the volatility of commodity prices, Fresh Subs has entered into a forward contract with the First Bank of Calgary. On April 1, Fresh Subs has locked the price of 100,000 kg of wheat at $0.75/kg. Upon its inception, Fresh Subs did not have to put forth any cash. All cash transfers will take place on settlement. As at December 31, the price of wheat is trading on the Chicago Board of Trade at $0.67/kg. Jenny and Jason have made no entries at year end and will record the cost of goods sold with a wheat price of $0.75 in the next fiscal year.

4. On August 1, the company reacquired and cancelled 1,500 of Jenny's and 1,500 of Jason shares at $2 per share. All 3,000 shares were re-issued to Khaled, a long-time friend, at a price of $5 per share. Jenny and Jason were unsure of how to account for these transactions.

   On January 1, Fresh Subs purchased a new roaster over. The purchase was financed though an "interest-free" five year vendor loan, whereby Fresh Subs is required to pay back $5,000 in each year. Jenny and Jason are excited about this financing promotion because they would have to pay 9% interest to borrow the money from the bank. Jason and Jenny recorded an asset and liability at $25,000. Fresh Subs uses the straight-line method to amortize the asset, which has a seven-year useful life.

To protect its investment, the First Bank of Calgary has included a restrictive covenant whereby Fresh Subs cannot have a debt to equity ratio in excess of 1:1. Upon inception, the debt to equity ratio is 0.83:1. Both Jenny and Jason have expressed their pleasure with the debt to equity ratio.

Required

The partner has asked you to prepare a memo that appropriately analyzes the accounting issues confronted by Fresh Sub, and provides a recommendation. Alternative treatments, where relevant, should also be discussed.

McDonnell Trucking Company

McDonnell Trucking Company (MTC) is a trucking company that operates in Ontario. The company is owned by Carl McDonnell. Carl is a successful businessperson and also a part owner of McDonnell Trucking Supplies (MTS), which services transport trucks and sells parts. The corporate structure is as follows:

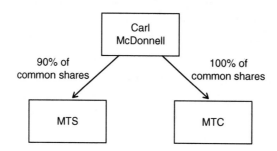

In January 2014, MTC has received a loan from a major bank to help finance an expansion of operations. The bank requires audited financial statements to be prepared and also prohibits the debt to equity ratio to exceed 2:1. Your firm has recently been engaged to complete the December 31, 2014 audit. As the audit senior, you recently met with Carl, who said that MTC will adopt ASPE. You also discover the following information:

1. MTC constructed a storage shed on land it leased for a five-year period on January 1, 2014. The company is required to remove the storage shed and restore the property to its original condition at the end of the lease term. The costs of removing the storage shed and restoring the property, at the end of the lease term, are estimated to be $200,000. MTC's credit-adjusted risk-free rate is 8%.

2. MTC completed construction of a new plant in Thunder Bay in November 2014. The cost of the plant was $1.2 million. The federal government provided a grant of $200,000 to aid in construction costs. It also announced a forgivable loan of $400,000 to be paid in installments of $100,000 per year, to offset wages paid. The loan must be repaid in its entirety if the business is sold or wound up within four years. The first installment was received in January 2015, just a few days after the year end of December 31, 2014.

3. During the year, MTC exchanged a parcel of land for a storage warehouse and $50,000 cash with MTS. The parcel of land had a carrying value of $150,000, and a fair value of $250,000. The storage warehouse received by MTC was being carried in MTS's books of account at $75,000, and has a fair value of $200,000. MTC has recorded a gain of $100,000 on the exchange.

4. On January 1, 2014, MTC raised additional financing by issuing 10,000 preferred shares for $20. The preferred shares have a cumulative dividend of $1 per share and are redeemable by MTC at any time for $12 per share. The preferred shares can be converted into a bond, at the option of the holder, repayable over a five-year period with a fixed interest rate of 7%.

Required

Prepare a report that discusses the accounting issues and provides recommended treatments. You have been asked to ignore any first-time audit adoption issues (e.g., opening balance issues with retained earnings) until later in the engagement.

Mitten Manufacturing Ltd.

Mitten Manufacturing Ltd. (MML) produces children's mittens and scarves, and sells their products to various large retailers in Canada. The company's sole shareholder and owner, Angela Mitten, is planning to pursue retirement in the near future and has decided to sell her ownership interest in the business.

John Kachurowski, a successful businessperson, has been in negotiations to purchase MML. John currently owns a company that manufactures winter jackets. He feels that an acquisition of MML would result in some synergies and economies of scale.

Angela has offered to sell the business to John for the book value of equity, calculated based on the December 31, 2014 balance sheet prepared in accordance with IFRS. John has approach the public accounting firm of Lebeau and Liang LLP (L&L) requesting assistance in determining an estimate of the purchase price.

The partner has assigned you, a recently qualified professional accountant, to this engagement. During an initial meeting with John, the following discussion took place:

> John: "I am not sure how much the business is going to cost me!"
>
> You: "Okay, well, I can help you with that."
>
> John: "When I look at the balance sheet, I see net equity of $3,517,789; however, I know that there are some accounting issues that need to be considered. In order to get started, I can give you MML's balance sheet (Exhibit I) and some notes that I took from my discussion with Angela, MML's management (Exhibit II)."
>
> You: "Okay, well, this should give me enough to get started on a report."
>
> John: "Sounds good. I look forward to your report. Please keep in mind that MML's financial statements were prepared for internal purposes and have not been audited."

After your meeting with John, you head back to your office and think about how to approach the engagement.

Required

It is now January 10, 2015. The partner has asked you to prepare a memo addressing John's concerns. The partner reminds you that the memo should provide adequate discussions of any alternative accounting treatments with IFRS. In addition, the partner has asked to provide as many journal entries as possible. The journal entries may be provided to Angela in order to update the financial statements.

EXHIBIT I – FINANCIAL STATEMENTS

MITTEN MANUFACTURING INC.
BALANCE SHEET

December 31	2014
Assets	
Current	
Cash and cash equivalents	
Receivables	$2,381,368
Inventories	2,352,949
Due from a shareholder	514,639
Prepaids	78,058
	5,327,014
Capital assets	3,917,157
	$9,244,171
Liabilities	
Current	
Bank indebtedness	$ 111,565
Payables and accruals	3,835,200
Deferred revenue	58,308
Current portion of long-term debt	129,368
	4,134,441
Long-term debt	1,137,161
Accrued benefit liability	169,969
Due to related company	—
Deferred credits	284,811
	5,726,382
Shareholders' equity	
Capital stock	510,010
Retained earnings	3,007,779
	3,517,789
	$9,244,171

EXHIBIT II – NOTES FROM MEETING WITH MML'S MANAGEMENT

The financial statements are prepared internally, and have not been audited. Based on a review of the financial information, the following accounting issues emerged:

» MML incurred a loss during the year of $500,000. The loss was the result of a one-time event that reduced operating profitability. The company is expected to return to profitability next year.

» On January 1, 2014, MML entered into a new lease agreement. The terms of the lease are as follow:

Annual lease payment (due at the beginning of year, starting Jan. 1)	$20,066.26
Bargain purchase option at the end of lease term	$4,500
Lease term	5 years
Economic life of lease equipment	10 years
Lessor's cost	$60,000
Fair value of asset at January 1, 2014	$88,000
Lessor's implicit rate	9%
Lessee's incremental borrowing rate	9%

The lease has not yet been recorded in the financial statements.

» The accrued benefit obligation of $163,969 is based on plan assets of $525,000 and plan liabilities of $694,969. No entries have been made to reflect changes in the plan asset and liability for the current year. A review of an actuary report reveals that the discount rate for the accrued benefit obligation (ABO) is 7%, while the expected and actual return on the plan assets is 7% and 10%, respectively. Service costs for the current year are $35,000, and the benefits paid to retirees were $40,000.

» The provision for income taxes included in the financial statements is recorded based on the taxes payable in the current period (i.e., the amount payable based on taxable income). Management has done this because there are very few differences between taxable income and accounting income. The only significant difference is related to the depreciation of capital assets. A review of Schedule 8 of the Corporate T2 reveals undepreciated capital cost (UCC) balances of $3,550,000. The average tax rate for MML is 30% on the current year's income.

» Management of MML made a comment regarding a $200,000 accounts receivable with Super Shopper, a large Canadian retailer. It appears that the receivable from Super Shopper is over 90 days old. Recent headlines shed some light into the financial difficulties confronting Super Shopper.

» MML is currently being sued by Tech Outerwear (TO) for patent infringement regarding the design of a new glove. The lawsuit was filed on December 15, 2014. MML's lawyers have not had enough time to properly assess the lawsuit, and therefore cannot determine the likelihood of losing the suit. Similar, past lawsuits have settled for anywhere between $200,000 and $700,000.

» Included in the $510,010 of capital stock is $50,000 of preferred shares. The preferred shares are retractable by the holders if there is a change in the ownership of the business.

» During the year, MM's management was issued employee stock options. The options can be exercised anytime during the next three years, which is the expected period of benefit. No options were exercised during the year. As such, the options are not reflected in the financial statements.

Precious Metals Exploration Ltd.

Precious Metals Exploration Ltd. (PME) is a precious metal exploration and development company. PME was established in 2013 by a management team and Board of Directors that has a successful history of creating shareholder value through the acquisition, exploration, financing, and development of gold projects. The company is traded on the Venture Exchange under the ticker PME. The shares are trading for $0.20 per share, which is in excess of the book value per share, based on expectations that management can reproduce their past results.

Currently, PME owns a small portfolio of prospective gold properties in Ontario and is currently exploring in the Beardmore-Geraldton gold belt. The company is looking to expand its portfolio by purchasing various properties that span across Canada. Accordingly, management would like to display a strong financial position in order to assist in their search for new debt or equity capital.

The first year of operations was geared mostly towards establishing the business, closing deals on two properties, and beginning exploration activities. The 2014 fiscal year has been much more hectic as PME acquired an additional property, and significantly ramped up exploration activities. Management has been too busy running the day-to-day operations to be able to devote a significant amount of time to the accounting duties.

Accordingly, they have just hired you, CA, as a controller in order to help management focus more of their time on property acquisition and development. It is now January 4, 2015, and you have been asked to help prepare the draft financial statements and year-end audit file. The draft balance sheet and income statement, along with excerpts from the notes, are found in Exhibit I. Exhibit II contains a summary of outstanding accounting issues from the current year-end file.

Required

Prepare a report that analyzes all of the accounting issues you have identified. Be sure to explore alternative accounting treatments, where appropriate, and to provide a reasoned conclusion.

EXHIBIT I – FINANCIAL STATEMENTS

PRECIOUS METALS EXPLORATION LTD.
(AN EXPLORATION STAGE COMPANY)
AS AT DECEMBER 31, 2014 AND 2013

	DRAFT	AUDITED
ASSETS	2014	2013
Current assets		
Cash and cash equivalents	$ 463,969	$ 941,020
Receivables	48,595	55,785
Marketable securities	370,000	370,000
Exploration tax credit receivable	55,275	22,750
Due from related party	19,000	21,000
Prepaid expense and deposit	35,450	14,725
	992,289	1,425,280
Mineral properties (note 1)	6,700,500	4,485,775
Property and equipment	14,070	16,780
	$7,706,859	$5,927,835
LIABILITIES AND SHAREHOLDERS' EQUITY		
Current liabilities		
Accounts payable and accrued liabilities	78,950	87,950
Due to related party	17,000	12,000
	95,950	99,950
Asset retirement obligation (note 2)	84,700	79,900
Shareholders' equity		
Share capital (note 3)	7,806,800	5,517,560
Contributed surplus (note 3)	478,550	468,550
Deficit	(750,296)	(234,080)
Accumulated other comprehensive income	75,855	75,855
	7,610,909	5,827,885
	$7,706,859	$5,927,835

EXHIBIT I CONTINUED – FINANCIAL STATEMENTS

PRECIOUS METALS EXPLORATION LTD.
(AN EXPLORATION STAGE COMPANY)
AS AT DECEMBER 31, 2014 AND 2013

	DRAFT 2014	AUDITED 2013
EXPENSES		
Accretion of retirement liability	$ 4,800	$ 0
Administrative services	131,275	54,700
Amortization	2,710	1,130
Consulting fees	105,000	43,750
Directors' fees	36,000	15,000
Investor relations and shareholder information	117,500	48,960
Office and miscellaneous	93,330	38,890
Professional fees	125,575	52,320
Property investigation	32,555	13,560
Property write downs	0	1,000
Rent	41,850	17,440
Salaries and wages	145,000	60,420
Stock-based compensation	0	0
Transfer agent and filing fees	11,450	4,770
Travel and promotion	13,450	3,960
	$860,495	$355,900
OTHER INCOME		
Interest income	175,225	51,540
Gain on sale of marketable security	40,000	11,760
	215,225	63,300
Loss for the year before income taxes	645,270	292,600
Future income tax recovery	(129,054)	(58,520)
Loss for the year	$516,216	$234,080
Deficit, beginning of the year	(234,080)	0
Deficit, end of the year	(750,296)	(234,080)

EXHIBIT I CONTINUED – EXCERPTS FROM THE NOTES TO THE FINANCIAL STATEMENTS

1. Mining Properties

The Company is in the process of exploring its mineral properties and has not yet determined whether these properties contain ore reserves that are economically recoverable. Mineral exploration and development costs are capitalized on an individual prospect basis until such time as an economic ore body is defined or the prospect is sold, abandoned, or determined to be impaired. Costs for a producing prospect are amortized on a unit-of-production method based on the estimated life of the ore reserves. Costs for prospects abandoned are written off.

The Company reviews the carrying value of mineral properties and deferred exploration costs when there are events or changes in circumstances that may indicate impairment. Where estimates of fair value are available, an impairment charge is recorded if the fair value is less than the carrying amount. Reductions in the carrying value of properties are recorded to the extent the carrying value of the property exceeds the greater of: (1) the discounted value of future cash flows; or (2) the net realizable value (proceeds less the costs to sell).

The following table shows the activity by property from January 1, 2014, to December 31, 2014:

Property	Dec. 31, 2013	Acquisitions	Explorations	Tax Credits	Write-downs	Dec. 31, 2014
Peter Lake	2,275,855	0	548,545	(27,855)	0	2,796,545
Wolf Gate	0	975,855	137,095	0	0	1,112,950
Mink Landing	2,209,920	0	585,755	(4,670)	0	2,791,005
	4,485,775	975,855	1,271,395	(32,525)	0	6,700,500

2. Asset retirement obligation

The Company's obligations with respect to asset retirement relate to reclamation of the Peter Lake Property site on which project operations are situated. The obligation is recognized in the period in which the obligation is created based on the estimated future reclamation costs using a credit-adjusted risk-free rate of 6 percent. The total undiscounted future obligation is $135,000. The Company estimates its obligations to be settled over approximately the next 10 years.

Balance - December 31, 2013	79,900
Accretion expense	4,800
Balance - December 31, 2014	84,700

EXHIBIT I CONTINUED – EXCERPTS FROM THE NOTES TO THE FINANCIAL STATEMENTS

3. Share Capital

Authorized: Unlimited common shares without par value

	Date	Number of Shares	Amount	Contributed Surplus
Balance, as at December 31, 2013		62,244,278	5,517,560	468,550
1) Shares issued for mineral properties	Jan. 31	30,000	6,000	
2) Shares issued for mineral properties	Jan. 31	200,000	40,000	
3) Shares issued for mineral properties	Mar. 31	50,000	7,500	
4) Shares issues for private placement	June 30	4,000,000	720,000	800
Share issuance costs			27,550	
5) Warrants exercised	June 30	115,000	17,250	9,200
6) Special shares issued for private placement	Nov. 30	6,000,000	600,000	
Share issuance costs			94,940	
7) Shares issued for mineral properties	Nov. 30	55,000	11,000	
8) Shares issues for private placement	Dec. 31	4,500,000	765,000	
		77,194,278	7,806,800	478,550

4. Related Party Transactions

a)   At December 31, 2014, the Company owed $17,000 (December 31, 2013: $12,000) to companies with directors and officers in common. This obligation does not have any repayment terms or interest.

b)   The following related party transactions were in the normal course of operations and are measured at fair value being their exchange amounts:

	December 31, 2013	December 31, 2014
1) Director fees	36,000	15,000
2) Management Salary	145,000	60,420
3) Toronto Capital Partners Inc. - professional fees		
(Company with a Director in Common)	25,000	15,000
4) Doug Pasulka – professional fees		
(Legal firm with a Partner and Company Director in Common)	17,500	22,500
Total	223,500	112,920

EXHIBIT II – NOTES OF OUTSTANDING ISSUES FROM THE YEAR-END FILE

1. Recent geological reports suggest that the Peter Lake property may not have as large a gold deposit as originally expected. Given this negative news, management hired an independent specialist to assess the ounces of gold that could be realistically mined from both the Peter Lake and Mink Landing properties. The following is a summary of the specialist's report:

Ounces	Year 1	Year 2	Year 3	Year 4	Year 5	Year 6	Year 7	Year 8	Year 9	Year 10
Peter Lake	0	130	265	400	425	535	535	475	475	265
Mink Landing	0	265	420	525	840	780	900	900	750	750

Current industry expectations are that the price of gold will retreat from its record highs and average approximately $1,250 per ounce, with expected extraction costs of $300 per ounce.

2. The Wolf Gate property was acquired by entering into a lease agreement with Geraldton Development Ltd. (GDL), a construction company. GDL owns the land, but has no intention of exploring and/or mining the property. Accordingly, a lease agreement was reached whereby PME has the rights to explore and mine any gold deposits found over a 10-year period of time.

The lease agreement required PME to pay an upfront fee of $575,855 to GDL. A royalty fee of 3% is payable for either: 1) the gross sales from mining any gold extracted from the land; or 2) the selling of the property in excess of $575,855 to a third party. The lease allows PME to require GDL to sell the land to a third party if a gold deposit is found with 2,500 ounces or more.

If the land is not sold to a third party, PME must restore the land to its original condition at the end of the 10-year period. Based on recent asset restorations of a similar size, it would cost PME approximately $500,000 to bring the land back up to its original condition. Management of PME feels that there is a 60% chance that they will find a gold deposit on the land in excess of 2,500, in which case, they will sell the land to a larger developer.

3. PME owns the following marketable securities:

Company	Shares	Dec. 31, 2014 Market Value	Dec. 31, 2013 Market Value
Wolfsteed Resources Ltd.	450,000	90,000	83,000
Premier Silver Mines Ltd.	375,000	56,250	65,000
Western Gold Inc.	175,000	70,000	50,000
Atlantic Eastern Miners	175,000	87,500	76,500
South Boreal Resources Ltd.	550,750	110,150	95,500
		413,900	370,000

PME has not made any adjustments to reflect the 2014 market values in the financial statements. During the year, PME sold their 200,000 shares of Kimberly Miners Ltd. for $0.40 per share. The shares' cost basis was $0.10 and were trading at $0.20 at the end of 2010. This transaction has not been recorded.

EXHIBIT II CONTINUED – NOTES OF OUTSTANDING ISSUES FROM THE YEAR-END FILE

4. PME implemented a stock-based compensation program during the current year as opposed to paying large cash salaries. The purpose of the compensation package is to allow to management to take on more of the risk and reward of ownership, with the ability to receive greater compensation in the long run if the company is successful. In addition, cash flow would be saved during this crucial time of start-up and exploration.

    The following combination of stock options and salary was awarded to the management team during the most recent year:

Name	Position	Salary	Director Fee	Stock Options
Brian Cambell, P. Eng., P.Geo.	President, CEO and Director	35,000	6,000	500,000
Scott Vanek, P. Eng., MBA	VP Exploration and Director	25,000	6,000	400,000
Daniel Marleau	Chairman of the Board	10,000	6,000	400,000
Fatima El-Atifi, CA	Chief Financial Officer and Director	25,000	6,000	400,000
Nareen Ghaffar, MBA	VP Corp. Development and Director	25,000	6,000	400,000
Jeffrey Rosenblatt	Corporate Secretary and Director	25,000	6,000	400,000
		145,000	36,000	2,500,000

    All of the options were issued on January 1, 2014, with a strike price of $0.35 per share when the shares were trading at $0.25 per share. The options could be exercised anytime during the next five years. Some additional information regarding the common shares of PME and market rates is as follows:

- Volatility (σ), calculated over the past month: 15%
- Volatility (σ), calculated over the past 6 months: 30%
- Volatility (σ), calculated over the past year: 45%
- 30-day Government of Canada treasury bill rate: 2%
- 1-year Government of Canada bond yield: 4%
- 5-year Government of Canada bond yield: 6%

5. The EPS for the current year has yet to be calculated.

6. During November 2014, the Company issued 6 million special common shares for $0.10 each. The common shares were issued to an investment bank in Toronto, and have the following characteristics:

    a) The shares have a retraction privilege that is in effect if PME's retained deficit balance exceeds $1 million. When the retained earnings are in a surplus position, the shares can be redeemed by the Company for $0.35 per share, regardless of the market price.

    b) The special common shares carry a 10%, non-cumulative dividend. In any given year, dividends must be paid on the special shares before any other dividend could be paid to the remaining common shares.

Sit-up Fitness Centre

Sit-up Fitness Centre (SFC) is a new athletic facility, located in Saskatoon, Saskatchewan. SFC is owned and operated by Calvin Power, a former Olympic gold medalist in weight-lifting. Calvin decided to make his passion his business by opening open a local gym. SFC has the following mission statement:

"SFC provides the residents of Saskatoon the opportunity to live a healthier, happier, and longer life by providing affordable access to athletic equipment, aerobic classes, and specialized dieticians."

Mr. Power borrowed $10 million from the bank in order finance the required start-up investments in working capital and capital assets. Mr. Power invested $2 million of his own money (that he earned through his career as a weightlifter and professional wrestler). The bank does not want the debt to equity ratio to exceed 5:1.

The first year of business has been a bit a rocky, as Mr. Power's expertise is in weight training, as opposed to running a business. However, SFC was able to attract 5,000 people to purchase full memberships.

It was difficult to attract new members during the first few months of operations. In order to attract more members, Mr. Power implemented the following creative marketing initiatives during the middle of the year:

» Power Points – SFC offers its members 1 point per visit to the gym (maximum of 1 point per day). Power Points can be redeemed for free passes for a guest or for a free protein drink.

» Initial Fee Return Guarantee – For three months, SFC provided new members with a guarantee period whereby their initial membership fee could be returned if they decide to discontinue their membership within the first year.

» Free Membership Challenge – "Members are entered into a draw every time they access the gym, and provided with a chance to win free membership fees for life."

Mr. Power has come to you, Badami and Lusamba LLP, for assistance regarding the preparation of the December 31, year-end financial statements in accordance with ASPE. Mr. Power knows how much cash came in from memberships, but is unsure about how much revenue should be recognized. In addition, Mr. Power needs help understanding how the marketing initiatives impact the financial statement. Additional details on the marketing initiatives can be found in Exhibit I, which outlines your most recent discussion with Mr. Power.

Required

Prepare a report that addresses Mr. Power's concerns. The partner would like you to do a good job this engagement as it may lead to more work, and the annual year-end audit. Therefore, the partner has asked you to prepare any journal entries to record your recommended accounting treatments.

EXHIBIT I – DISCUSSION WITH MR. POWER

» Memberships require a non-refundable $500 initiation fee, followed by a monthly fee of $50. The monthly fee must be paid at the beginning of each month. The following is a monthly breakdown of the new memberships.

Jan	Feb	Mar	Apr	May	June	July	Aug	Sept	Oct	Nov	Dec
200	250	350	200	250	400	850	900	800	300	300	200

» SFC offered new members an Initial Fee Return Guarantee during the months of July, August, and September. The program was well received, and resulted in significant increases in membership. Mr. Power believes the program is so successful because it provides people with a risk-free opportunity to see what SFC has to offer. Mr. Power is confident that once a member has a chance to work out at the gym, and take advantage of all it has to offer, no one will discontinue their membership. As of December 31, not a single person has taken advantage of the Initial Fee Return Guarantee. Revenue has been recorded on a cash basis by Mr. Power.

» The Power Points can be redeemed as follows:

  • A total of 10 Power Points can be redeemed for a free pass for a guest. With a free pass, a member can bring a guest into the gym to use all of the facilities for free. The only condition is that a free pass guest cannot partake in any aerobic classes if they are full (i.e., they cannot bump out a paying customer). Anyone can purchase a day pass to SFC for $5, which will entitle them to full access to the gym, including all classes.

  • A total of 15 Power Points can be redeemed for a free protein shake. The shake can be purchased from SFC for $6.50. It costs SFC a total of $2.50, including all overhead allocations, to prepare the shake.

  During the year, a total of 30,255 Power Points were issued. Members took favourably to this promotion; the Points were redeemed for 60 free guest passes and 75 free protein shakes. Industry standards suggest that a total of 20% of all Points will not be redeemed. The only journal entries recorded in regards to the Power Points was a debit to cost of goods sold and credit to inventory for the protein shakes.

» Every time a member swipes their membership card to access the gym they are electronically entered into a random draw. The winner of the draw will then have a chance to win free membership fees for life. In order to win the challenge, the member must do more push-ups than Mr. Power. The draw will take place on February 5 of the following fiscal year, and the push-up challenge will take place on February 25.

Boreal Farms and Nursery

Jenny Kinnear just completed a university degree in natural resource sciences. Given the tough economic times, it has been difficult to find any form of meaningful employment. Prior to moving to Montreal in order to attend university, Jenny lived with her parents in a small farming community. Accordingly, Jenny has been thinking about acquiring some farm land on the outskirts of Montreal and establishing a farm and nursery. Farm land can now be obtained for a reduced price. Jenny has discussed the idea with her retired parents, and they suggested they would move to Montreal if she decides to pursue the business in order to assist her to get the business up and running.

On January 1, 2013, Jenny decided to go into business by incorporating Boreal Farms and Nursery (BFN). BFN immediately purchased a plot of farm land from a family of retiring farmers. The land was obtained for the bargain price of $1 million. A bank loan, with an interest rate of 5%, was obtained in order to help finance the land acquisition cost.

Jenny and her parents decided to segregate the farm land in order to be able to grow seasonal produce (strawberries, beans, peas, corn, etc.), Christmas trees, and raise chicken and cattle. A storefront is also included on the land. A map of the land can be found in Exhibit I.

It is now December 2014, and Jenny is beginning to worry about BFN's financial statements. She knows that the bank loan requires BFN to file audited annual financial statements. BFN has engaged Abdillahi and Blouin LLP to perform the audit. In order to prepare for the upcoming audit, Jenny has hired you, CMA, for a special consulting contract. Specifically, Jenny provides you with the terms of the consulting project:

> "I feel that the nature of BFN's business is fairly straightforward, except for inventory. Therefore, I would like you to prepare a report that discusses all theoretically possible measurement bases of inventory, along with the resulting impact of each measure on revenue recognition. Based on your theoretical discussion, I would like your report to focus in on the actual accounting standards. Because the bank will accept either ASPE or IFRS financial statements, I would like you to discuss how my inventory should be accounted for under both standards."

Jenny provides you with some additional information regarding the operations of BFN (Exhibit II), along with some financial information related to the inventory (Exhibit III).

Required

Prepare the report for Jenny.

EXHIBIT I – MAP OF FARMLAND

Various seasonal produce (24%)	Christmas trees (26%)	
	Corn field (5%)	
Farm yard (26%)	Vacant land (8%)
	Storefront (11%)

EXHIBIT II – INFORMATION FROM BFN'S OPERATIONS

Year end

» Jenny selected the fiscal year to run from January 1 to December 31 in order to capture a full season of the seasonal produce and corn field activities.

Seasonal produce

» BFN grows a variety of seasonal produce, including peas, strawberries, cucumbers, and peppers.

» At the end of the season, BFN sells produce through various means: (1) in bundles through their storefront; (2) through local retailers that promote local produce; (3) through farmer's markets; and (4) by allowing customers to pick their own basket of produce on site.

» The corn field is a component of the seasonal produce. The corn is grown and then sold through the same outlets as the rest of the seasonal produce. During the month of October, the corn field is turned into a Halloween corn field, whereby customers walk through for $10. The Halloween corn field was a huge success this year, and a great source of supplemental income. Jenny paid $7,500 to design the layout of the corn field, and to purchase the required accessories.

Christmas trees

» The Christmas tree market can be classified as pure competition. There is an abundant supply of trees, such that any individual supplier cannot impact the price. In addition, there are an abundant number of purchasers, such that any single purchaser cannot impact the price. Finally, the product is considered to be homogenous as well, aside from the type of tree (e.g., Douglas fir, white pine). Although trees may come in different shapes and colours, the value of a tree is based solely on its height (the shape can be altered through pruning while colour can be adjusted through dyes).

» A Christmas tree is priced similar to any commodity that trades in a market. The market price of a Christmas tree is determined based on its equivalent of a commodity spot price. The following are the current Christmas tree prices for white pine:

3 Feet:	$30	7 Feet:	$45	Note: estimated selling costs are 10% of the sales price.
4 Feet:	$35	8 Feet:	$47	
5 Feet:	$38	9 Feet:	$55	
6 Feet:	$40			

» Generally, white pine trees are not grown to exceed 9 feet as their retail commercial value disappears at this level.

» Trees are scrapped as soon as it becomes apparent that they no longer have any value. Aside from any weather calamities or insect infestation outbreaks, the scrappage rate is fairly consistent from year to year.

» The growth rate for white pine depends a lot on whether trees are free to grow or are suppressed under a canopy. Average height growth for young suppressed white pine is often less than 6 inches per year. However, with free-to-grow trees on the better sites, height growth is normally 2 to 3 feet per year.

Farm yard

» During the past year, BFN set up a chicken pen. The chickens are used to produce eggs, which are sold through retailers and at farmers' markets. Eventually, the chickens will be sold as poultry.

» A hen's reproduction cycle is set by the length of the day. During the summer months, a hen usually produces one egg per day. A hen will lay fewer eggs as the day shortens, eventually skipping days between laying eggs. Many hens stop laying eggs all together until the spring arrives because winter is a bad time to raise chicks given that cold weather decreases a chick's chance of survival.

» BFN is planning to purchase cattle next year, and offer dairy products as well (milk, cheese, etc.). No expenses have been incurred in this regard for the current year.

EXHIBIT III – FINANCIAL INFORMATION RELATED TO INVENTORY

»   During the year, BFN started its Christmas tree farm by purchasing 8,000 white pine seedlings for $8 each. The seedlings are just below one foot tall when planted this year. Approximately 3% of all seedlings do not survive their first year.

»   BFN purchased and installed a sprinkler system that covers farm land area (seasonal and Christmas trees) for a total of $175,000. The system has an expected useful life of 8 years.

»   BFN consumed $55,000 in water directly related to the use of the sprinkler system.

»   BFN hired two student employees to work directly to maintain (prune, weed, water, etc.) the seasonal produce and Christmas trees. The two employees earned $35,000 in total over the course of the summer months.

»   BFN incurred costs of $13,000 for seeds related to the seasonal produce items.

»   BFN utilized fertilizers during the past year in order to aid with the growth process. Super Grow fertilized was used for both the seasonal produce and trees, and cost $29,000. In addition, a total of $17,500 worth of Tree Booster was purchased during the year. A total of $2,500 worth of the product remained at year end.

»   An organic pesticide was used during the year as well. A total of $27,000 and $34,000 was spent on Tree Bug Zapper and Pest Be Gone, respectively. The ending balance of Tree Bug Zapper and Pest Be Gone was $3,500 and $2,500, respectively.

»   In order to help aerate the soil, BFN purchased a land cultivator for $55,000. The equipment is expected to have a useful life of six years, and was used for the land around both the seasonal produce and trees.

»   BFN purchased 100 chickens (87 hens able to lay eggs, 10 chicks, and 3 roosters) for a total cost of $950 from a local farm. The hens are expected to be able to lay eggs for the next five years, at which point the hens will be sold for $8 each to a local grocery store.

»   BFN purchased $6,500 of chicken feed during the year. The year-end inventory of chicken feed is $2,250. In addition, BFN purchased a cage for $2,500, which is expected to last 12 years.

»   A dozen eggs are sold for $4.00, which reflects a premium as they are sold as organic eggs.

»   Hens can be sold in the open market for $9 per hen.

Forgurt Ice Creams

Forgurt Ice Creams (FIC) was established in 1995, in Edmonton, Alberta by Raj Swaminathan to produce natural ice creams using only milk, sugar, chocolate, and fruits. The company prides itself on its wide selection of varieties and the fact that it uses no preservatives or stabilizers.

Mr. Swaminathan is planning to take the company public within the next few years; however, he is having doubts given the recent turbulence in the equity markets as a result of the global economic slowdown. The IPO market has become much more competitive as investors are hesitant to take on the risks associated with small cap companies. Only companies with strong a financial position and earnings growth have been greeted positively by the equity markets.

The controller of FIC is preparing the year-end financial statements and external audit working paper file. The controller is reviewing the following transactions that took place during the year (all figures are in '000s):

1. The company agreed to sell a large order of ice cream to a retailer in exchange for $10,000 cash and a note receivable for $50,000 at 3%. The note is repayable at the end of a two-year period. Interest must be paid at the end of each year. The retailer's normal borrowing rate is prime plus 3%. At the time of the sale, prime was 3%. FIC recorded revenues of $60,000.

2. Given the recent volatility in the market, FIC decided to enter into a futures contract to lock in the price of milk on April 1. The contract is traded on the Chicago Mercantile Exchange, under the symbol DC, and is for the standard contract size of 200,000 lbs. The contract was entered into at a price of $21.22 per hundredweight. As at year end, milk was trading at $19.54 per hundredweight. FIC has not recognized this futures contract in the accounts.

3. On July 1, the company received a $150,000 patent infringement settlement regarding a competitor's use of FIC's special recipe. The funds are going to be used to reinvest in the business's capital assets and expand operations within the next two years. Because the expansion is not taking place until next year, management decided to invest funds into an exchange traded fund that invests in a mixture of short and long-term bonds. The bond fund was trading at $12.50 per share on July 1, and at $13.38 on December 31. This bond fund is being carried at its historical cost.

4. On January 1, the company purchased for $150,000 a newly issued, five-year bond that was yielding 6%, when the market rate was 6%. Interest is paid annually. As of year end, global economic turmoil resulted in a flight to safety, pushing market yields down. The market rate for this bond is now 5%. Management plans to use the funds from the bonds to help finance the future expansion plans. The bond is currently being measured at amortized cost.

5. During the prior year, FIC purchased 10% of the common shares of Crispy Cones (CC), a producer of waffle ice cream cones, for $200,000. The shares of CC are not publicly traded, and the purchase price was established as 5 times net income of $40,000. The past fiscal year has proved to be a challenge for CC due to increased competition, commodity price inflation, and an inability to raise prices due to limits on consumer discretionary spending. CC's most recent financial statements report reveals net income of $27,500.

Prior to the above-noted transactions, pre-tax net income was $225,000. The management team is happy about the current year results as they will obtain a bonus of $11,250, or 5% of net income.

Required

Assume the role of the controller and prepare a report that discusses the recognition and measurement of the financial instruments noted above. The company uses IFRS.

Generally Accepted Accounting Principles or Generally Prescribed Accounting Rules?

As you prepare for graduation, you are excited to make the transition from an academic accounting student to a professional accounting student. You have applied to various accounting firms, and received an interview offer from three different firms.

On your first interview with a major firm, the following dialogue takes place between you and a managing partner:

Managing Partner: "I always enjoy recruiting season. It is refreshing to see all of the young and ambitious accounting students with a thirst to apply their knowledge in practice."

You: "I am very excited to begin working full-time towards my professional accounting designation."

Managing Partner: "Well, that is great to hear. I hope that you understand what this profession entails. It is a dynamic profession that is constantly changing and evolving."

You: "I am ready for the challenge, and look forward to constantly learning."

Managing Partner: "I most certainly have seen many changes in the Canadian financial reporting landscape since I obtained my designation. Specifically, the concept of generally acceptable accounting principles has evolved tremendously over the past 20 years. Back in the day, generally accepted meant that a few accountants thought it was appropriate. Now, there is much more guidance on the concept of generally accepted. What is your understanding of generally accepted, and who decides what is generally accepted?"

You: "My understanding of generally accepted is that _____ "

Managing Partner: "You should also know that the *Handbook* used to be a small compilation of principles. Now, it's a large collection of detailed standards covered in four different parts. I am wondering if we have transitioned to Generally Accepted Accounting Rules! What are your thoughts on the rules versus principles approach to standard setting, and do you believe that our current GAAP really is principle based?"

You: "Well, I believe that _____ "

Managing Partner: "Okay, now, what would you do if you were confronted with an accounting issue that is not explicitly dealt with by GAAP?"

You: "I would _____ "

Managing Partner: "I have one final question. The presentation of financial statements has also changed significantly, especially with the recent introduction of Part I GAAP. However, even prior to IFRS, Canadian standards offered explicit guidance on the presentation of financial statements. What is your understanding of the presentation of financial statements?"

You: "I recall studying this in my advanced accounting course. Specifically, _____ "

Required

Prepare the responses to the partner's interview questions.

Gem Shine Car Wash

Gem Shine Car Wash (GSCW) is a car wash in a busy residential suburb of Saint John, NB. GSCW offers coin-operated, self serve car wash, along with a full service car wash. Recently, the company obtained a bank loan in order to upgrade its equipment and spruce up the exterior of the building and signage. The bank loan includes a covenant stipulating that total debt (current and long-term) to equity is not to exceed 3:1.

The covenant has GSCW's owner, Joshua Savoie, concerned about the company's total liabilities at year end. Specifically, Joshua is unsure about the impact on the bank covenant of the following:

» Joshua received a customer complaint regarding a recent full service car wash. The customer alleges that the washer scratched the car, causing damage of $2,000. The customer would like GSCW to incur the costs to repair the vehicle, or else he will proceed to small claims court. Joshua has experience with these situations. He estimates that, based on the terms and conditions of the cash wash agreement, there is only a 10% chance that the customer will receive a $2,000 reward. There is a 50% chance that the customer will be awarded $500.

» In the community, it is standard practice that all businesses donate $5,000 to a local community charity with the mandate of eliminating homelessness. GSCW has always donated in the past. The fundraising campaign was delayed in the current year and is scheduled to take place during the days just after the year end. During the current year, Joshua has pledged to contribute again this year.

» When decommissioning the car wash, the company will be required to incur various clean-up costs. Joshua expects that it may cost upwards of $10,000 to decommission the car wash, but he is unsure of an exact amount. The car wash is expected to last at least another 20 years.

» Although the GSCW just completed an upgrade of the machinery, it is likely that some maintenance will be required on the equipment within the next three years. In addition, a major overhaul will be required in another eight years.

» GSCW implemented a loyalty program in order to help increase customer loyalty, and boost earnings over the long run. Customers receive one "Clean Point" for every full service car wash. Ten Clean Points can be redeemed for a free car wash (retail value of $24.99).

  Financial records indicate that a total of 8,750 Clean Points have been issued since the inception of the program, with 545 free car washes provided. Industry statistics suggest that 10% to 20% of all loyalty points issued will not be received. GSCW has never recorded the loyalty points in the financial statements in the past.

» GSCW sells non-refundable gift certificates that can be used for full service car washes. The company's policy is to record all gift certificates as deferred revenue and write off all unused gift certificates after two years. The gift certificates do not expire. The following is a summary of the gift card issued, used, and written off:

	Six Years Ago	Five Years Ago	Four Years Ago	Three Years Ago	Two Years Ago	Last Year	This Year
Amount issued	3,650	3,375	2,675	3,480	2,870	3,455	2,980
Amount used	3,250	2,850	2,250	2,950	2,210	2,560	1,175
Written off	400	525	425	530	660	0	0

Currently, GSCW has a deferred revenue balance of $2,700. Given the capital intensive nature of car washes, GSCW will incur little variable cost to provide the services to settle the gift certificates. Specifically, GSCW has a contribution margin of 70%.

Joshua has hired you, an independent professional accountant, to prepare a report that discusses alternative accounting treatments for the above-noted issued. The financial statements must be prepared in accordance with ASPE; however, Joshua would like you to discuss any differences that would arise if the statements are prepared in accordance with IFRS.

Required

Prepare the report for Joshua.

Marko Pharma Ltd.

Marko Pharma Ltd. (MPL) is a biotech company that is involved in research and commercialization of products to treat a variety of human diseases and to boost human health. The company issued an IPO in the current year, and is traded on the Toronto Stock Exchange under the ticker MPL. The company also has bonds issued in the public market, which are currently yielding 8%.

Given the recent market volatility and global economic conditions, the share price of MPL has been under significant pressure. During its first year on the TSX, MPL's stock price has performed as follows:

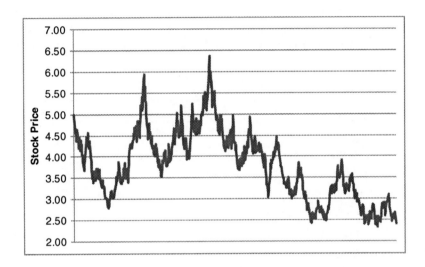

The stock price peaked at around $6.50 per share, but has steadily declined since the company announced second-quarter earnings that missed analysts' expectations. Third-quarter earnings met analysts' expectations; however, this did not prove to be a catalyst for share price appreciation.

Shareholders were upset with the weak IPO issuing and are again becoming restless with the slumping share price. Shareholders are looking for management to generate shareholder wealth and there have been rumblings that a shareholder activist group is looking to change top management at the upcoming annual meeting. The low share price has also led to speculation that MPL will be taken over by a larger biotech company through a hostile bid.

The CFO is now preparing the annual financial statements for the year ended December 31, 2014, and considering the following transactions during the most recent quarter:

» MPL recently attracted two new researchers to the company. The researchers were paid an upfront signing bonus of $350,000 each. The researchers come from a larger company and have a proven track record of developing profitable products. For example, the researchers recently developed (in their previous employment) a highly profitable testing procedure that detects early stages of prostate cancer. The procedure is estimated to generate in excess of $5 million in discounted cash flows. The researchers must work for MPL for a minimum of three years, or else the bonus must be repaid.

» MPL purchased a patented pharmaceutical drug for $3.4 million from a smaller company that does not have the resources to commercialize the product. The product treats kidney disease and is named BlockXs. Generally, drug patents last for 20 years. However, the patent was applied for three years ago when clinical trials began.

The product has been recently approved by both Health Canada and the US Food and Drug Administration (FDA), and will be available to the market next year. BlockXs is expected to earn the following net cash flows:

- Fiscal 2015 - $1,250,000
- Fiscal 2016 - $750,000
- Fiscal 2017 - $750,000
- Fiscal 2018 - $750,000

- Fiscal 2019 - $750,000
- Fiscal 2020 - $750,000
- Fiscal 2021 - $750,000
- Fiscal 2022 - $750,000

» During the most recent quarter, MPL had a breakthrough in its research and development of a new protein supplement called $Protein^2$. $Protein^2$ successfully merges the benefits of whey and casein proteins in an ultra absorptive formula. The following costs were incurred on the project during the past quarter:

$Protein^2$ – Costs Incurred	
Costs incurred in order to obtain government approvals and patents:	$ 33,000
Purchase of equipment to be used to manufacture the protein supplement:	550,000
Materials and services consumed in development of formula:	345,000
Payroll and consulting expenses incurred in the design of a logo and packaging:	37,800
Marketing of the product in fitness magazines:	34,750
Cost of efforts to refine, improve, and enhance the formula:	177,500
Materials used in pre-production pilot testing:	88,000
	$1,266,050

Management is excited to launch this product as the protein supplement industry is large, and growing. Both Health Canada and the US FDA have approved the product, and a patent for the formula has been filed and approved. $Protien^2$ is expected to generate net cash flows of $450,000 per year over the next five years.

» MPL purchased a non-transferable right to distribute its products through a direct-to-doctor sales company. The company visits doctors and hospitals and directly promotes the benefits of the products in order to sell the product. MPL paid $1.2 million to acquire the distribution rights for a four-year period, and must pay a royalty of 2% of all products sold through this outlet.

Management expects that there is a 55% chance that this new distribution arrangement will increase total sales by 5%. Total revenue in the current fiscal year is $5,150,000. However, there is a 25% probability that sales could increase by as much as 10%, and a 20% probability that sales could increase by as little as 2%.

Required

You have been hired as part of the accounting group. The CFO has asked you to prepare a report that discusses the appropriate accounting treatment of the transactions noted above. The CFO would like you to not only address recognition and initial measurement, but, also subsequent measurement.

Munich IT Solutions

Munich IT Solutions (MITS) is a fast growing, medium-sized business that primarily provides integrated server solutions that manage the storage, organization, and retrieval of information. MITS provides IT solutions by offering both server hardware and database management software.

MITS' CEO, CFO and COO are compensated with based on a 10% bonus of pre-tax net income if revenues exceed $4 million. The net income and revenue measures are based on the financial statements prepared in accordance with IFRS. The Board of Directors implemented such a bonus structure in order to help align the goals of top management and shareholders, and also ensure that executives do not cut discretionary spending in order to reach a net income bonus threshold.

MITS' top management team is excited about the current year's results because the draft financial statements reveal revenues in excess of the $4 million threshold and a bonus of $156,390 will be payable. The draft financial statements are to be reviewed by the internal audit department, in anticipation of the external auditor's field work next week.

You have just been hired as an internal auditor, reporting directly to the internal audit manager. The manager has called you into her office to discuss your first engagement:

Manager: "Welcome to the team. We are very happy that you decided to accept our offer of employment."

You: "Thank you. I am very excited to be here, and look forward to being a part of the team."

Manager: "Excellent. Well, your first engagement is a very important task. I would like you to review our draft income statement prior to the external audit next week. Specifically, I would like to you focus on the revenue line item. Please prepare a report that outlines any concerns that you have, and addresses any accounting issues."

You: "Okay, sounds interesting. How can I start?"

Manager: "Well, here is a copy of the draft income statement (Exhibit I). In addition, I have prepared the following notes of the current year's operations for your review (Exhibit II). This should be enough to get you started on your report. We can meet again once you have prepared your report."

You: "Sounds good. I'll get started right away."

Required

Prepare the report.

EXHIBIT I – DRAFT INCOME STATEMENT

For the year ended December 31 (unaudited)

Sales

Mainframe server sales	2,200,000	
Small business solution sales	2,625,000	
		4,825,000

Cost of sales

Mainframe server	1,200,000	
Small business solutions	1,350,000	
		2,550,000
Gross profit		2,275,000

Expenses

Advertising and promotion	187,950
Amortization	98,000
Insurance	16,540
Interest	19,560
Legal and accounting	8,900
Lease expense	44,500
Office and general expenses	25,000
Repairs and maintenance	17,000
Utilities	34,000
Wages and benefits	272,000
	723,450
	1,551,550

Operating income	
Other service income	12,350
Income before taxes and bonus	1,563,900
Bonus (10%)	156,390
Income before taxes	1,407,510
Current taxes (30%)	469,170
Net income	$1,094,730

EXHIBIT II – INFORMATION REGARDING THE CURRENT YEAR'S OPERATIONS

1. <u>Mainframe Servers:</u> MITS sells large mainframe servers for $550,000. The cost of the server is $300,000. MITS delivers and installs the server at the customer's site. The customer signs off on an acceptance form once the server is installed and tested. MITS has never had a customer reject the installation of a mainframe server.

   In order to help promote sales, MITS began to offer a two-year warranty with all mainframe servers. The warranty is expected to cost an average of $45,000 per server to service the warranty over the two-year period. Industry competitors that offer similar warranties set the warranty price as two times expected cost.

   MITS has received orders for four mainframe servers during the current year, of which all four have been delivered and three have been accepted by the customer. MITS has provided warranty coverage for a total of 13 months during the year.

2. <u>Small Business Solutions:</u> MITS's typical small business solution customer is a growing business without a designated information technology department that purchases server hardware. MITS sells a small business solution of $175,000, with payment in advance to allow MITS to order the servers. The small business servers cost $90,000.

   Included with the purchase of a server is one year of database management services. If a customer does not want the database management services, MITS provides a discount of $25,000 from the mainframe purchase price. All customers wanted the services in the current fiscal year and MITS provided a total of 47 months of DMS services as a result of these sales.

3. <u>Database Management Services (DMS):</u> MITS recently began marketing its DMS on a stand-alone basis for $3,500 per month. As of year end, the company has not received any orders for only DMS; however, management expects orders to begin to pick up shortly.

4. The gross margin percentage on the small business server and mainframe server is expected to be the same.

5. Mainframe server revenue is recorded upon delivery and installation.

6. Small business solutions server revenue is recorded when the cash is received.

North American Gold and Silver

North American Gold and Silver (NAGS) is a start-up company, closely held by a small group of successful businesspeople, geologists, and engineers. NAGS is a junior mining company that explores for gold and silver. During its first year of operations, the company focused on raising capital and purchasing assets.

Jack Gerikyan, the CFO, is preparing the financial statements for the December 31, 2014 year end. Jack is determining whether the company should adopt ASPE or IFRS. Management does not expect to go public anytime in the near future. However, management is working with a major financial institution in the hopes of securing long-term debt. Therefore, Jack would like to present a strong balance sheet and favourable debt to equity ratio.

During the year, the company financed initial operations by issuing the following instruments:

1. At the beginning of the year, the company issued $500,000 10-year bonds. The holder of the bonds can convert $10,000 in bonds into cash based on the performance of the company. Specifically, each $10,000 bond can be converted into cash at the rate of 10% of net income. Draft financial statements reveal net income of $250,000.

2. On January 1, the company issued $2.5 million of six-year, zero-interest-bearing notes along with warrants to buy 1.25 million common shares for $10 per share. The company received $1.9 million for the notes and warrants. If offered alone, the notes would have been issued to yield 9% to the creditor. The warrants are valued at $550,000 with an option pricing model.

3. On January 1, the company issued $1.5 million of five-year, 6% convertible bonds at par value. Each $1,000 bond is convertible into 100 common shares. A similar bond (without conversion feature) would have been issued at a market yield of 9%. On December 31, $200,000 worth of bonds were converted to common shares.

4. On April 1, the company issued 15,000 8% non-cumulative, retractable preferred shares for $100 per share. The shares are retractable by the holder on or after September 1 of the current year, and redeemable at the option of the company on or after September 2 of the current year. Commencing on September 2 the company is required to purchase 10% annually of the total outstanding preferred shares at $105 per share.

5. On March 1, the company issued 50,000 preferred shares with a 5% cumulative dividend for $10 per share. The preferred shares are redeemable, but not retractable. In addition, the preferred shares can be converted into common shares at any time, at a ratio of 1-to-1.

6. During the year, the company issued 200,000 common shares for $5 per share.

Required

Assume the role of Jack Gerikyan, and prepare a report to the Board of Directors that discusses the recognition, measurement, and presentation of the financial instruments issued.

North Shore Car Dealers

North Shore Car Dealers (NSCD) is a holding company that owns two car dealerships in Ontario. One dealership services the city of Barrie, while the other dealership operates out of Orillia. Both dealerships sell new and used vehicles, and have a full mechanic and body shop. The corporate structure is as follows:

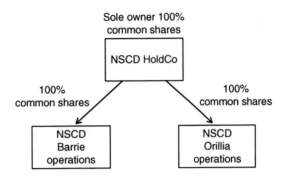

The owner of NSCD is planning to retire in the near future, and is looking to sell the NSCD Barrie dealership. Preliminary negotiations suggest that the dealership will be sold for tangible net worth plus 2 times net earnings, calculated in accordance with ASPE.

The financial statements of all three corporations have never been audited, as they have been prepared with a Notice to Reader report (compilation). Recently, a dispute has emerged between the owner of NSCD and the potential purchaser regarding the treatment of certain related-party and non-monetary transactions. Accordingly, the owner of NSCD has approached your accounting firm seeking assistance with the proper accounting treatment of the following transactions:

1. On June 30, 2014, NSCD Orillia sold a building to NSCD Barrie for $600,000 cash. This amount has not been supported by an independent appraisal. NSCD Orillia had purchased the building for $1 million on January 1, 2004. NSCD Orillia used straight-line depreciation over the estimated 20-year life of the building. NSCD Orillia's contributed surplus account contains a credit balance of $100,000 from previous related-party transactions. NSCD Barrie does not have a balance in its contributed surplus account.

2. During the year, NSCF Orillia traded three used cars with a cost of $35,000 and a blue book value of $44,000 to NSCF Barrie for two used trucks with a cost of $33,000 and a blue book value of $43,000.

3. The controller's duties for both dealerships are performed by a single employee, who is paid from the Orillia operations. The controller is paid an annual salary of $75,000. The wage expense is included in only NCSD Orillia, although she spends her time equally between the Orillia and Barrie operations.

4. NSCD Orillia has guaranteed a long-term mortgage of $450,000 taken by NSCD Barrie. The Barrie dealership is experiencing some financial difficulties; however, it is difficult to predict where there is any risk of loan default.

Required

Prepare the report that discusses the appropriate accounting treatment of the above-noted transactions.

Pro-Tops
The Initial Meeting

Pro-Tops is a manufacturer and distributor of sports jerseys, including baseball, basketball, football, and hockey jerseys. Pro-Tops is owned equally by Wayne Jordan, a former professional hockey player, and Michael Getzinger, a former professional basketball player. Wayne has always been involved in the administration of the company, including the preparation of internal financial statements. Michael's role has always been in regards to product development and marketing.

Recently, Wayne and Michael were involved in an argument regarding the strategic direction of the company. Wayne would like to focus on hockey jerseys, divest the company of all other sports jerseys, and move into the hockey equipment market. Alternatively, Michael would like to keep the company's jersey offering, and add hats to its product offering.

The disagreement has escalated to the point that Wayne has decided to leave the company. The shareholders' agreement provides the remaining shareholder the right of first refusal in regards to purchasing the outgoing shareholder's shares. The shareholders' agreement stipulates that the company's value is to be determined as three times maintainable earnings, whereby maintainable earnings are the earnings expected to be earned into the foreseeable future.

Draft internal financial statements were prepared by Wayne. Wayne has estimated that his shares are worth $1,427,640, calculated as 50% of net income times the multiple of three.

Michael has hired Piccini and Warwick, LLP to provide an estimate of maintainable earnings, comment on the riskiness of the earnings, and provide a preliminary indication of the shares' value. The partner has recently met with Michael and would like you to prepare a report that addresses the client's concerns. The partner has provided you with a copy of the internally prepared income statement (Exhibit I).

Required

Prepare the report requested by the partner for the client.

EXHIBIT I – INTERNALLY PREPARED INCOME STATEMENT

INCOME STATEMENT
For the year ended December 31 (unaudited)   **2014**

Revenue and income	$5,400,750
Cost of sales	2,430,337
Gross profit	2,970,413
Expenses	
Advertising and promotion	255,000
Amortization	445,330
Insurance	22,500
Interest	1,250
Legal and accounting	12,100
Lease expense	34,500
Office and general expenses	255,000
Repairs and maintenance	97,500
Utilities	112,575
Wages and benefits	375,000
	1,610,755
Operating income, before taxes	1,359,657
Income taxes (30%)	407,897
Net income	951,761

Pro-Tops
The Audited Financial Statements

You have met with Michael, and provided him with your draft report. Michael reviews the report, and the following dialogue proceeds:

Michael: "Thank you for providing you report. During the time it took you to prepare the report, our company's audited financial statements have become available. The net income figure in the audited statements is the same as in the draft statements. Do you still think that the audited statements could lead to a different conclusion?"

You: "Well, the audited statements are likely to provide more information, including the appropriate note disclosure, which could lead to a different conclusion."

Michael: "Okay, well, I can provide you with a copy of the audited financial statements. Sorry for any inconvenience that this has caused, but I will be happy to pay you for the extra time it will take to revise your report. This is an important decision for me."

You: "Not a problem, it should not take a great deal of time to review the statements and make any necessary revisions."

Michael: "Okay. I wanted to mention something as well. As I was reviewing the income statement, I noticed that the $250,000 of income our company realized as a result of a key person life insurance payment has not been separated on the income statement. I understand that in the past, there was some requirement to break out what were called 'extraordinary items', however, recent changes to the accounting standards no longer allow for this. I believe this is included in other income, along with interest income."

You: "Yes, you are correct. Thank you for the information. I will consider this in my report as well. I will get back to you within a week."

Michael: "Sounds good, I hope to hear from you soon."

Michael provides you with the audited financial statements (excerpts in Exhibit I), and you head back to the office.

Required

Review the financial statements and make any necessary adjustments to your report.

EXHIBIT I – EXCERPTS FROM THE FINANCIAL STATEMENTS

INCOME STATEMENT

For the year ended December 31 (audited)	2014	2013
Revenue and income	$4,875,200	$4,643,048
Cost of sales	2,162,537	2,059,560
Gross profit	2,712,663	2,583,488
Expenses		
Advertising and promotion	255,000	242,858
Amortization	445,330	424,124
Insurance	22,500	21,429
Interest and bank charges	27,040	25,752
Legal and accounting	12,100	11,524
Lease expense	34,500	32,857
Office and general expenses	255,000	242,857
Repairs and maintenance	97,500	92,857
Utilities	112,575	107,214
Wages and benefits	625,000	595,238
	1,886,545	1,796,710
Operating income	826,118	786,779
Other income	275,790	262,657
Government assistance (note 1)	150,000	142,857
Earnings from continuing operations before taxes	1,251,908	1,192,293
Provision for income taxes	(375,572)	(357,688)
Earnings from discontinued operations, net of taxes (note 2)	75,424	71,833
Net income	951,760	906,438

1. GOVERNMENT ASSISTANCE

The Company applied for, and received, a one-time loan of $150,000. The loan is forgivable based on Pro-Tops maintaining a certain level of employment in certain urban areas. The Company maintained the employment levels and therefore considered the loan as government assistance and is included as income.

2. DISCONTINUED OPERATIONS

During the year, the Company announced the sale of CCP, an operating segment that produces replicate hockey jerseys, to Mega Mart for $350,000.

3. MEASUREMENT UNCERTAINTY

The Company's provision for income tax includes both the current and future tax expense. The Company's taxes are paid to various governments. The preparation of tax filings in various jurisdictions and estimating the future tax expense requires considerable judgement and the use of assumptions. Accordingly, the amounts reported could vary in the future.

4. ECONOMIC DEPENDENCE

Approximately 35% of the Company's total revenue is generated from two customers.

Realty Income Ltd.
Construction Phase

Realty Income Ltd. is a young company, established with the intent of earning rental income from apartment complexes. The company is owned by Jeff Florescu. During the most recent year, the company built a 24-unit apartment complex. The construction commenced on March 1, and was completed by December 31, 2014 (year end).

The following is a detailed breakdown of the construction costs incurred (it is safe to assume that the costs were incurred evenly throughout the year):

	Cost	Useful Life
Appliances	10,749	8
Asphalt driveway	9,249	8
Building permit fees	12,792	40
Cabinets and countertops	37,332	10
Drywall	33,996	40
Electrical wiring	24,927	20
Excavation, foundation and backfill	47,634	40
Exterior doors	5,790	15
Framing and trusses	104,415	40
Gutter and downspouts	2,847	15
HVAC	26,580	10
Insulation	9,996	20
Interior doors and hardware	10,068	15
Landscaping and sod	21,264	8
Lighting and fixtures	7,116	15
Other	57,255	40
Other fees and inspections	9,495	40
Painting	22,914	8
Plumbing	35,259	20
Roof shingles	25,416	8
Sheathing	11,607	40
Siding	38,574	8
Stairs	5,028	40
Steel	4,911	40
Tiles and carpet	34,308	15
Trim material	22,182	15
Water and sewer inspection	11,283	40
Windows	18,708	10
Wood deck	5,844	20
Total	667,539	

On March 1, 2014, the company issued a $500,000 bond payable at a rate of 10% to finance a significant portion of the construction costs. Details of other interest-bearing debt outstanding during the year are as follows:

8% 15-year bonds, issued September 1, 2003	350,000
6% 5-year bonds, issued July 1, 2009	175,000

Given the recent expansion with the company, Jeff has hired you as a controller. The company has adopted the cost model (CM) for its investment properties.

Required

Jeff has asked you to determine the cost-basis of the apartment complex, and prepare an estimate of the annual amortization. The company reports under IFRS.

Realty Income Ltd.
Operating Phase

Seven years have transpired since the construction of the 24-unit apartment complex. Currently, the 24 units are fully rented, and operations are running smoothly. The company is getting ready to prepare the 2021 year-end financial statements. Again, Jeff has asked for your assistance with certain transactions related to the apartment building. Specifically, the following transactions must be accounted for:

1. During the year, the following repairs and maintenance took place:

    a. On April 1, 2021, the roof and shingles were removed and replaced with a new and improved shingle design. The total cost of the new shingles was $26,500. The new shingles are expected to have a useful life of eight years.

    b. On October 1, 2021, the entire apartment was repainted for a cost of $18,000. At the same time, the landscaping was redone, including laying new sod, for a total of $29,000. Both the painting and the landscaping are expected to have a useful life of eight years.

    c. Prior to these transactions, no repairs or maintenance were required on the building.

2. At December 31, 2021, 24 new alarm systems were installed, one in each unit. The total cost of the new alarm system was $35,000. The building did not include an alarm system prior to this installation.

In addition to the above transactions, Jeff is contemplating the use of either the fair value model (FVM) under IAS 40 or the revaluation model (RVM) under IAS 16. He is wondering how the financial statements would be impacted if the either of the FVM or RVM was implemented since inception (ignore any retroactive adjustments). Based on various valuation reports and industry standards, Jeff estimates the following fair values:

»	2014	$850,000
»	2015	$665,000
»	2016	$750,000
»	2017	$835,000
»	2018	$900,000
»	2019	$900,000

The sharp declines in 2015 and 2016 are a result of a global economic recession, with a rebound in 2017.

Required

Prepare a report that addresses Jeff's concerns.

Rosetta Inc.

Rosetta Inc. (RI) is a new corporation that just acquired the assets of an unincorporated technology business on September 1, 2013, from Jess Stone. Extracts from the purchase and sale agreement entered into by RI and Jess Stone are provided in Exhibit I. RI is owned by three shareholders: Carlos Guevara, the CEO of RI, who owns 20% of the shares of RI; and two investors, who each own 40% of the shares. Jess Stone is not a shareholder of RI.

Jess Stone developed new touch screen technology but lacked the financial resources necessary to benefit commercially from this technology. The touch screen technology is far superior to the current technology, and has many potential uses, ranging from mobile devices, computer screens, and laptops.

RI put the technology it purchased to work immediately by entering into a licensing agreement with Mica (Exhibit II). In addition, RI has developed a new PC computer monitor with the touch screen, and entered into an agreement Ferrous Inc. to distribute the technology.

You, CA, have been recently employed by RI as the special assistant to Carlos Guevara. On July 3, 2014, Carlos Guevara calls you into his office and says he has an assignment for you:

> "The financial statements of RI for the fiscal year ending August 31, 2014 are required to be
> audited. I want you to address the significant financial accounting issues pertaining to the
> preparation of RI's financial statements for its first fiscal year ending August 31, 2014 and provide
> your recommendations on the accounting treatments to be used."

As you leave Mr. Guevara's office, he provides you with a file that includes some additional information about the operations of RI (Exhibit III).

Required

Prepare a report that addresses the requests of Carlos Guevara.

EXHIBIT I – EXTRACTS FROM THE PURCHASE AND SALE AGREEMENT BETWEEN RI AND JESS STONE

Purchase and Sale of the Business Assets of Jess Stone

- » RI will purchase the technology and the research findings of Jess Stone as at September 1, 2013
- » RI agrees to purchase the equipment owned by Jess Stone as at September 1, 2013
- » Jess Stone agrees to be responsible for all liabilities as at September 1, 2013

Purchase and Sale Price

- » RI will pay to Jess Stone an amount of $3,500,000 for the technology and the research findings
- » RI agrees to pay to Jess Stone the appraised value of $420,000 for the equipment

Contingent Consideration

- » RI agrees to pay to Jess Stone an amount equal to 50% of net income (determined in accordance with generally accepted accounting principles) in excess of $500,000 for the fiscal year ending August 31, 2014

Employment Contract with Jess Stone

- » RI and Jess Stone agree to enter into a two-year employment contract, and RI agrees to pay to Jess Stone an annual salary of $200,000
- » Jess Stone agrees that all research findings during the employment are the property of RI

EXHIBIT II – EXTRACTS FROM THE LICENSING AGREEMENT BETWEEN RI AND MICA INC.

Licensing Arrangement

- » RI agrees to provide to Mica the exclusive right to use the touch screen technology referred to as FeldsparX for a term of three years commencing on December 1, 2013
- » RI agrees to deliver the technology to Mica on December 1, 2013
- » Mica agrees to pay to RI a licensing fee in the amount of $900,000, with the first payment of $300,000 due on December 1, 2013; and, agrees to make payments in the amount of $300,000 plus interest of $36,000 on December 1, 2014, and $300,000 plus interest of $18,000 on December 1, 2015

Royalty

- » Mica agrees to pay to RI a royalty fee in the amount of 15% of the gross margin (determined in accordance with generally accepted accounting principles) realized by Mica from sales of goods that use the FeldsparX technology
- » Mica agrees to provide to RI a quarterly statement of gross margin realized by Mica that is subject to the royalty payable to RI
- » RI, or its representative, has the right of access to the records and information of Mica necessary to audit the gross margin reported by Mica to RI

EXHIBIT III – INFORMATION OBTAINED ABOUT THE OPERATIONS OF RI

Licensing arrangement with Mica

» Revenue in the amount of $300,000 has been recognized in the accounting records

» Royalty revenue in the amount of $135,000 has been recognized in the accounting records based on a gross margin of $900,000 reported by Mica for the six months from December 1, 2013 to May 31, 2014

» Mica is a financially sound entity

Research and Development

RI acquired the following technology and research findings from Jess Stone:

Project Technology/ Assigned Name	Fair Value	Current Status
» FeldsparX	$700,000	licensed to Mica for three years (see Note 1)
» QuartZ	1,500,000	used in the commercial production of goods (see Note 2)
» BasalT	900,000	used in the commercial production of goods (see Note 3)
» Grandiorite	400,000	testing use in a possible product
	$3,500,000	

» *Note 1 - FeldsparX Technology:* Management of RI decided to license use of the FeldsparX technology rather than to produce goods using this technology itself. Management expects that this technology will have a useful life of three years.

» *Note 2 - QuartZ Technology:* Management of RI estimates that the QuartZ technology will generate total revenue in the amount of $7,500,000 over a four-year period commencing December 1, 2013

» *Note 3 – BasalT Technology:* Management estimates that the BasalT technology will generate total revenue in the amount of $2,700,000 over a three-year period commencing March 1, 2014.

Jess Stone has started work on a new project, Kryptonite, after becoming an employee of RI and this project is presently in the conceptual formulation state of a possible product that uses the technology.

A research and development asset in the amount of $3,500,000 is reported on RI's balance sheet as at May 31, 2014. All research and development costs incurred by RI have been expensed in the accounting records.

EXHIBIT III CONTINUED – INFORMATION OBTAINED ABOUT THE OPERATIONS OF RI

Sales Arrangement with Ferrous Inc.

Ferrous Inc. has placed a large order for PC touch screen monitors produced by RI that uses the QuartZ technology. The sales agreement requires RI to have the goods available for delivery to Ferrous by August 31, 2014, and to make deliveries to Ferrous as requested during September and October 2014. Ferrous will be holding a special sales event during these months. Ferrous has requested that the goods are not to be delivered until September and October as they do not have the warehouse space to store all of the items for the special sale. Revenue pertaining to this agreement is $2,500,000 and the related direct production costs are estimated to total $1,350,000. These goods will be covered by RI's inventory insurance.

Ferrous made the non-refundable fee payment of $1,250,000 required by this agreement on June 1, 2014. This amount has been recognized as sales revenue. The final $1,250,000 is to be paid by Ferrous on October 31, 2014. Ferrous is a financially sound entity.

Sales Arrangement with Mega Mart Ltd.

RI entered into an agreement with Mega Mart Ltd., a large global retailer, to distribute a lower-end touch screen for price sensitive customers. This touch screen makes use of the BasalT technology. The sales agreement requires RI to deliver units of the touch screen to Mega Mart. Mega Mart will display the screens in a prime location, and retain 20% of the per-unit sales price ($50 per unit), with the remaining 80% of the sales price to be sent to RI. In addition, Mega Mart will provide RI an upfront payment of $250,000 in order to help offset working capital requirements.

According to the sales agreement, RI shipped 30,000 units to Mega Mart Ltd. in April 2014. At the time of delivery, RI recorded revenue of $1,200,000, debited cash for $250,000, and set up an accounts receivable for the remaining $950,000.

Taiga Pulp and Paper Ltd.

Taiga Pulp and Paper Ltd. (TPP) is an integrated pulp and paper company, with operations in Canada. TPP operates four market pulp, paper, and wood product manufacturing units and has sales offices in Canada, China, and the United States. The four operating segments are as follows:

» Pulp mills: The pulp mills convert wood chips (plant fibre source) into a thick fibre board (pulp). The pulp is then shipped to paper mills for further processing. Some pulp is transferred internally, while some pulp is sold to external customers.

» Newsprint and paper mill: The paper mills convert wood, pulp, and other fibres or ingredients into paper by using a Fourdrinier machine. The newsprint is sold to major newspaper companies, while the paper is sold through various outlets.

» Sawmills: The sawmills' main operation is to turn logs into boards. The boards are dried, dyed, and smoothed. The finished products are shipped to the lumber market.

» Coated and specialty paper: The coated and specialty paper mills are essentially the same as the newsprint and paper mills, except that the finishing equipment is enhanced in order to create coated and specialty papers. The coated and specialty paper division had an impairment loss two years ago when market conditions were much worse. The market conditions have reversed and are now more favourable.

The pulp and paper industry in Canada has come under significant pressure in recent years due to increased competition from global markets, a rapidly appreciating Canadian dollar, and more scarce and distant sources of fibre supply.

The following are the quarterly earnings reported by TPP over the past two years:

('000s)	Current Year				Prior Year			
Quarter	4th	3rd	2nd	1st	4th	3rd	2nd	1st
Revenue	2,355	2,877	2,756	2,987	2,765	3,987	3,359	3,456
Earnings	(277)	(199)	(165)	177	212	388	375	455

Based on internal and external sources indicators, the auditors plan to conduct a comprehensive impairment test on the operating assets. The auditors know that the bank relies upon the statements in order to assess compliance with various loan covenants, including a tangible net worth test.

In order to assist with the impairment testing, the CFO has compiled detailed information regarding the cost bases of the capital and intangible assets (Exhibit I), future cash flow information (Exhibit II), and liquidating values for the capital assets (Exhibit III).

Required

Assume the role of the senior auditor in charge of the TPP year end, and prepare a report that discusses the asset impairment tests of the operating assets under both ASPE and IFRS. An appropriate discount rate for the company is 7%.

EXHIBIT I – INFORMATION REGARDING CAPITAL AND INTANGIBLE ASSETS COST BASES

» The breakdown of the capital and intangible assets is as follows:

('000s)	Cost	Acc. Amort.	NBV
Land	1,235	0	1,235
Production buildings and equipment			
Pulp mills	7,655	3,455	4,200
Newsprint and paper mills	2,870	1,780	1,090
Sawmills	2,360	1,245	1,115
Coated and specialty papers	2,755	1,275	1,480
Roads and timber holdings	765	550	215
Other buildings and equipment	1,243	780	463
	18,883	9,085	9,798

('000s)	Cost	Acc. Amort.	NBV
Water rights	300	108	192
Power purchase agreements	1,780	641	1,139
Forest Stewardship Council (FSC) and other licensing	350	126	224
Supplier agreements	275	99	176
	2,705	974	1,731

» The combined NBV of the capital and intangible assets is $11,529.

» The following is a breakdown of the pulp mills' NBV:

Pulp mills selling to external customers	NBV
Thunder Bay, Ontario, Mill	965
St. Andrews, Quebec, Mill	855
Terrace Bay, Ontario, Mill	775
Pulp mills transferring internally	
Vancouver Island, B.C., Mill	730
Pine Falls, Manitoba, Mill	875
	4,200

The Vancouver Island mill ships solely to the newsprint paper mills, while the Pine Falls mill ships only to the coated and specialty paper mills.

» The roads and timber holdings, the other building and equipment, power purchase agreement, and FSC/licensing asset classes are used equally by the four operating segments. (Note, 25% is used by the pulp mills that sell externally, while the internally transferring pulp mills percentage is included with their respective division.)

» The supplier agreements are used exclusively by the specialty papers segment.

» The water rights are used exclusively by the sawmills.

EXHIBIT I CONTINUED – INFORMATION REGARDING CAPITAL AND INTANGIBLE ASSET COST BASES

» The land is used throughout all four operating segments. The land is broken out as follows:

Pulp mills	
Thunder Bay, Ontario, Mill	175
St. Andrews, Quebec, Mill	155
Terrace Bay, Ontario, Mill	120
Vancouver Island, B.C., Mill	95
Pine Falls, Manitoba, Mill	105
Newsprint and paper mills	225
Sawmills	195
Coated and specialty papers	165
	1,235

» The Thunder Bay, St. Andrews, and Terrace Bay mills use the road and timber holdings, other building and equipment, power purchase agreements, and FSC/licences equally.

EXHIBIT II – CASH FLOW INFORMATION REGARDING CAPITAL AND INTANGIBLE ASSETS

» The cash flows from the pulp mills that sell to external customers are expected to be as follows:

- Combined unit $600 annually for the next 10 years
  - Thunder Bay Mill $150 annually for the next 10 years
  - St. Andrew Mill $250 annually for the next 10 years
  - Terrace Bay Mill $200 annually for the next 10 years

» The cash flows from the newsprint and paper mills are expected to be as follows:

	Years Out:						
	1	2	3	4	5	6	7
Incremental Cash Flows	450	550	655	600	500	375	150

» The cash flows from the sawmills are expected to be as follows:

	Years Out:				
	1	2	3	4	5
Incremental Cash Flows	350	300	250	200	150

» The cash flows from the coated and specialty papers are expected to be as follows:

	Years Out:									
	1	2	3	4	5	6	7	8	9	10
Incremental Cash Flows	550	600	600	650	650	700	600	550	500	250

EXHIBIT III – LIQUIDATING VALUES OF CAPITAL ASSETS

» The liquidating values of the segments are estimated to be as follows:

- Combined unit $2,500
  - Thunder Bay Mill $550
  - St. Andrews Mill $1,000
  - Terrace Bay Mill $950
- Newsprint and paper mills $2,250
- Sawmills $1,500
- Coated and specialty papers $2,500

Canadian Airborn Technologies (CAT)

You, CA, recently hired by Blackrock Investment Ltd.'s (BIL) internal audit department, are sitting in your office planning for your upcoming meeting with the head of internal audit. It is January 20, 2015. You just returned from a week visiting Canadian Airborn Technologies (CAT), BIL's newest subsidiary.

CAT has been part of the BIL group of companies since late in 2013 and up to now had never been visited by internal auditors. As is standard practice at BIL, the internal audit department visits the subsidiary companies once a year to check on the functioning of the accounting systems and internal controls, and to make sure that policies and procedures are being adhered to.

This was your first assignment and you thought it was a tough one because you have to prepare a report discussing the financial reporting issues you found related to IFRS.

As you sit down to write your report, you once again review the material gathered in your investigation. Exhibit I is a brief history of CAT; Exhibit II contains notes from your meeting with Mike Peterson, CAT's president; Exhibit III is a summary of the development costs incurred during 2014; Exhibit IV provides CAT's financial statements for the year ended December 31, 2014; and Exhibit V contains other information you gathered.

Required

Prepare the report.

EXHIBIT I

BRIEF HISTORY OF CANADIAN AIRBORN TECHNOLOGIES (CAT)

Mike Peterson is an amateur inventor. He developed a new technology for air cleaning that is especially useful for spaces that do not have central forced air heating and cooling. The technology is more effective at removing airborn pollutants than any existing technology. CAT was formed in 2010. Mike's goal for the company was to develop and market a new method for residential and commercial air cleaning. In 2005, Mike built and tested commercial prototypes for the new technology, which performed very well under difficult conditions. Because of the increase in asthma in children and the perceived decrease in air quality in many parts of Canada, Mike knew his technology would be very successful.

EXHIBIT I (CONTINUED) – BRIEF HISTORY OF CANADIAN AIRBORN TECHNOLOGIES (CAT)

While Mike was convinced that the product would be successful, he did not have the resources to take the project any further. He was unsuccessful in obtaining financing from banks or venture capitalists and could not find anyone interested in purchasing an equity stake in CAT. Mike was about to give up when, in November 2012, he had a chance meeting with the chief executive officer of BIL, Mirko Bracovic, at a local meeting of the asthma association. Mr. Bracovic is the father of two children who have severe asthma and Mike was demonstrating his product. Mr. Bracovic took an immediate interest. Mike loaned Mr. Bracovic his prototypes; Mr. Bracovic was very pleased that they helped improve his children's symptoms. Based on his personal experiences with the prototypes, Mr. Bracovic saw that the product had significant market potential and agreed to get involved in developing and marketing it.

In late 2013, Mike sold all the outstanding shares in CAT to BIL for $250,000. BIL agreed to finance the remaining research and development necessary to complete the product and bring it to market. The sale agreement required that Mike remain as president of CAT until December 31, 2014, to complete development of the product and launch it. Mr. Bracovic believed that Mike's knowledge was vital for the product's success. Mike' agreement with BIL stipulates that he receive a salary of $50,000 per year. In addition, he is to receive a bonus of $1 million if (1) the product is successfully brought to market, (2) at least 10,000 units of the product are sold at a minimum average price of $65 per unit by December 31, 2014, and (3) CAT generates a profit for the year ended December 31, 2014.

EXHIBIT II

NOTES FROM MEETING WITH MIKE PETERSON

Mike explained that, from the time BIL acquired CAT until the end of 2013, his effort was directed towards refining the product. During that time, $300,000 was spent on improvements to the product and the full amount was expensed. CAT reported a loss for tax purposes of $424,000.

In early 2014, everything came together. All the glitches with the product were solved, and testing results were consistent and met the specifications. Sure that the product would be successful, Mike then turned all of his attention to selling the product.

In January and February 2014, marketing studies and production feasibility studies were carried out. In late April, Mike made a presentation to Mirko Bracovic and received commitment of the funds required to get production underway. The manufacturing process is quite straightforward and relatively inexpensive, requiring only about $800,000 for manufacturing and assembly equipment. Despite a number of initial problems, the first full production run occurred in July. The first 900 units produced did not meet specifications and could not be shipped. The first shipment of units to customers was in August. Mike explained that the 900 units with specification problems are currently in inventory and he expects that, when time permits, they will be repaired and sold.

Mike said that he agreed to stay on with CAT for an additional three months (until March 31, 2015) by which time a new president for CAT should be hired. He said that Mirko Bracovic did all he could to convince him to stay on longer but Mike explained that he is an inventor at heart, not a manager, and that, with the right president, CAT would continue its success.

Mike was very satisfied with initial demand for the product. He had arranged contracts with a number of national and local distributors, and early feedback from the distributors was favourable. However, Mike thought that the initial orders made by the distributors were unrealistically low and that they would quickly run out of inventory, which would cost CAT significant sales because customers might buy a competitor's product.

Mike thinks that market penetration is key and he is not prepared to miss any sales. As a result, he often shipped significantly more units to distributors than ordered. While Mike assured any distributors that objected that they would see that the extra units were merited, he allowed them to delay payment until six months after delivery. At that time, they have to pay in full or return any unsold units shipped in excess of the initial amount ordered. Mike's first priority is getting product out the door. Once orders are sent to the shipping department, Mike wants the goods shipped within a day or two. Mike keeps production operating at full capacity to ensure there is enough inventory in place to meet the anticipated demand.

Mike acknowledged that paperwork was a bit sloppy. Because of the strong demand for CAT's product, Mike had little time to pay attention to administrative tasks, devoting his time instead to selling, and to making sure production was kept on schedule and orders were shipped on time. He pointed out that BIL had kept CAT on a fairly tight budget and, as a result, he was understaffed in the office.

Mike expects the paperwork to flow better once everyone gets used to the computer system and its glitches are fixed. The computer system was mandated by BIL and was installed by a small company recommended by BIL. The system was installed in May 2014. Mike complained that the computer company simply showed up one day, installed the system without any discussion of what was wanted or needed, and then left. It was never heard from again, except to render the bill.

EXHIBIT III

SUMMARY OF DEVELOPMENT COSTS DURING 2014

Costs incurred from January to March, 2014:	
Marketing surveys	$ 65,000
Consultant's report on air quality issues	80,000
Search costs for production facility	70,000
Feasibility study for production facility	92,000
Costs incurred from April to July, 2014:	
Cost of setting up production facility	37,000
Training of production staff	48,000
Costs incurred from August to December, 2014:	
Production cost overruns during first three months of production	97,000
Selling, marketing, and promotion costs	118,000
Total development costs incurred	$607,000

EXHIBIT IV – CANADIAN AIRBORN TECHNOLOGIES EXTRACTS FROM THE INTERNAL FINANCIAL STATEMENTS

BALANCE SHEET

As at December 31, 2014

Assets	
Current assets	
Cash	$ 75,000
Accounts receivable	475,000
Inventory	303,620
Other current assets	35,000
	888,620
Property, plant, and equipment	767,650
Development costs	607,000
	$2,263,270
Liabilities	
Current liabilities	
Accounts payable and accrued liabilities	$ 302,000
Loan from parent company	2,500,000
	2,802,000
Shareholder's deficiency	
Share capital	278,670
Deficit	(817,400)
	(538,730)
	$2,263,270

EXHIBIT IV (CONTINUED) – CANADIAN AIRBORN TECHNOLOGIES EXTRACTS FROM THE INTERNAL FINANCIAL STATEMENTS

INCOME STATEMENT

For the year ended December 31, 2014

Revenue	$770,352
Cost of goods sold	295,352
Gross margin	475,000
Amortization of equipment	32,000
Selling, general, and administrative costs	201,000
Income before income taxes	242,000
Income taxes	75,400
Net income	$166,600

» CAT recognizes revenue when merchandise is shipped to customers. This method is consistent with BIL's standard accounting policy for other manufactured products.

» Amortization of the equipment began in August 2014 and is calculated on a straight-line basis over 10 years.

EXHIBIT V – OTHER FINDINGS

CAT shipped the first units to customers in August 2014. Total units shipped during 2014 were 11,672. No other products are produced by CAT. During 2014, CAT shipped 500 units as demonstration models to potential customers, and to a variety of lung and asthma associations. The units were treated as sales with a selling price of $0.

Discussion with the accounts receivable clerk found considerable dissatisfaction with CAT's computer accounting system. When the clerk tried to reconcile the receivables list to the general ledger, she found that the listing sometimes had the same invoice number assigned to more than one shipment. The clerk said that she knows "for a fact" that different numbers were assigned but the computer seems to have its own ideas.

Other members of CAT's staff complained that they weren't consulted in the development of the computer system and that they didn't receive any training. It seemed they were supposed to figure it out for themselves. Some people complained that the system doesn't produce the information they need to do their jobs properly, generating useless reports instead. Some of these people have figured out how to circumvent the system to obtain the information they need.

From discussions with the shipper, there appear to be significant problems in the shipping department. The shipper seems overworked and extremely dissatisfied with the way shipping is managed. The shipper has been involved in shipping for 15 years and has never seen a mess like CAT's. It's virtually impossible for him to keep up with the orders that have to be shipped. "I'd say I'm two to three weeks behind getting orders out." The shipper said that he could use more help in the department, but he could probably get the job done if Mr. Peterson didn't get involved in what gets sent out. "It seems he's down here every day telling me to add a few more units to this order and to that order. The shipping documents are almost useless. I'd say that most orders go out of here with a different number of units than what is recorded on the shipping documents I receive from sales. In fact, they're so useless I don't even bother filing them anymore. I just toss them into that box in the corner."

EXHIBIT V (CONTINUED) – OTHER FINDINGS

Review of the accounting system showed that the billing process is initiated as soon as an order is confirmed and sent to the shipping department. Trade receivables and sales are recorded at that time.

Inventory records are perpetual. The inventory is reduced when goods are shipped. The shipper maintains a log of units shipped and the log is used to update the inventory records each day.

CAT operates in a rented facility. The production department occupies about 45% of the building, storage 25%, and offices and administration the rest. The full amount of rent is treated as a product cost and included in inventory. BIL's accounting policies state that only the rental cost associated with production should be inventoried. CAT also includes the cost of office staff, managers, and production supervisors in the cost of inventory.

Crank Games Ltd.

Crank Games Ltd. (CGL) is relatively new company that designs video games and applications for mobile devices. Users are able to download a game or application onto a mobile device for a fee that normally ranges from 99 cents to $4.99. In addition, users can play the company's games over the internet at www. crankgames.com.

The company was established by Hong Nguyen and Olga Hyszka, one year after they completed a degree in computer sciences. Hong and Olga are excellent programmers, and have been playing video games since they were children. After designing a mobile device game for an undergraduate course assignment, the two friends decided to start up CGL. The company's games have been well received by the market, and have been downloaded by over 5 million users across the globe. In addition, the company's applications are also considered to be high quality.

The company experienced significant growth in its first five years of operations, and decided to go public. Two analysts are currently following CGL's shares, which are trading at $13, and are preparing their first recommendation. CGL is scheduled to release its financial results in two weeks during a conference call. Based on the results released by industry competitors, analysts are expecting the company to report revenue of $7 million and earnings of $1.5 million in the current year.

You are the senior manager with Whiteduck and Hellen, LLP, the auditors of CGL. Recently, you met with Hong and Olga to discuss the following transactions that took place during the year:

» CGL entered into an agreement with Virtual Applications Ltd. (VAL). The terms of the agreement required CGL to provide in-game advertising to VAL in exchange for VAL providing CGL with in-game advertising on its website. CGL normally does not sell advertising space in its games, and likely would not have been able to sell the advertising for cash. Since this is a new transaction for CGL, the fair value is difficult to estimate, but management believes the advertising is worth $200,000. VAL normally sells in-game advertising, and estimates the fair value of the advertising provided is $250,000. It is unlikely that CGL management would have paid cash for the advertising received. The transaction has been recorded as a credit to revenue and a debit to advertising expense for $200,000.

» The company recently began selling the games of smaller companies on its website. The games are sold for $1 (credit card payments only), with 95 cents going to the game designing company and 5 cents being retained by CGL. The selling price of the game is established by the game designer. The game designer retains any continuing commitment to the customer after the game is purchased (e.g., game updates, modifications). During the year, 1 million games were downloaded, resulting in CGL recording $1 million in revenue and $950,000 in cost of goods sold.

» CGL began selling 2-year, non-refundable memberships. The memberships are sold for $75 and allow users to download any 100 games during the two-year period. During the year, 15,000 memberships were sold. Accordingly, members can download up to a maximum of 1.5 million games under the membership. On average, a member downloads 85 games. During the current year, a total of 475,000 games were downloaded under the agreement. Management decided to record revenue $1,125,000 during the current year as CGL has no further work required to service the memberships. Currently, CGL has over 100 games in its library available for download.

» During the year, the company purchased the rights to develop a game based on a popular comic book hero. CGL paid $175,000 for this exclusive right, and incurred an additional $475,000 in programming costs to create the game, and $205,000 in promotional costs. CGL capitalized $855,000 as an intangible asset. The following are the expected downloads for the game, which will be sold for $1.99.

| | | Downloads | | |
	Probability	Year 1	Year 2	Year 3
Optimistic	25%	300,000	200,000	55,000
Average	60%	165,000	90,000	20,000
Pessimistic	15%	75,000	50,000	5,000

» CGL purchased 30-year bonds of another public company for $500,000. The bonds were purchased in the prior year, and classified as FV-NI as the fair value was increasing as rates decreased. During the current year, the bonds declined in value by $40,000 as central banks began to raise rates in order to combat inflation. At the beginning of the year, management reclassified the bonds to amortized cost as the company plans on holding the bonds until maturity, and the bond is a pure debt instrument.

» At the beginning of the year, CGL issued 100,000, redeemable preferred shares to the public for $5 each. The preferred shares have a dividend yield of 7%. The preferred shares must be redeemed if the common share price exceeds $20 per share. Dividends of $35,000 were declared and paid during the year.

» During the year, CGL was named in a patent infringement lawsuit in regards to the use of various trademarked logos. The Company's lawyers believe that there is a 50% chance that the case will be settled with no damages to be paid by CGL. However, there is a chance that the company may have to pay between $100,000 and $200,000 in damages. As of year end, both the $100,000 and $200,000 amounts are equally likely (50% each).

Draft financial statements reveal revenue and earnings of $7,478,000 and $2,257,000, respectively. Management displayed their excitement for their ability to meet analysts' revenue and earnings expectation. The partner has asked you to prepare a memo for the audit file that discusses the appropriate accounting treatment of the above-noted transactions. The memo will be used as part of the audit planning process.

Required

Prepare the memo.

Eagle Bay Community Museum

Eagle Bay Community Museum (EBCM) is a non-profit organization that operates a community museum in Eagle Bay, Manitoba. EBCM was created in 1918 with the mandate of preserving and interpreting the history of Eagle Bay, and the surrounding area. The museum has a large collection of art, artifacts, and monuments from the Eagle Bay area. In addition, EBCM generally has two to three major exhibits a year that showcase collections from around Canada, and provides a free lecture series to the community.

EBCM receives most of its funding primarily from government grants and contributions from wealthy individuals. In addition, funding is received from membership fees, investment income from endowments, and admission fees. The museum also holds an annual muscle car raffle to generate additional funds.

As a recently qualified professional accountant, you decide that it is time to give back to the community and volunteer your specialized services. You have always maintained an interest in art and history, and feel that being a member of the EBCM Board of Directors would be an interesting experience for a worthwhile cause.

At your first board meeting, the chair of the board welcomes you and expresses her happiness about your decision to join. The chair explains to you that the financial statements of EBCM have never been audited in the past, and have always been prepared solely for internal purposes. Special reports on financial information have been prepared and audited annually for restricted contributions.

However, the board is feeling increasing pressure to prepare general purpose financial statements. Accordingly, the chair has asked you to prepare a report that discusses the alternatives available for recognizing the funding received. Exhibit I presents some additional information on the sources of funding. Given the poor economic conditions, the board would like to keep the cost of preparing the financial statements as low as possible.

Aside from the revenue recognition issues, the chair has asked you to assist with the selection of accounting policies for the various other aspects of the museum's operations. Additional details are provided in Exhibit II.

You have agreed to prepare a report for the next board meeting that outlines the specific accounting policies recommended. The chair has made it clear that the financial statements should comply with Part III of the *CICA Handbook*.

Required

Prepare the report for the board of directors.

EXHIBIT I – SOURCES OF FUNDING

Revenue for 2014 included the following:

Memberships	$200,000 (note 1)
Admission fees	$75,000 (note 2)
Government grants	$1,250,000
Contributions	$285,000 (note 3)
Endowment fund revenue	$35,000 (note 4)

Note 1 – Membership fees are recognized as revenue when money is collected.

Note 2 - Admission fees are recognized as money is collected.

Note 3 - Contributions are recognized when a pledge is made by the donor. Internal reports segregate the number of restricted and unrestricted contributions. Restricted funds include amounts contributed for a specific purpose and amounts segregated by the board for specific projects or purposes.

Note 4 – Endowment fund revenue is recorded as the investment income accrues.

EXHIBIT II – ADDITIONAL INFORMATION

1. All capital assets are recorded at $1 to have a nominal amount provided on the financial statements. No amortization is taken on the assets. A recent review of the capital assets indicated the following items. The amounts were estimated by one of the board of directors:

Automobiles	$70,000
Artwork	unable to estimate
Building	$375,000
Office equipment	$55,000

2. During 2014, the flooring was replaced. The cost of new flooring was $35,000. This amount was expensed. In addition, a new HVAC unit was installed to protect the artwork from damages due to temperature. The cost was $65,000. To finance the purchase of the new HVAC system, a piece of artwork was sold.

3. Volunteer services are not recorded.

General Household Appliances

General Household Appliances (GHA) is a closely held company owned by the Hillis family. The company has a long history dating back to the early 1900s. The company manufactures small household appliances, such as toasters, blenders, coffee makers, and indoor grills. GHA's products are well known for their quality and affordability.

Recently, the company has been experiencing poor financial results due increased competition, lack of new product development, and the increasing power of the retailers in the supply chain. As a result, Larry Hillis, the former CEO, was recently relieved of his duties.

On September 1, 2014, the Board of Directors elected to hire Martha Blazeski as the new CEO. Martha is a well known turnaround specialist and is the first person outside of the Hillis family to become CEO of GHA.

It is now January 7, 2015, and GHA is preparing for its December 31, 2014 year-end financial statement audit. GHA is a long standing client of the public accounting firm of Lebeau and Liang, LLP. You are the senior accountant with Lebeau and Liang, LLP who is responsible for GHA's audit. The partner in charge of the audit recently met with Martha, and has provided you with a copy of the draft financial statements (Exhibit I) and notes from her meeting with Martha (Exhibit II). The partner has asked you to prepare a memo to the audit file that addresses your concerns regarding any financial accounting issues.

Required

Prepare the report for the audit file.

EXHIBIT I – DRAFT FINANCIAL STATEMENTS

GENERAL HOUSEHOLD APPLIANCES
BALANCE SHEET

As at December 31 (unaudited)	2014
Assets	
Current	
Cash	$ 50,675
Marketable securities	115,200
Accounts receivable	174,930
Inventory	837,040
Other assets	250,000
	1,427,845
Property and equipment, net	1,300,000
	$2,727,845
Liabilities and shareholders' equity	
Current	
Accounts payable	$ 104,305
Accrued and other liabilities	267,595
Deferred revenue	345,900
	717,800
Long-term debt	659,000
Common shares	1,098,258
Retained earnings	252,787
	1,351,045
	$2,727,845

EXHIBIT I CONTINUED – DRAFT FINANCIAL STATEMENTS

GENERAL HOUSEHOLD APPLIANCES
INCOME STATEMENT

For the year ended December 31 (unaudited)	2014
Sales	$2,775,990
Cost of sales	1,499,035
Gross profit	1,276,955
Expenses	
Amortization	155,490
General and administrative	534,500
Marketing and sales	459,704
Office Expense	395,980
Wages and benefits, administration	515,000
Total operating expenses	$1,905,184
Operating income (loss)	$(628,229)
Gain (losses) on marketable securities	12,455
Impairment loss on capital assets	(327,900)
Income (loss) before taxes	(943,674)
Provision for (benefit from) income taxes	(264,229)
Net income (loss)	(679,445)
Opening balance—retained earnings	932,232
Net income	(679,445)
Dividends	0
Closing balance—retained earnings	$252,787

EXHIBIT II – NOTES FROM THE PARTNERS' MEETING WITH MARTHA

» Martha signed a 16-month contract on September 1, 2014. Martha was paid an upfront signing bonus of $80,000, a monthly salary of $2,000, and a bonus of 15% of 2015 net income. The signing bonus was paid in September, and expensed in fiscal 2014 as part of the wages and benefits, administration. The bonus is not repayable if Martha leaves prior to the 16 months.

» On August 1, 2014, GHA entered into a sales agreement with SuperMart, a large Canadian retailer. Under the terms of the agreement, GHA shipped 70,000 coffee makers to SuperMart, which placed the products in special display booths throughout its stores in Canada. SuperMart is able to return any unsold appliances to GHA up to February 1, 2015 (just after the holiday season). The coffee markers are sold to retailers for $22 each and have a cost of $10 each.

Past history under similar arrangements suggests that at least 60% of the appliances are sold during the holiday season (i.e., just before New Year's Eve). Martha has decided not to record any revenue until the right of return period lapses.

» On July 1, 2014, GHA exchanged 10,000 coffee makers to TeleCo, a large telecom company, in exchange for $280,000 worth of telecom services. The coffee makers have a cost of $14 and a retail value that ranges between $25 and $30 per unit. TeleCo plans to use the coffee makers in the staffrooms of its offices across North America. Martha posted the following journal entry:

Other Assets	250,000	
Inventory		250,000

» Given the recent poor financial performance, Martha decided to conduct an asset impairment test. The controller estimated that the following net cash flows are expected to be generated from the property and equipment (a reasonable discount rate is 8%):

Year:	1	2	3	4	5	6	7
Cash Flow:	350,000	350,000	450,000	450,000	300,000	300,000	250,000

The fair value of the capital assets, less costs to sell, is estimated to be $1.3 million. The NBV of the property, plant, and equipment was $1,627,900 prior to Martha recording an impairment loss of $327,900.

» GHA operates a small number of outlet stores that distribute their products. Martha has accrued a $100,000 liability for the closing of two unprofitable stores. Martha is currently unsure which stores will be closed, but, is very sure that two stores will be closed in 2015, resulting in severance pay and other closing costs. The expense has been included in the general and administrative expenses.

EXHIBIT II CONTINUED – NOTES FROM THE PARTNERS' MEETING WITH MARTHA

» In fiscal 2013, 10,000 can openers held in inventory were written down from their historical cost of $5.50 each to their net realizable value of $4.00. The writedown was a result of a decrease in demand for the product due to child safety concerns. In fiscal 2014, a total of 5,000 of these can openers were sold. The can openers were sold for $7.50 each as it appears that the child safety concerns have subsided.

» On December 1, the company paid $250,000 in order to undertake a large marketing campaign. The marketing campaign is intended to help re-brand the company's products and to increase customer awareness of the company's product offering. The marketing campaign began in December and will run for four months over the Internet, television, radio, and on billboards. The entire $250,000 is included in the marketing and sales expense.

» There were no additions or dispositions in the marketable securities from 2013. The marketable securities are being held until 2015, at which point they will be used to help fund an expansion of the company's product offering. The following additional details are available regarding the marketable securities, with no entries posted in the current year:

	2014 FV	2013 FV
Equities	155,788	145,788
Fixed-income	81,665	78,665
Short-term treasuries	41,244	40,747
	278,697	265,200

» During the year, GHA designed and developed a new technology for a toaster that toasts bread more evenly than the toasters on the market. The following costs were incurred during the year related to the toaster:

New Toaster Technology - Costs expensed	
• Developing heat insulation technology:	35,450
• Developing inner toaster technology:	95,900
• Design of toaster outer casing:	37,500
• Patenting of toaster technology:	21,500
• Testing the prototypes prior to commercialization:	48,000
	238,350

The toaster technology is expected to generate additional net cash flows of $35,000 for the next five years. Martha has expensed all of the costs as part of general and administrative expenses.

» On November 1, GHA was sued by a competitor for a patent infringement suit. Legal counsel suggests that GHA will be liable to make a payment. There is a 30% chance of a $50,000, a 50% chance of a $100,000 payment, and a 20% chance of a $150,000 payment. Martha recorded a $150,000 contingent liability.

Northeast Community College

Northeast Community College, located in northeastern Ontario, was established in 1965 by a group of local citizens. It is governed by a Board of Governors, which consists of student representatives, faculty members, the Ontario Ministry of Training, Colleges and Universities (the Ministry), appointees and community representatives.

The college receives most of its revenue from student tuition and grants from the Ministry. The operating grants from the Ministry are based on the number of students enrolled and the types of programs offered. Capital grants are based on specific proposals. Due to recent provincial government cutbacks, operating grants have been reduced and capital grants virtually eliminated. The college also receives donations from individuals and businesses. Most donations carry restrictions on the use of funds. The most common types of restrictions are that the funds must be used for scholarships, research, or capital improvements.

At the last meeting of the college's Board of Governors, they requested that the auditors submit a report discussing whether the current accounting policies best meet the reporting objectives of the college and what other alternatives exist. In previous years, your firm issued a qualified audit report for the college since the accounting policies were not in accordance with GAAP.

The Board would also like the report to discuss any other important financial and reporting issues, together with recommendations for improvements. A new Board member has specifically asked you to include in the report a brief explanation of what the Board's role is compared to the Audit Committee's and the relationship of each to the external auditor.

It is now April 25, 2014, and your firm is working on the report. Your firm will be presenting your findings at the next Board meeting. It will be an open meeting and various interested parties have been invited to attend. To assist your firm in conducting the review, the college has provided the following information:

4. Draft financial statements for the year ended March 31, 2014, and audited comparative figures for 2012 (Exhibit I).

5. Information on accounting procedures and policies (Exhibit II).

Required

Prepare a draft report to be presented to the Board of Governors.

EXHIBIT I – NORTHEAST COMMUNITY COLLEGE
STATEMENT OF FINANCIAL POSITION

	2014 Draft	2013 Audited (with qualification)
Assets		
Current assets		
Cash	$13,606	$13,234
Grant receivable	564	456
Donations receivable	500	-
Accounts receivable	2,445	3,446
Inventory	1,162	1,345
Other assets	82	62
	18,359	18,543
Capital assets	25,381	23,361
	$43,740	$41,904
Liabilities and Fund Balances		
Current liabilities		
Accounts payable and accrued liabilities	$ 2,175	$ 1,722
Deferred revenue	1,028	1,122
Due to students' association	852	846
Current portion of long-term debt	400	400
	4,455	4,190
Long-term debt	3,607	4,196
	8,062	8,386
Fund balances		
Operating	1,136	1,632
Capital	20,733	18,943
Scholarship	1,712	1,032
Research	930	844
Endowment	11,167	11,167
	35,678	33,618
	$43,740	$41,904

EXHIBIT I – NORTHEAST COMMUNITY COLLEGE
STATEMENT OF OPERATION AND CHANGES IN FUND BALANCES

	Operating Fund	Capital Fund	Scholarship Fund	Research Fund	Endowment Fund	2014	2013*
Revenue							
Grants and reimbursement	33,128	500	710	840	0	35,178	38,440
Student tuition	12,981	0	0	0	0	12,981	12,192
Ancillary operations profit	1,040	0	0	0	0	1,040	960
Donations	440	1,090	910	740	0	3,180	2,710
Transfer from endowment	480	40	310	280	0	1,110	1,310
Investment	40	0	0	0	1,110	1,150	1,410
Other	400	50	40	70	0	560	410
	48,509	1,680	1,970	1,930	1,110	55,199	57,432
Expenditures							
Academic programs	38,114	0	0	0	0	38,114	38,242
Student services	3,117	0	0	0	0	3,117	2,893
Administration	3,114	0	0	0	0	3,114	3,240
Property	3,640	0	0	0	0	3,640	3,981
Scholarship awarded	0	0	1,430	0	0	1,430	1,399
Research grants awarded	0	0	0	1,974	0	1,974	1,780
Early retirement costs	640	0	0	0	0	640	511
Transfers out of endowment funds	0	0	0	0	1,110	1,110	3,350
	48,625	0	1,430	1,974	1,110	53,139	55,396
Excess (deficiency) of revenue over expenditure for the year	(116)	1,680	540	(44)	0	2,060	2,036
Fund balances, beginning	1,632	18,943	1,032	844	11,167	33,618	31,582
	1,516	20,623	1,572	800	11,167	35,678	33,618
Net transfers approved by Board of Governors	(380)	110	140	130	0	0	0
Fund balance, ending	1,136	20,733	1,712	930	11,167	35,678	33,618

* Audited with qualification

EXHIBIT II – INFORMATION ON NORTHEAST'S ACCOUNTING PROCEDURES AND POLICIES

The College's controller has provided you with the following information:

1. The College uses the restricted fund method in accounting for and presenting contributions. The financial statements include a statement of financial position that combines all funds, as well as a statement of operations and changes in fund balances for each fund. The following funds exist:

    Operating Fund

    This fund accounts for all revenue and expenditure relating to current operations of the College, including its ancillary operations (see item 4). The main sources of revenue for this fund are government grants and tuition fees. Government operating grants and tuition fees are treated as revenue evenly over the semester to which the funding or tuition fees relate. Grants and tuition fees received in advance of or after a semester are treated as deferred revenue or receivables, respectively. Expenditures are recognized in the period to which they relate.

    Capital Fund

    This fund is used to account for all capital assets of the College. All contributions received for the purchase of capital assets are recognized as revenue of this fund.

    Scholarship Fund

    This fund is used to account for all amounts received that are specifically designated by the donor for scholarships and bursaries. All amounts received for these purposes are treated as revenue when received. Expenditures are recognized at the time the scholarship or bursary is awarded.

    In many cases, the scholarships are for a number of years and a portion of the scholarship is paid at the beginning of each semester provided the student maintains prescribed minimum grades. In most cases, these minimum grades are achieved. In these cases, amounts relating to future periods that are unpaid at year end are treated as liabilities. Amounts forfeited due to poor marks are treated as a reduction in scholarships paid in that year.

    Research Fund

    This fund is used to account for all amounts received for research. Revenue is recognized when received. Expenditures are recognized at the time each research grant is awarded to a specific professor or organization. In many cases, the research occurs over a number of years and the grants are paid in installments after the submission and approval of progress reports. It is rare for progress reports to not be approved by College officials. For research grants paid in installments, amounts relating to future periods that are unpaid at year end are treated as liabilities.

    Endowment Fund

    This fund is used to account for all contributions that require the original principal to remain intact. Contributions are treated as increases in the fund's balance. The earnings on the investment of the original contributions are recognized as revenue each year. In most cases, the endowments have a restriction that the earnings be used for a specific purpose, such as operations, capital, scholarships, or research. Therefore, when earnings are transferred to other funds, the endowment fund recognizes these transfers as expenditures and the other funds recognize them as revenue.

2. In 2013, the College entered into an agreement with its students' association to build a student centre. Construction of the student centre is expected to begin in 2016. Under the terms of the agreement, the College has agreed to provide the land for the student centre and to levy a surcharge of $15 per course commencing in the fall 2013 semester.

EXHIBIT II CONTINUED – INFORMATION ON NORTHEAST'S ACCOUNTING PROCEDURES AND POLICIES

Under the agreement with the students' association, all contributions collected for the student centre are to be remitted to the students' association annually. The students' association will then supervise construction of the building, which, on completion, will be owned 50% by the College and 50% by the students' association.

The surcharge revenue will be turned over to the students' association on December 31 of each year. It is expected that the surcharge revenue will total $10 million by the end of 2016. The total cost of the student centre is expected to be $13 million. In 2013, the College and the students' association began a public campaign to raise the additional $3 million. Donations received by the College are to be turned over to the students' association on December 31 of each year.

The agreement provides that once construction has begun, the College and the students' association will share equally in the title to the land and building, and in the revenues and costs of the student centre. Revenues will consist of rent from merchants and food outlets. Maintenance of the facility will be conducted by the College and recorded at actual cost. Upon completion of construction, the students' association will donate 50% of the building to the College.

The surcharge revenue received to date has been accounted for as a liability to the students' association. No recognition of the surcharge revenue has been made in the College's statement of revenue and expenditures. Once the building is completed, the College will record 50% of the value as donation revenue and debit capital assets. Disclosure of the details of the agreement has been made in the notes to the financial statements.

3. The College owns all of the shares of Northeast Publishing Inc. (NPI), which rents premises in the basement of the College. The company publishes and sells textbooks of professors whose textbooks cannot get published by larger textbook publishers. NPI's Board of Directors consists of three representatives of the College and three faculty members.

    NPI's objectives are to minimize textbook costs for students and to maximize royalties for authors. As a result, it has operated at close to a break-even point since its inception. However, during NPI's fiscal year 2014, the College decided to raise textbook prices and royalties paid to faculty as a concession in contract negotiations to avert a faculty strike. For the year ended December 31, 2014, revenue was $3.9 million and net income was $500,000 (2013 - $80,000). NPI had total assets of $2.8 million and total liabilities of $1.4 million.

    The College has always considered its ownership of NPI as being ownership held in trust for its faculty members and does not intend to derive any profit from NPI. As a result, no recognition is made of NPI's revenue, expenses, assets, or liabilities in the College's financial statements.

4. Ancillary operations of the College include bookstore sales, facility rentals, student residence fees and other non-academic activities. Each of these operations is treated as a division in the accounting records of the College. For the year ended March 31, 2014, total revenues from ancillary operations were $8,180,000 and total expenditures were $7,140,000. Only the net profit is reported on the financial statements of the College.

5. Due to recent government cutbacks, the College has been forced to reduce the size of its academic and administrative staffs. In January 2013, the College entered into an agreement with its unions that provides for voluntary early retirement incentives. Many employees have indicated that they will accept this package. To date, the College has paid $1,151,000 (2014 - $640,000, 2013 - $511,000) in early retirement incentives, which were treated as expenses when paid. During fiscal 2015, the College expects that it will pay $1.7 million in early retirement incentives and an additional $0.8 million in severance payments to employees who do not accept the package and who are laid off. No provision has been made for these costs in the College's financial statements, although they are disclosed in the notes to the financial statements.

    The Ontario Ministry of Training, Colleges and Universities has indicated that it will reimburse approximately $1.4 million of the early retirement incentive costs from a special downsizing adjustment fund, provided that further cuts to education are not made in an upcoming provincial budget.

EXHIBIT II CONTINUED – INFORMATION ON NORTHEAST'S ACCOUNTING PROCEDURES AND POLICIES

6. Purchased capital assets are recorded at cost and donated capital assets are recorded at fair value. The College amortizes all capital assets over their useful lives, except buildings. The College adopted this policy because it believes that if the buildings are properly maintained, they will have a life in excess of one hundred years and also because the replacement cost of the buildings rises each year. The College receives funding annually from the Ministry to maintain the buildings.

    The College's capital asset policy was implemented in 1995. Prior to 1995, the College recorded purchased capital assets at cost but had not recorded any donated assets or amortization expense. When the accounting policy was changed, the College increased the value of its capital assets by $12.4 million. The $12.4 million represented the approximate fair value of its unrecorded donated assets, at the time of their donation, less $1.4 million accumulated amortization of all its capital assets except buildings.

    This adjustment did not include the value of land donated to the College by the Government of Ontario when the College was built in 1965. The controller had not recorded a value for the land because valuations of $2.0 million and $3.2 million, performed by appraisers in 1965, were significantly different. As a result, the controller felt that any value allocated to the land would be subjective and should not be recorded.

    The College's equipment leases are accounted for as operating leases. Lease payments in the 2014 fiscal year totalled $22,300.

7. The Public Sector Salary Disclosure Act requires the College to disclose the names and salaries of those employees whose annual salary exceeds $100,000. The College's Board of Governors is upset about this issue as the Board and the faculty association feel that disclosure of these amounts violates the employees' privacy. Since only a few employees' salaries exceed the $100,000 threshold, the College has decided not to make the required disclosures this year. Failure to make these disclosures can result in the Ministry withholding grant monies.

8. In March 2014, a local entrepreneur and alumnus, Phil Bloess, announced his intention to donate $1.5 million cash towards the construction of a new computer centre. Phil plans to provide $0.5 million per year for the next three years commencing June 2014.

    Only the first installment of $0.5 million has been recorded as a receivable on the statement of financial position and as revenue in the capital fund. The Board of Governors is hopeful that Phil will fulfill his pledge. The College's past experience with these types of promises has not been good.

    The total cost of the computer centre is expected to be $4.0 million. In order to help fund the construction, Northeast's Board of Governors is considering selling 100 acres of land at the back of its campus. Expected proceeds from the sale are $2.5 million to $3.0 million. As a requirement of the original donation of the land, the Government of Ontario must approve this proposal.

Overlook Video Stores Inc. (OVS)

Overlook Video Stores Inc. (OVS) is a privately held chain of DVD rental stores headquartered in Toronto. The company was incorporated in 1992 and has gone from a single store in Toronto to over 30 stores throughout Ontario. Hietkamp & Hijazi, LLP (H&H), a mid-sized professional services firm, have been the auditors for OVS since its inception. You are the audit senior on the OVS audit for the year ending December 31, 2014. On December 1, 2014, Alice Hietkamp, the partner, calls you into her office to explain that the audit will need to begin in early January 2015, because OVS's bank is eager to see the audited financial statements.

"I met with Victor Ziegler, the controlling shareholder of OVS, a few months ago and he told me about OVS's new directions. Here are my notes from that meeting (Exhibit I). There are some new accounting issues that have arisen since last year end. I would like you to look at them and provide your recommendations on the accounting treatments to adopt. The controller of OVS has sent us the interim financial statements for the 11 months ended November 30, 2014 (Exhibit II)."

Required

Prepare the report requested by Alice Hietkamp.

EXHIBIT I
NOTES FROM MEETING WITH VICTOR ZIEGLER

After years of slow and steady growth, OVS began expanding in two directions. First, OVS opened 10 new video stores in 2014. In the past, OVS had only opened one store per year. Second, OVS moved into the Internet-based DVD rental business by launching a new website, www.MoviesByMail.ca. The expansion was financed by a 10-year term loan from OVS's bank. Victor noted that the bank now seems concerned with the profitability of the company. Given all the extra hours worked this year, Victor will be receiving a bonus of 2% of net income.

No Late Fees

OVS introduced a new program called "No Late Fees" during 2014. Since people are often reluctant to rent movies because they cannot return them on time, OVS eliminated late fees for its customers. However, to prevent abuse of this program, after 30 days if the movie is not returned, the outstanding movie is considered sold to the customer who rented it. The next time the customer comes to the store, there will be a charge of $25, the price of purchasing a new DVD, on the customer's account and they have the right to keep the DVD.

The program has been "tremendously successful," according to Victor. It has both increased rental revenue and increased sales of DVDs, since many customers keep their DVDs beyond the 30 days. However, Victor conceded that it has upset some customers who believed that OVS had truly eliminated all forms of late fees. Most customers who were charged for an over-30-day DVD have refused to pay for it and simply returned the DVD to an OVS store. Others have yet to pay for the DVD and have yet to return it.

Previously Viewed DVDs

In the past, a wholesaler purchased all of OVS's previously viewed DVDs. Now, due to its expansion, OVS first sells all the previously viewed DVDs it can to the wholesaler. OVS then offers the remaining previously viewed DVDs for sale to its customers at discounted prices. Each of these remaining DVDs is scanned and its cost is transferred from "Inventory–DVDs for Rent" to "Inventory–Previously Viewed DVDs for Sale." When a new movie is released on DVD, OVS must order at least 20 copies of it for each store, at an average cost of $20 per DVD. Within two months, demand for the movie has diminished so that only five copies per store are necessary. As a result, OVS must sell off 15 copies per store for about $10 each.

EXHIBIT I (CONTINUED)
NOTES FROM MEETING WITH VICTOR ZIEGLER

Exchange with Blockster Home Video

During the year, OVS exchanged $1,000 cash and various new DVD inventory with a cost of $85,000 and a fair value of $96,000 with Blockster Home Video in exchange for 3,000 Model XT500 DVD players. OVS is going to sell the DVD players to its customers. The XT500s can be purchased from various suppliers, with a price range of $25 to $38 per unit. OVS sold DVDs similar to those traded to its customers for $15 per unit last month. OVS has not recorded this transaction, as "it's really like nothing happened," Victor tells you. "We gave them inventory and they gave us inventory. That's why I didn't record anything."

Movies by Mail – Rental Program

When customers first subscribe to the Movies By Mail service at the store, they supply their credit card number and agree that it will be charged $30 at the end of each month until they cancel their subscription. To rent a DVD, customers log on to the website using a user ID and password provided to them. Once logged on, customers can choose up to 40 movies to have in their "wish list." Customers can flag as urgent certain DVDs.

The customer is mailed his or her initial four DVDs from the OVS warehouse in Toronto. These are selected automatically by the system based on availability of DVDs in the rental inventory, while giving priority to those DVDs marked as urgent by the customer. Once the customer is finished watching a particular DVD, he or she returns it by mail in a postage-paid envelope. OVS then sends the customer the next DVD on the list. During the introduction period of May 2014, OVS offered new customers the option of paying $500 up front for three years of DVD rentals by mail and 5,000 customers took advantage of this option due to its substantial savings.

Movies By Mail – Database Development

OVS has spent more than $425,000 to date researching and developing a patented database used to track orders and returns of DVDs from Movies by Mail. The database is fully integrated with the website. Victor Ziegler has determined that other companies, in various lines of business, could make use of this technology. Essentially, OVS has developed an off-the-shelf packaged inventory tracking database that other businesses can purchase. It seems that OVS has spent $175,000 on research and an additional $250,000 on development. OVS capitalized the full $425,000 as an asset on the balance sheet. A breakdown of the costs is as follows:

Development Costs:	
Salaries of researchers	$ 50,000
Salaries of office administration staff	$ 20,000
Allocation of direct overhead utility cost	$ 20,000
Allocation of building amortization (Note 1)	$ 50,000
Amortization of equipment used in development process	$ 60,000
Materials used in the lab during development	$ 50,000
	$250,000

Note 1 – the amortization of the building was based on a 20% allocation, since the development lab accounts for approximately 20% of the building.

The present value of the revenues and expenses from database are $1.35 and $1.13 million, respectively.

RentPoints

In January 2014, OVS introduced a customer reward program called RentPoints. For every dollar a customer spends with OVS, they get one RentPoint added to their OVS account. The point-of-sale system in OVS's stores automatically tracks the points each time a customer rents or purchases DVDs.

Customers can then redeem RentPoints for selected rewards. For example, 1,000 RentPoints can be redeemed for a new DVD, or 250,000 RentPoints can be redeemed for a trip for two to Hollywood. Although Victor believes the program has been very popular, to date, only 92,000 RentPoints have been redeemed. Victor has faith that more people will eventually redeem their points since the points do not expire. However, he is now wondering if he should continue the program, since so few people have taken advantage of it.

One-Time Federal Government Funding Program

On April 1, 2014, OVS received a $50,000 grant from a one-time special federal government funding program. The grant was provided to help offset the capital costs associated with opening up various new stores. The capital assets are expected to have a useful life of 5 years. Victor Ziegler stated, "We were so happy to receive the grant. We have recorded the entire amount in revenue because we received the cheque in May." OVS amortizes all assets on a straight-line basis.

EXHIBIT II
OVERLOOK VIDEO STORES INC.EXCERPTS FROM THE BALANCE SHEET

(in thousands of dollars)

	Nov. 30 2014 (unaudited)	Dec. 31 2013 (audited)
Assets		
Current assets		
Cash	$ 21	$ 35
Accounts receivable (No Late Fees)	3,210	—
Inventory—DVDs for rent	7,935	6,545
Inventory—New DVDs for sale	2,315	2,119
Inventory—Previously viewed DVDs for sale	3,526	—
Other inventory	598	412
Prepaid expenses	1,251	1,105
	18,856	10,216
Property, plant, and equipment	40,355	31,105
Database development costs	425	—
Website	8,512	—
	68,148	41,321
Liabilities		
Current liabilities		
Accounts payable	652	3,569
Current portion of long-term debt	2,937	—
	3,589	3,569
Long-term debt	26,430	—
Due to shareholders	4,532	6,483
	34,551	10,052
Shareholders' Equity		
Common shares	100	100
Retained earnings	33,497	31,169
	33,597	31,269
	$68,148	$41,321

EXHIBIT II (CONTINUED)
OVERLOOK VIDEO STORES INC.EXCERPTS FROM THE BALANCE SHEET
(in thousands of dollars)

	Nov. 30 2014 (unaudited)	Dec. 31 2013 (audited)
Revenues		
Rentals	$15,477	$14,613
Sales	6,321	5,946
Movies by Mail	7,432	—
No Late Fees	3,539	—
Government grant	50	—
Other	537	419
	33,356	20,978
Expenses		
Advertising	3,124	2,460
Amortization	659	450
Bank charges and interest	1,325	11
Business and property taxes	151	149
Cost of movies sold	8,797	4,757
Insurance	125	105
Professional and consulting fees	691	710
Rent and office	1,286	1,246
Repairs and maintenance	569	498
Utilities	1,542	1,612
Wages and benefits	10,540	8,465
	28,809	20,463
Income before taxes	4,547	515
Income taxes	2,219	206
Net income	$ 2,328	$ 309
Retained earnings, beginning of period	31,169	30,860
Retained earnings, end of period	33,497	31,169

QUBI Entertainment Ltd.

QUBI Entertainment Ltd. (QUBI) is a developer and distributor of video games. The company became public three years ago, and now trades on the Toronto Stock Exchange under the ticker QUBI. Its main source of revenue is from packaged video games, although the company has begun to earn more significant revenues from mobile device games and online gaming.

The video game industry is characterized by its many participants frequently launching new games, which may be new game concepts or sequels of popular game franchises. QUBI has five popular sports game franchises, and two role-playing franchises. In addition, QUBI is always developing and offering new products in the hopes that it too will become a franchise title. The fierce competition in the industry is based on product quality and features, timing of product releases, brand-name recognition, availability and quality of in-game content, access to distribution channels, effectiveness of marketing, and price.

Many analysts have been following QUBI's stock since its initial public offering. The following are the analysts' expectation of QUBI's EPS, along with the reported earnings:

	2014	2013	2012
Expectation	0.07	0.05	(0.15)
Actual	?	(0.03)	(0.11)
Surprise	?	(0.08)	0.04

QUBI missed earnings expectations in 2013, but exceeded expectations in 2012. QUBI's share price reacts significantly to the earnings surprise. The following chart outlines QUBI's share price over the past three years, and highlights the earnings announcement dates:

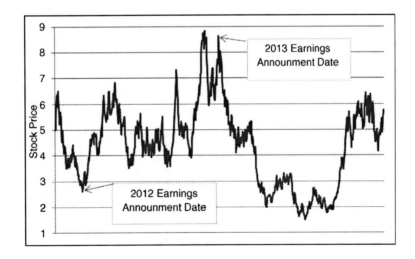

Management of QUBI does not want to disappoint the analysts again this year, following fiscal 2013's large, negative earnings surprise. The most recent run-up in share price is the result of analysts' expectations that QUBI can continue to grow earnings and report positive earnings. These expectations are based on a combination of management issuing positive earnings guidance, positive earnings surprises reported by many industry competitors, and the growth potential offered by the mobile gaming industry.

Olivares and Samson, LLP has been QUBI's auditor since inception and you have been the audit senior on the file for the past three years. Recently, Juan Olivares, the partner in charge of the audit, met with management of QUBI to discuss the upcoming year-end audit. Management displayed their pleasure with the current year's financial performance as EPS exceeded the analysts' estimate.

Juan has called you into his office to discuss the results of his meeting. He has provided you with the draft financial statements (Exhibit I), along with his notes from the meeting (Exhibit II). Juan has asked that you prepare a report addressing the accounting issues that can be used at the next meeting between Juan and QUBI management.

Required

Prepare the report.

EXHIBIT I – DRAFT FINANCIAL STATEMENTS

QUBI ENTERTAINMENT LTD.
BALANCE SHEET

As At December 31 (unaudited)	2014
Assets	
Current	
Cash	$ 129,870
Marketable securities	342,110
Accounts receivable	225,660
Inventory	176,780
Other assets	34,210
	908,630
Goodwill	125,780
Property and equipment, net	1,455,000
Intangible assets, net	10,231,508
	$12,720,918
Liabilities and shareholders' equity	
Current	
Accounts payable	134,550
Accrued and other liabilities	345,200
Deferred net revenue (packaged goods and digital content)	2,456,880
	2,936,630
Bonds outstanding (7%), issued at par	4,956,780
Common shares	5,035,850
Retained earnings (accumulated deficit)	(208,343)
	4,827,508
	$12,720,918

EXHIBIT I CONTINUED – DRAFT FINANCIAL STATEMENTS

QUBI ENTERTAINMENT LTD.

INCOME STATEMENT

For the year ended December 31	2014 (unaudited)	2013 (audited)	2012 (audited)
Sales	$3,475,690	$2,780,552	$1,946,386
Cost of sales	1,459,790	1,195,637	836,946
Gross profit	2,015,900	1,584,915	1,109,440
Expenses			
Marketing and sales	524,134	570,569	513,512
General and administrative	161,272	158,047	154,886
Research and development	463,657	459,020	440,660
Amortization of intangibles	533,297	522,631	517,405
Acquisition-related contingent consideration (note 1)	(28,000)	8,000	0
Goodwill impairment	0	5,000	0
Total operating expenses	1,654,360	1,723,268	1,626,463
Operating income (loss)	361,540	(138,353)	(517,022)
Gain (losses) on marketable securities	12,455	(4,400)	1,200
Income (loss) before taxes	373,995	(142,753)	(515,822)
Provision for (benefit from) income taxes	104,719	(39,971)	(144,430)
Net income (loss)	269,276	(102,782)	(371,392)
EPS	0.08	(0.03)	(0.11)
Weighted-average number of shares outstanding	3,500,000	3,430,000	3,361,400
Opening balance—retained earnings	(477,619)	(374,837)	(3,445)
Net income	269,276	(102,782)	(371,392)
Dividends	0	0	0
Closing balance—retained earnings	$(208,343)	$(477,619)	$(374,837)

Note 1 – Contingent consideration for a wrestling game franchise purchased in 2013.

EXHIBIT II – NOTES FROM MEETING WITH QUBI'S MANAGEMENT

» During the year, the Board of Directors approved a new compensation package for management. The new package moves away from cash-based compensation towards stock-based compensation. Details on the new stock-based compensation program will be provided to Juan at the next meeting.

» The intangible asset breakdown is as follows:

	Gross amount	Accumulated Amortization	Net
Acquired technology	1,924,560	213,840	1,710,720
Licences	765,000	85,000	680,000
Software	8,960,900	1,120,113	7,840,788
	11,650,460	1,418,953	10,231,508

» The software intangible asset is broken-down as follows:

Hockey game franchise	1,004,567
Golf game franchise	780,976
Wrestling game franchise	756,780
Baseball game franchise	765,890
Soccer game franchise	556,662
Mobile strategy game	490,500
Mythical Legend game franchise	1,750,890
Antique Legacy game franchise	1,734,523
	7,840,788

» The NBV of the property, plant, and equipment is utilized in operations as follows:

Acquired technology	260,597
Sports game franchise	588,744
Mobile games	74,719
Role playing game franchise	530,940
	1,455,000

» The sporting games, as a combined unit, are expected to sell the following copies:

Year	1	2	3	4	5	6	7
Copies sold	120,000	110,000	100,000	100,000	100,000	90,000	90,000

The sporting games have sold for an average of $50 per copy, and generally result in costs of $750,000 annually for updates.

» Management believes that the licences are used by each unit based on the extent of their intangible assets.

EXHIBIT II CONTINUED – NOTES FROM MEETING WITH QUBI'S MANAGEMENT

» The role playing games, as a combined unit, are expected to sell the following copies:

Year	1	2	3	4	5	6	7
Copies sold	45,000	20,000	15,000	125,000	85,000	35,000	15,000

The role playing games have sold for an average of $35 per copy, and with no annual costs required for upgrades. The large increase in sales in Year 4 is based on the expectation that both role playing games will have developed and published a sequel game in the continuing storyline. The cost of developing the sequel is $1,750,000.

» During the year, QUBI capitalized costs related to the development of a new strategy game concept for mobile devices. The following expenses were capitalized:

New Mobile Device Game - Capitalized Costs

• Market research related to popular military game features:	75,000
• Design of characters and writing story line:	115,000
• Programming and coding of game play:	235,000
• Pilot testing and error analysis:	17,500
• Marketing and promotional material:	48,000
	490,500

Given the fierce competition in the mobile device gaming industry, combined with a short gaming life span, management is uncertain about the future revenues to be earned by the new game; however, management does believe that the game will be successful if priced at $1.99 per download. Management has developed the following forecast of downloads:

		Downloads		
	Probability	Year 1	Year 2	Year 3
Optimistic	10%	300,000	200,000	55,000
Average	65%	165,000	90,000	20,000
Pessimistic	25%	75,000	50,000	5,000
	Average	156,000	91,000	19,750

» The acquired technology resulted from the acquisition of a successful professional football game franchise from SQUARE CUBE Software (SCS). QUBI purchased the software for $1,924,560 cash on the assumption that 30,000 copies would be sold annually. The agreement includes a contingent consideration clause whereby QUBI must pay SCS a royalty of 5% of sales on any copy sold in excess of 30,000. Conversely, SCS must pay QUBI a 5% fee if 30,000 copies are not sold. The 5% fee is calculated based on the difference between 30,000 and the number of copies sold, assuming that each copy would sell at $40.

EXHIBIT II CONTINUED – NOTES FROM MEETING WITH QUBI'S MANAGEMENT

»   Given a recent lockout in professional football, the popularity of the sport has declined. Only 23,000 copies were sold during the past year. The following forecast is available for future sales:

Year	1	2	3	4	5	6	7
Copies sold	25,000	27,500	30,000	30,000	30,000	30,000	30,000

Each copy is expected to sell for an average of $40 per game. In addition, it is expected to cost $300,000 each year in maintenance in order to upgrade the game play, rosters, functionality, cover design, etc.

»   QUBI shipped 10,000 copies of the above noted football game to a new retailer. The games were shipped in early December in hopes that the retailer could promote and sell the units over the holiday season. In order to entice the retailer to take on such a large number of units, QUBI provided a general right of return on any unsold copies up to January 15, 2015. As a result of the right of return, QUBI did not recognize any revenue on the sale. Based on experience with other retailers, it is very likely that at least half of the order will be sold to customers.

»   Included in the inventory balance are 7,500 units of QUBI's basketball franchise game with a cost of $17.50 per game. The cover of the basketball game is a superstar who is known for his great on-court play, along with his "bad boy" attitude. Just prior to the year-end, the superstar was arrested as a result of a domestic disturbance. It is unclear if the superstar will miss any time on the court as a result of this incident; however, many parent groups have began protesting the fact that the superstar is included on the cover of the game. The impact of this event on the resale value of the game is unknown.

»   The marketable security breakdown is as follows:

	2014 FV
Equities	245,788
Fixed-income	78,665
Short-term treasuries	17,657
	342,110

The marketable securities are classified as fair value through profit or loss. During the year, QUBI realized gains of $12,455 on securities that were sold. The fair value of the securities still held by QUBI at the beginning of the period was $306,978.

Toronto Mavericks

Today is March 15, 2015. Your partner called you, CA, into her office to discuss a new, special engagement. Your firm has been engaged to assist a group of investors, led by Bryan Sahota, with a business acquisition. Bryan Sahota is interested in buying the Toronto Mavericks Inc. (TM), a wholly owned subsidiary of Maple Lodge Entertainment and Sports (MLES). TM owns a minor-league professional hockey team. The hockey team has been rather successful on the ice, winning three championships in its first five years in the league.

The partner tells you that she and Mr. Sahota have scheduled a meeting with the rest of the investors next week to finalize an offer to be presented to MLES for the purchase of TM's shares. At an initial meeting a week ago, Mr. Sahota dropped off excerpts from the purchase price calculation agreement (Exhibit I) and financial statements (Exhibit II). Subsequent to the meeting, the partner, with the consent of MLES and the investor group, met with the management and staff of TM. Notes from both meetings are collected in Exhibit III.

Based on the financial statements obtained, and the purchase price equation, Mr. Sahota said to your partner: "MLES's management expressed that it is expecting to receive between approximately $1.4 to 1.8 million for TM. I'm not sure whether the investor group will continue to run TM the same way that MLES did, but MLES's management used the 2014 financial statements as a starting point in determining their expected price."

The partner tells you: "Our primary task is to review the financial statements of TM to determine compliance with GAAP. Based on the information we have obtained thus far, please prepare a report outlining any GAAP issues and a recommended treatment, along with any reasonable alternative treatments where applicable. Because of the relatively small size of TM, its financial statements have never been audited. Secondly, can you please calculate purchase price based on the GAAP adjusted net income that Mr. Sahota can use in the meeting next week."

Required

Prepare the report for the partner.

EXHIBIT I
PURCHASE PRICE AGREEMENT EXCERPTS

Purchase Price Calculation

The final purchase price is to be determined based on using an earnings multiple approach, whereby the total net income for the most recent fiscal year is multiplied by the earnings multiple as follows:

$$\text{Net Income}^1 \times \text{Earnings Multiple} = \text{Purchase Price}$$

Earnings Multiple

An earnings multiple of between 3 and 4 is common for companies owning minor-league professional baseball teams.

Net Income

Net income must be determined based on Generally Accepted Accounting Principles.

---

[1]Calculated in accordance with Part II of the *CICA Handbook*

EXHIBIT II
FINANCIAL STATEMENTS
TM INC.
BALANCE SHEET

As at December 31

(unaudited)

	2014	2013
Current assets		
Cash	29,400	27,000
Temporary investments	120,000	120,000
Accounts receivable	271,400	163,400
Employee receivable	70,000	45,000
Prepaid insurance	25,000	0
	515,800	355,400
Property, plant, and equipment (net)	237,600	93,000
Franchise rights	1,000,000	950,000
	1,753,400	1,398,400
Current liabilities		
Accounts payable	20,000	31,000
Due to MC Corp.	55,280	150,000
	75,280	181,000
Share capital (common shares)	7,000	7,000
Share capital (preferred shares)	3,000	3,000
Retained earnings	1,668,120	1,207,400
	1,678,120	1,217,400
	1,753,400	1,398,400

TM INC.
EXCERPT FROM THE INCOME STATEMENT

For the year ended December 31

(unaudited)

	2014	2013
Income before taxes	768,720	860,386
Income taxes	307,400	344,200
	40%	40%
Net income	461,320	516,186
Dividends	$600	

EXHIBIT III

NOTES FROM MEETING WITH BRYAN SAHOTA AND EMPLOYEES AT TM INC.

1. In 2006, MLES purchased a minor-league professional hockey franchise in Toronto and paid $800,000 in initial league fees. The hockey operations were immediately incorporated in a new subsidiary company, TM Inc. Recently, MLES made a decision to return to its core business of major league sports and to sell TM. TM's year end is the same as MLES's year end, December 31.

2. The hockey season runs from September to April, with the team playing 80 games—40 at home and 40 away. Attendance in the first part of the season is low but, by January, attendance for home games is usually close to capacity of 6,000 seats. About half of the home games are played by the end of December of each year.

3. All tickets are general admission tickets, with single game seats selling for $6.00. Season ticket holders, which number around 2,000, pay $200 for the 40 home games in August and September. Any season tickets not used cannot be transferred for another game, no refunds are offered, and the tickets are non-transferable and non-refundable. Jeffrey Tardif, the team's general manager, has instructed the bookkeeper to record all season ticket sales as revenue when the customer pays for the tickets. Play-off tickets are sold apart from the season ticket package, although season ticket holders are given the right of first refusal to purchase playoff tickets for their seats.

4. Jeffrey describes his relationship with advertisers as excellent, although he admits that the approaches he uses are sometimes unique. Some of the advertising revenue comes in through the exchange of products or services instead of cash. Advertising revenue is generated through the sale of space on the rink boards, displays on the ice surface, and announcements during the game, etc.

   For example, one advertiser, TorontoTech, supplied 15 laptops, with a carrying value of $10,000, on the condition that they be given away at specifically scheduled home games during the season, in exchange for an advertising sign on the boards behind the goalie net. The fair value of the advertising given was $15,000. Jeffrey credited $15,000 of revenue and debited $15,000 prepaid advertising on this sale when the transfer took place. As at December 31, there were 10 laptops still on hand. The laptops are expensed, and the prepaid advertising reduced, as they are given away.

5. TM's largest advertiser is MLES. It has the premier advertising space in centre ice. MLES pays $60,000 per year for this advertising space, which is about $40,000 more than what the space would cost in other minor-league arenas. TM records advertising revenue each year in the amount of $60,000.

6. Jeffrey believes that the value of the franchise has increased over the years that TM has owned the team. Consequently, Jeffrey has asked the bookkeeper to increase the value of the franchise on the balance sheet each year to reflect his estimate of the increase in market value. The journal entry's credit has been posted to gain on intangible asset.

7. On January 1, 2013, TM issued 3,000 redeemable and retractable preferred shares at a value of $1 per share. The shares are redeemable by TM at any time after January 2017. The shares are retractable for the original $1 per share at the discretion of the holder at any time up to January 2017, after which the retractable feature expires. The preferred shares require the payment of a mandatory $2 per share during the retraction period, after which, the dividends become non-cumulative and are paid at the discretion of the board only.

EXHIBIT III (CONTINUED)

NOTES FROM MEETING WITH BRYAN SAHOTA AND EMPLOYEES AT TM INC.

8. The arena where the team plays is owned by the city and leased by TM. The lease expires on June 30, 2017. TM is responsible for all operating expenses, including maintaining the ice surface and all equipment necessary to maintain the arena and parking lot. While the lease payments are relatively low ($100,000 per year), the facility desperately needed about $250,000 in renovations, particularly the concession stands and the home and visitors dressing rooms. TM had been pushing the city to do the renovations for several years, but the city was reluctant to spend the money and had not done anything.

   Jeffrey got tired of waiting. On July 1, 2014, he took it upon himself to spend about $150,000 on improvements, which have been set up as a receivable. Since the work should have been done by the city, he is now battling with the city to recoup this 'receivable' from them. He is frustrated because there is still another $100,000 of upgrades to go. If the arena is not completely upgraded, Jeffrey is fearful the league will step in and force the franchise to move to another city. It is unlikely that the city will reimburse TM for any incurred or future upgrade costs.

9. TM has temporary investments that are being carried at cost. Jeffrey has confessed that he has not adopted the accounting standards for financial instruments. The temporary investments are being carried at cost on the financial statements. The market value of the investments are as follows:

2014		2013	
Cost	**Market value**	**Cost**	**Market value**
$100,000	$150,000	$100,000	$110,000
100,000	150,000	100,000	110,000

Vulcanzap Inc. (VZAP)

Vulcanzap Inc. (VZAP) is a high-technology company that develops, designs, and manufactures telecommunications equipment. VZAP was founded in 2004 by the former assistant head of research and development at a major telephone company, Dr. Alec Zander. He and the director of marketing left the company to found VZAP. VZAP has been very successful. Sales reached $8.3 million in its first year and have grown by 80% annually since then. The key to VZAP's success has been the sophisticated software contained in the equipment it sells.

VZAP's board of directors recently decided to issue shares to raise funds for strategic objectives through an initial public offering of common shares. The shares will be listed on a major Canadian stock exchange. VZAP's underwriter, Mitchell Securities, believes that an offering price of 18 to 20 times the most recent fiscal year's earnings per share can be achieved. This opinion is based on selected industry comparisons.

VZAP has announced its intention to go public, and work has begun on the preparation of a preliminary prospectus. It should be filed with the relevant securities commissions in 40 days. The offering is expected to close in about 75 days. The company has a July 31 year end. It is now September 8, 2014. You, CA, work for Olariu Chathan, Chartered Accountants, the auditors of VZAP since its inception.

You have just been put in charge of VZAP's audit, due to the sudden illness of the senior. VZAP's year-end audit has just commenced. At the same time, VZAP's staff and the underwriters are working 15-hour days trying to write the prospectus, complete the required legal work, and prepare for the public offering. The client says that the audit must be completed so that the financial statements can go to the printer in 22 days. VZAP plans to hire a qualified chief financial officer as soon as possible.

An extract from VZAP's accounting records is found in Exhibit I. You have gathered the information in Exhibit II from the client, and your staff has gathered the information in Exhibit III. You have been asked by the audit partner to prepare a memo dealing with the key financial accounting issues.

Required

Prepare the memo.

EXHIBIT I
EXTRACT FROM ACCOUNTING RECORDS

(in thousands of dollars)

Product	Revenue Month of July	Revenue Total fiscal 2014	Deferred development costs[1]
Zibor	$ 815	$ 8,802	$ 9,463
Resale components	540	4,715	—
Webstar	700	4,241	359
IDSL 600	—	2,104	1,431
Transact training	2,077	2,077	—
Firewall Plus	402	1,640	1,500
Transact	670	1,350	2,159
700J	—	400	725
ATM 4000	—	394	1,825
Photon phasing project	—	—	691
	$5,204	$25,723	$18,153

EXHIBIT II
INFORMATION GATHERED FROM THE CLIENT

1. The job market for top software and hardware engineering talent is very tight. As a result, VZAP has turned to information technology "head hunters" to attract key personnel from other high-technology companies. During the year, VZAP paid $178,000 in placement fees, and the company is amortizing the payments over five years. The search firm offers a one-year money-back guarantee if any of the people hired leaves the company or proves to be unsatisfactory.

2. On July 29, 2014, the company made a payment of $100,000 to a computer hacker. The hacker had given the company 10 days to pay her the funds. Otherwise, she said she would post a security flaw she had detected in the VZAP's Firewall Plus software, on the Internet.

3. Alec Zander had been working on a photon phasing project when he left the telephone company. He has moved this technology ahead significantly at VZAP, and a prototype was built at a cost of $691,000. The project has been delayed pending a decision on the direction it will take.

4. VZAP defers and amortizes software and other development costs using the following formula:

$$\text{Annual amortization rate} = \frac{\text{sales in units for the year}}{\text{total expected sales in units during product life}}$$

---

[1]Cumulative costs for each product that have been deferred and recorded on the balance sheet.

EXHIBIT II (CONTINUED)

INFORMATION GATHERED FROM THE CLIENT

5. In line with normal software company practice, VZAP releases software upgrades that correct certain bugs in previously released software, via the Internet.

6. During a routine visit to the AC&C Advanced Telecommunications laboratory in southern California, a VZAP engineer discovered that nearly 600 lines of code in an AC&C program were identical to those of some VZAP software written in 2012—right down to two spelling mistakes and a programming error.

7. The ATM 4000 has been the company's only product flop. High rates of field failures and customer dissatisfaction led VZAP to issue an offer, dated July 30, 2014, to buy back all units currently in service for a total of $467,500. Southwestern Utah Telephone is suing VZAP for $4 million for damages related to two ATM 4000 devices that it had purchased through a distributor. The devices broke down, affecting telephone traffic for two weeks before they were replaced.

8. VZAP also resells components manufactured by a Japanese company. The effort required to make these sales to existing customers is minimal, but the gross margin is only 12% versus an average of 60% for the company's other products, excluding the Transact and 700J lines.

9. During its first two years, VZAP expensed all desktop computers when purchased, on the grounds that they become obsolete so fast that their value after one year is almost negligible. In the current year, VZAP bought $429,000 worth of PCs and plans to write them off over two years.

10. Revenue is recognized on shipment for all equipment sold. Terms are FOB VZAP's shipping location.

11. VZAP's Director of Marketing, Albert Brezar, has come up with a novel method of maximizing profits on the Transact product line. Transact is one of the few VZAP products that has direct competition. Transact routes telephone calls 20% faster than competing products but sells for 30% less. VZAP actually sells the product at a loss. However, without a special training course offered by VZAP, field efficiency cannot be maximized. Customers usually realize that they need the special training a couple of months after purchase. Brezar estimates that the average telephone company will spend three dollars on training for every dollar spent on the product. Because of the way telephone companies budget and account for capital and training expenditures, most will not realize that they are spending three times as much on training as on the product.

EXHIBIT III
INFORMATION GATHERED DURING THE AUDIT

1. Materiality has been set at $300,000.

2. The IDSL 600 equipment was sold to customers in May 2014. In September 2014, VZAP provided the custom software required to operate the IDSL 600 equipment. The software was "shipped" via the Internet.

3. On June 30, 2014, VZAP issued from treasury 50,000 common shares, with a stated capital of one cent each, to another high tech company. On the basis of an oral agreement that company provided design services to VZAP in exchange for the shares.

4. In 2004, VZAP introduced a new model of telecommunication equipment that was popular with consumers because its reduced energy consumption. The equipment design has remained virtually unchanged since it was introduced. The equipment is sold with 10-year warranties on parts and labour. Historically, claims have been minimal thus far.

   In the summer of 2014, several warranty claims were made against VZAP. Routine inspections by telephone company employees revealed cracked cables, which could create various inefficiencies, and possibly fire risks. Thirty claims were made, and VZAP paid for repairs. The cost of repairing each cable was $150, which was expensed by VZAP.

   Management believes that the cables were damaged because of poor installation by contractors. They cannot see more than an additional 40 or 50 units being damaged. The 30 repaired cables were manufactured in 2009 and 2010. Over 10,000 units of this model have been sold over the three years.

   Later, in a discussion with the chief engineer, you learn that she had examined the cables in the telecommunication equipment in question and saw no evidence of a design flaw. However, she expressed concern that the problem might be due to heavy use of the cables lines, combined with cold weather. She noted that the 30 reported problems were in northern locations where the demands on the equipment are considerable, and the weather can be extreme. Between 1,500 and 2,000 cables were installed in homes in those locations.

5. After lengthy negotiation, VZAP received a $900,000 grant from the provincial government to help finance a new facility. The terms of the grant require VZAP to maintain certain employment levels in that province over the next three years or the grant must be repaid. The new facilities became operational on May 1, 2014, and VZAP has recorded the entire $900,000 as revenue in the current fiscal year.

6. During the year, Vulcanzap was involved in various transactions with JDP. JDP is controlled by the same shareholder group as Vulcanzap.

Xtreme Go-Karts Inc.

Xtreme Go-Karts Inc. ("XGK"), a private Canadian company, began operations in 2008. XGK manufactures and markets various high-speed go-karts used by extreme thrill seekers. XGK also wholesales specialized go-karting accessories, such as helmets, gloves, and protective eyewear. Two friends, Abdule Olawale and Jennifer Woods, own XGK. Abdule and Jennifer were go-kart racing competitors. Their passion for improving the performance and safety of go-karts resulted in their decision to start XGK.

XGK dominates the Canadian market for go-karts, with a market share of approximately 90%. Over the years, North Americans have grown more and more interested in go-karting. Recently, extreme sport fans have expanded into the world of go-karting and are finding new thrills through the use of high-speed go-karts and challenging tracks. For example, annual go-kart grand prix events are appearing across the nation. XGK go-karts are manufactured in a specialized facility owned by XGK. XGK builds the frame, then installs 2-stroke or 4-stroke engines, customized transmissions, and tires.

Because the specialized manufacturing process is so capital intensive, XGK has had to borrow funds from a large bank to finance operations. XGK was able to reduce its debt load over the years but still relies heavily on its suppliers and bank for continued support and growth. The bank did not require audited financial statements in the past. However, in a recent routine meeting with the bank, Abdule and Jennifer were told they would have to provide audited statements for the year ended December 31, 2014. Specifically, the bank now requires XGK to provide audited financial statements within 90 days of the December 31 year end. The bank also stipulated that XGK must maintain a debt to equity ratio of no more than 1 to 1 (i.e., for every $1 in equity, there should be no more than $1 in debt).

Arthurs & Partners LLP (A&P) has been XGK's accountants for many years. It is now November 2014, and you are the senior accountant at A&P responsible for XGK's year end in the past. Abdule and Jennifer asked you to come in before year end to help their controller establish accounting policies. You meet the owners and the controller and note the following:

1. Speed and durability are the two most important aspects of go-kart engine. XGK has spent more than $425,000 to date researching and developing new equipment to manufacture new engine designs for its race go-karts. Abdule and Jennifer are also aware that many opportunities exist to supply efficient small 2- or 4-stroke engines to non-competing manufacturers. For example, lawnmower manufacturers outsource the production of 2-stroke engines and mini-bike manufacturers outsource the production of 4-stroke engines. Abdule and Jennifer are sure that the $175,000 spent on research and the additional $250,000 spent on development of patented engine designs will result in long-term financial security. XGK capitalized the full $425,000 as an asset on the balance sheet. A break down of the costs is as follows:

Research Costs:	
Salary of mechanical engineer	$ 75,000
Materials	100,000
	175,000
Development Costs:	
Salaries of mechanical engineer and mechanics	50,000
Salaries of office administration staff	20,000
Allocation of direct overhead utility cost	20,000
Allocation of building amortization (Note 1)	50,000
Amortization of equipment used in development process	60,000
Materials used in the lab during development	50,000
	250,000
	$425,000

Note 1 – the amortization of the building was based on a 20% allocation, since the development lab accounts for approximately 20% of the building.

The total future expected revenues in the next 5 years from this project are $1,350,000, while the costs expected to be incurred are $1,130,000.

2. During the year, XGK exchanged $1,000 cash and go-kart helmet inventory with Karting Supplies Ltd. The inventory given up cost $85,000 and had a fair value of $96,000. XGK received 3,000 Model XT500 helmets that XGK could otherwise have purchased from its regular suppliers. The purchase price can range from $25 to $38 per unit. XGK sold similar helmets to its customers for $28 per unit last month. The controller has not recorded this transaction because he doesn't know how. "It's really like nothing happened," he tells you. "We gave them inventory and they gave us inventory. That's why I didn't record anything except a debit to inventory and a credit to cash for $1,000."

3. In September 2014, XGK shipped a truckload of go-karts to Point Peek Karting (PPK), a new customer in the United States. To make the terms of the sale attractive and to encourage future purchases, XGK structured this deal so that no payment is required until the karts were sold to PPK customers. For this transaction, XGK recorded a sale of $223,000 and reduced inventory by $188,000. As of today, PPK has sold 20% of the truckload.

4. Sales of $450,000 were made to another American company, Off Road Go Karting (ORGK). Just as it had with PPK, XGK sweetened the deal with ORGK by offering a six-month money-back guarantee for the full $450,000. Most of the sales to ORGK were made in November, so the return period will not have expired by XGK's year end (December 31). XGK has recognized all $450,000 of revenue for the above transaction.

5. On March 31, 2014, XGK received a $50,000 grant from a special federal government funding program. The grant was provided to help offset the costs incurred to purchase a machine used in the manufacturing process. The machine is expected to have a useful life of 5 years. "We were so happy to receive the grant. I have recorded the entire amount in revenue because we received the cheque in May," the controller told you. XGK amortizes all assets on a straight-line basis.

6. XGK has 1,000 go-kart gloves in inventory with an original cost of $20 per glove. These gloves were written down to their net realizable value of $15,000 in June when a competitor released the TecTrek glove, which was widely marketed as a superior model. "It is too bad that we had to take a writedown," the controller complained, "because three months after the release of the TecTrek, a significant design defect was revealed and the TecTrek gloves are no longer on the market. Our go-kart gloves now have a net realizable value of $27." A review of XGK's inventory reveals that 750 of the gloves are still in stock at year end.

7. XGK also has four remaining GT-1111 go-karts in inventory at a cost of $20,000. The karts may be banned in the near future, pending a regulator's review of the crash safety characteristics of the kart. If the karts are banned from being sold, they will have no value any longer. At this point, it is unclear whether the karts will be banned. The karts are under review because a customer is suing XGK for an undetermined amount, claiming that the kart's lack of safety features resulted in undue physical harm during a go-kart accident. The controller said, "Our lawyer said she intends to vigoursly defend us against this action, so we trust that XGK will not lose the case."

8. XGK purchased, for $25,000, a lifetime exclusivity agreement with two of the largest go-kart retailers in Canada. The entire amount was expensed in 2014. "We looked at the cost-benefit of setting up our payment for this agreement as an intangible asset and decided that the required annual impairment testing would be too difficult and costly to comply with. Furthermore, we were not sure if it would be considered an asset to begin with," the controller said, "so, we just expensed the $25,000. We do not mind expensing the cost because we are quite pleased with our current debt to equity ratio of 0.80 to 1."

XGK's balance sheet reveals that the corporation has $800,000 in debt and $1 million in equity.

Required

Prepare the report to Abdule, Jennifer, and the controller that addresses the accounting issues.